Lecture Notes in Computer Science   9398

Commenced Publication in 1973
Founding and Former Series Editors:
Gerhard Goos, Juris Hartmanis, and Jan van Leeuwen

More information about this series at http://www.springer.com/series/7409

Jorge Cardoso · Francesco Guerra
Geert-Jan Houben · Alexandre Miguel Pinto
Yannis Velegrakis (Eds.)

Semantic Keyword-Based Search on Structured Data Sources

First COST Action IC1302
International KEYSTONE Conference, IKC 2015
Coimbra, Portugal, September 8–9, 2015
Revised Selected Papers

Springer

Editors
Jorge Cardoso
University of Coimbra
Coimbra
Portugal

and

Huawei European Research Center
Munich
Germany

Francesco Guerra
Dipartimento di Ingegneria "Enzo Ferrari"
Università di Modena e Reggio Emilia
Modena
Italy

Geert-Jan Houben
Delft University of Technology
Delft, Zuid-Holland
The Netherlands

Alexandre Miguel Pinto
University of Coimbra
Coimbra
Portugal

Yannis Velegrakis
Università degli Studi di Trento
Trento
Italy

ISSN 0302-9743   ISSN 1611-3349   (electronic)
Lecture Notes in Computer Science
ISBN 978-3-319-27931-2   ISBN 978-3-319-27932-9   (eBook)
DOI 10.1007/978-3-319-27932-9

Library of Congress Control Number: 2015957235

LNCS Sublibrary: SL3 – Information Systems and Applications, incl. Internet/Web, and HCI

This Springer imprint is published by SpringerNature
The registered company is Springer International Publishing AG Switzerland

Preface

These proceedings contain the papers presented at the First International KEYSTONE Conference (IKC 2015), which was held in Coimbra, Portugal, during September 8–9, 2015. The conference was organized by the COST Action IC1302 KEYSTONE (semantic *key*word-based *s*earch on *s*tructured data *s*ources – http://www.keystone-cost.eu).

The main objective of the KEYSTONE Action is to launch and establish a cooperative network of researchers, practitioners, and application domain specialists working in fields related to semantic data management, the Semantic Web, information retrieval, artificial intelligence, machine learning, and natural language processing. The action coordinates the collaboration among these actors to foster research activities and technology transfers in the area of keyword-based search over structured data sources. Coordination efforts will promote the development of a new revolutionary paradigm that provides users with keyword-based search capabilities for structured data sources as they currently do with documents. Furthermore, it will exploit the structured nature of data sources in defining complex query execution plans by combining partial contributions from different sources. The action started to operate in October 2013 and today includes more than 200 researchers from 28 countries who seek to analyze, design, develop, and evaluate techniques to enable keyword-based search over large amounts of structured data.

The First International KEYSTONE Conference was open to the research community and was organized in tracks. The research track was oriented to scientific outcomes. The challenge track accepted preliminary ideas prepared by teams from at least two countries and the in-use track explored techniques, tools, and libraries in the topic. The goal was to collect and analyze the main results achieved by the research areas covered by KEYSTONE. For action members, it was also the place to discuss the results obtained during the first two years of activity. The research theme of IKC 2015 was "Keyword-search on massive datasets." It is an emerging and challenging theme. In particular, since large-scale data sources usually comprise very large schema and billions of instances, keyword search over such datasets can suffer from several challenges related to scalability and interpretation of the keyword query intended meaning. Whereas state-of-the-art keyword search techniques work well for small or medium-sized databases in a particular domain, many of them fail to scale on heterogeneous databases that are composed of thousands of instances. The discovery of suitable semantically related data sources is another critical issue, hindered by the lack of sufficient information on available datasets and endpoints. Browsing and searching for data at this scale is not an easy task for users. Semantic search can support the process aiming at leveraging semantics to improve the accuracy and recall of search mechanisms. The following is a non-exhaustive list of topics that were of special interest:

- Highly scalable techniques for keyword search
- Keyword search on large graphs
- Keyword search semantics
- Open data exploitation for information discovery at large
- Interplay between analytics and search
- Semantic similarity, management, disambiguation, and indexing
- Social Web and social media
- Keyword search over privacy preserving data
- Modern interfaces for keyword search and result presentation on big data
- Benchmarking for search on big data
- Knowledge/ontology exploitation for efficient and effective search

The research track of the conference received 22 submissions from 16 countries. Each submission was reviewed by three Program Committee members and evaluated by research track chairs. Thirteen papers were accepted as full papers (an acceptance rate of 59 %) and three as short papers. The proceedings also include two invited talks. The first one was delivered by Dr. Veli Bicer (Research Scientist at the Smarter Cities Technology Center Ireland Research Lab, Dublin, Ireland) on "Handling City Data Deluge Challenges and Applications." The second talk was delivered by Prof. Dr. Andreas Nuernberger (Otto-von-Güricke-Universität Magdeburg, Magdeburg, Germany) on "Collaborative Information Seeking: On Traceability, Sensemaking, and Recommendation."

Finally, we would like to thank the authors for their submissions, the members of the Program Committee for reviewing the papers, and the Department of Informatics Engineering (University of Coimbra, Coimbra, Portugal) and the Instituto Pedro Nunes for the local organization of the workshop. A special thanks also to the COST Association that supported the networking and coordination activities promoted by KEYSTONE. We hope that you will enjoy and benefit from reading the conference proceedings.

September 2015

Jorge Cardoso
Francesco Guerra
Geert-Jan Houben
Alexandre Miguel Pinto
Yannis Velegrakis

Organization

Program Committee

Charlie Abela	University of Malta, Malta
Khalid Belhajjame	Université Paris-Dauphine, France
Mária Bieliková	Slovak University of Technology in Bratislava, Slovakia
Angela Bonifati	Lyon 1 University, France
Omar Boucelma	Aix-Marseille University, France
Peter Butka	Technical University Kosice, Slovakia
Andrea Cali	University of London, Birkbeck College, UK
Jorge Cardoso	University of Coimbra, Portugal
Bogdan Cautis	University of Paris-Sud 11, France
Elena Demidova	L3S Research Center, Germany
Stefan Dietze	L3S Research Center, Germany
Dorian Gorgan	Technical University of Cluj-Napoca, Romania
Francesco Guerra	University of Modena and Reggio Emilia, Italy
Yaakov Hacohen-Kerner	Jerusalem College of Technology - Machon Lev, Israel
Claudia Hauff	Delft University of Technology, The Netherlands
Marko Horvat	Polytechnic of Zagreb, Croatia
Dragan Ivanovic	University of Novi Sad, Serbia
Georgia Kapitsaki	University of Cyprus, Cyprus
Innar Liiv	Tallinn University of Technology, Estonia
Mihai Lupu	Vienna University of Technology, Austria
Gjorgji Madjarov	Ss. Cyril and Methodius University, FYROM
Sanda Martinčić - Ipšić	University of Rijeka, Croatia
Ana Mestrovic	University of Rijeka, Croatia
Loizos Michael	Open University of Cyprus, Cyprus
Paolo Missier	Newcastle University, UK
Jelena Mitrovic	University of Belgrade, Serbia
Ngoc-Thanh Nguyen	Wroclaw University of Technology, Poland
Andreas Nuernberger	Otto von Güricke University of Magdeburg, Germany
Vesna Pajic	University of Belgrade, Serbia
Norman W Paton	The University of Manchester, UK
Rok Piltaver	Jozef Stefan Institute, Slovenia
Alexandre Miguel Pinto	University of Coimbra, Portugal
Laura Po	Universitá di Modena e Reggio Emilia, Italy
Florin Pop	University Politehnica of Bucharest, Romania
José Ramón Ríos Viqueira	University of Santiago de Compostela, Spain
Mohand Said-Hacid	Université Claude Bernard Lyon 1 - UCBL, France

Gianmaria Silvello	University of Padua, Italy
Piotr Szpryngier	Gdansk University of Technology, Poland
Julian Szymanski	Gdansk University of Technology, Poland
Martin Theobald	Ulm University, Germany
Ljupco Todorovski	University of Ljubljana, Slovenia
Raquel Trillo Lado	University of Zaragoza, Spain
Genoveva Vargas	CNRS-LIG-LAFMIA, France
Yannis Velegrakis	University of Trento, Italy
Manolis Wallace	University of the Peloponnese, Greece
Hubert Zarzycki	Wroclaw School of Information Technology, Poland

Additional Reviewer

Spina, Cinzia Incoronata

Handling City Data Deluge: Challenges and Applications

(Invited Talk)

Veli Bicer

IBM Research, Ireland
velibice@ie.ibm.com

Due to world-wide urbanization, major problems of cities such as urban congestion, accessibility, liveability, air quality or traffic safety become more apparent and innovative techniques are sought to make the cities more comfortable and enjoyable to its citizens. With the emergence of Smart Cities, the steps leading on this path are paved with partial data and the need to make a lot of detail out of less than complete input. Instead, in order to better understand the city problems and status, available city data need to be harvested in a hollistic way and so called city data deluge needs to be handled for a better "sensing" of the city. In particular, the urban data provides insight considering all types of data (retrieved from mobility, sensors, mobile devices, social network messages, governmental applications, or utility services). However, as the nature of such data is of being large, heterogeneous, multi-domain, continuous and disconnected, it poses novel research challenges which importantly, are open to the investigation of a broad community of researchers in various fields. Recently the novel and innovative techniques have been developed in order to better analyze the data and provide important insights about the cities.

This talk mainly outlines some of the recent works in terms of processing the city data at scale and extract useful information out of it for the use of city operators, stakeholders, and citizens. In particular, there are many research streams which aim to find answers to some of the difficult questions: (i) Could multiple sources of City data be linked together at scale to uncover new behaviours and provide new insights?. (ii) What technologies will enable contextual query across massive volumes of heterogeneous data, for applications and people?. (iii) How could we protect the City – and Citizens – from harm as well as protecting their privacy?. (iv) How can we use computer reasoning to simplify City Operations through diagnosis and prediction?. (v) How can we incorporate human & social data sources to interpret and predict emergent behavior?. (vi) How can the emergent technologies such as cloud computing or enterprise mobility can help to address city data deluge?. As answers to those questions, many applications are developed by the acquisition, integration, search and mining of the city data and applying it to particular domains in terms of, e.g., traffic management, safety, social life and many more.

This work is supported by the PETRA project, funded by the European Commission 7th Framework Programme under project number 609042.

Contents

Professional Collaborative Information Seeking: On Traceability
and Creative Sensemaking   1
   Andreas Nürnberger, Dominic Stange, and Michael Kotzyba

Recommending Web Pages Using Item-Based Collaborative Filtering
Approaches   17
   Sara Cadegnani, Francesco Guerra, Sergio Ilarri,
   María del Carmen Rodríguez-Hernández, Raquel Trillo-Lado,
   and Yannis Velegrakis

Processing Keyword Queries Under Access Limitations   30
   Andrea Calì, Thomas W. Lynch, Davide Martinenghi,
   and Riccardo Torlone

Balanced Large Scale Knowledge Matching Using LSH Forest   36
   Michael Cochez, Vagan Terziyan, and Vadim Ermolayev

Improving css-KNN Classification Performance by Shifts
in Training Data   51
   Karol Draszawka, Julian Szymański, and Francesco Guerra

Classification Using Various Machine Learning Methods and Combinations
of Key-Phrases and Visual Features.   64
   Yaakov HaCohen-Kerner, Asaf Sabag, Dimitris Liparas,
   Anastasia Moumtzidou, Stefanos Vrochidis, and Ioannis Kompatsiaris

Mining Workflow Repositories for Improving Fragments Reuse   76
   Mariem Harmassi, Daniela Grigori, and Khalid Belhajjame

AgileDBLP: A Search-Based Mobile Application for Structured Digital
Libraries   88
   Claudia Ifrim, Florin Pop, Mariana Mocanu, and Valentin Cristea

Support of Part-Whole Relations in Query Answering   94
   Piotr Kozikowski, Ekaterini Ioannou, Yannis Velegrakis,
   and Francesco Guerra

Key-Phrases as Means to Estimate Birth and Death Years
of Jewish Text Authors   108
   Dror Mughaz, Yaakov HaCohen-Kerner, and Dov Gabbay

Visualization of Uncertainty in Tag Clouds   127
   Nikos Platis, Manolis Wallace, and Thanos Triantos

Multimodal Image Retrieval Based on Keywords and Low-Level
Image Features   133
     Miran Pobar and Marina Ivašić-Kos

Toward Optimized Multimodal Concept Indexing   141
     Navid Rekabsaz, Ralf Bierig, Mihai Lupu, and Allan Hanbury

Semantic URL Analytics to Support Efficient Annotation
of Large Scale Web Archives   153
     Tarcisio Souza, Elena Demidova, Thomas Risse, Helge Holzmann,
     Gerhard Gossen, and Julian Szymanski

Indexing of Textual Databases Based on Lexical Resources:
A Case Study for Serbian.   167
     Ranka Stanković, Cvetana Krstev, Ivan Obradović,
     and Olivera Kitanović

Domain-Specific Modeling: Towards a Food and Drink Gazetteer.   182
     Andrey Tagarev, Laura Toloşi, and Vladimir Alexiev

Analysing Entity Context in Multilingual Wikipedia to Support
Entity-Centric Retrieval Applications   197
     Yiwei Zhou, Elena Demidova, and Alexandra I. Cristea

Author Index   209

Professional Collaborative Information Seeking: On Traceability and Creative Sensemaking

Andreas Nürnberger[1]([✉]), Dominic Stange[2], and Michael Kotzyba[1]

[1] DKE Group, Faculty of Computer Science, University of Magdeburg,
Magdeburg, Germany
{andreas.nuernberger,michael.kotzyba}@ovgu.de
[2] Volkswagen AG, Berliner Ring 2, Wolfsburg, Germany
dominic.stange@volkswagen.de

Abstract. The development of systems to support collaborative information seeking is a challenging issue for many reasons. Besides the support expected for an individual user, such as query formulation, relevance judgement, result set organization and summarization, the smooth exchange of search related information within the team of users seeking information has to be supported. This imposes strong requirements on visualization and interaction to enable user to easily trace and interpret the search activities of other team members and to jointly make sense of gathered information in order to solve the initial information need. In this paper, we briefly motivate specific requirements with a focus on collaborative professional search, review existing work and point out major challenges. In addition, we briefly introduce a system that has been specifically developed to support collaborative technology search.

Keywords: Collaborative search · Information behaviour · Search user interface

1 Introduction

With the increasing amount of digitally stored data and information the requirements and expectations on information search systems, in particular web search engines, steadily grow. To achieve an appropriate user experience, search systems not only have to retrieve web documents related to the explicit given (keyword) search query, but also have to consider the user's context and ideally support the whole search process, i.e., all steps from query formulation over relevance judgement to result set organization and summarization. Current search engines already provide several features to support users regarding context, e.g., by considering the location, previously used search queries or already visited result pages, to adapt query suggestions or the search result set. But if the user's information need gets more complex and the search goes beyond a simple fact finding task the support provided by existing systems is still rather limited.

In this paper, we focus on search systems for domain experts, also called professionals. This group of users usually not only need to retrieve simple facts

© Springer International Publishing Switzerland 2015
J. Cardoso et al. (Eds.): KEYWORD 2015, LNCS 9398, pp. 1–16, 2015.
DOI: 10.1007/978-3-319-27932-9_1

or explore an area of interest, but have to satisfy a complex information need. For professionals the search is rather a creative process in which domain specific information is collected and very often used to derive solutions for an application domain. For example, a frequent task in the business area is to perform an extensive technology research to keep up to date, know about state-of-the-art methods and hence to be competitive. In addition, since the tasks to be solved by professionals are usually complex, they often have to be processed by a team of experts in order to solve the task in reasonable time and appropriate quality. Therefore, adequate support methods for collaborative information seeking (CIS) tasks are needed. Unfortunately, we still lack tools and methods to support complex search tasks [11] and collaborative search tasks [14], especially for professional searchers.

Different (theoretical) models for information seeking, or more general information behaviour, have been proposed [17,35]. These models underline the complexity of the search process, describe essential components and consider the search process from different perspectives. However, the majority of the models rather consider information seeking as a process that is performed by an individual and not a group of users. Therefore these models have to be adapted and extended to be applicable to support design and evaluation of search systems that enable collaborative information seeking by a team of professionals. To make collaborative information seeking feasible, a search user interface (SUI) is required that covers all steps of the search process and its phases, such as planning, exploration, sensemaking and summarization. That is, the search system should enable the team of searchers to trace the seeking process and to collaborate in understanding structure and meaning of the revealed information [11]. Hence, we start in the following with a discussion of aspects and issues of complex information seeking processes and then propose two SUI concepts that focus on supporting traceability and creative sensemaking in collaborative search. Section 2 provides a brief overview of information seeking, established models and illustrates their relation to collaborative search. In Sect. 3 we address the process of collaborative information seeking from different perspectives and describe important aspects. Afterwards, we provide two suggestions for SUIs, that support traceability (Sect. 4) and creative sensemaking (Sect. 5). The last section summarizes the paper and provides an outlook towards prospective, collaborative search systems.

2   Related Work

Information behaviour models provide the most general approach to describe a user during information acquisition and exploration. The models are used to characterize and formalize seeking behaviour, context information, possible dialog partners and the search system itself. The literature provides a huge variety of models that address different levels and aspects of information behaviour. In Wilson [35] several models are summarized. A more recent overview can be found in Knight and Spink [17]. Wilson's nested model of information behaviour

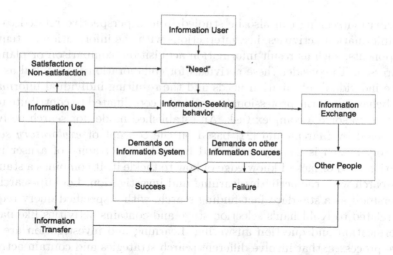

Fig. 1. Wilson's model of information behaviour from 1981 [35].

(as proposed in [35]) defines information seeking behaviour in the framework of information behaviour and considers these models as a subset. That is, information behaviour models additionally describe intervening variables, activating mechanisms and different information sources to embed information seeking behaviour. Models of information seeking behaviour cover all methods describing a user who is conducting a search to discover and yield access to information sources, i. e., all used strategies and tactics. In Wilson's first model of information behaviour [34] (see Fig. 1), the user recognizes an information need and starts seeking for information on different formal or informal information sources. Alternatively, the user can seek for information exchange with other people. If successful, the user may use the gained information to further refine his or her information seeking behaviour or to transfer information to other people. Furthermore, successfully gained information may be used to evaluate the current state of satisfaction and to (re-)formulate the information need. However, the model considers information (seeking) behaviour rather as an individual process: The user has an individual information need, seeks individually for information and merely exchanges or transfers information with other users, but not the need itself nor is the seeking process linked or synchronized with others.

Information-seeking can also be considered from other perspectives than proposed by Wilson. The cognitive or mental perspective allows to describe information seeking in several phases. For example, Kuhlthau [19,20] proposed a phenomenological model with six *stages*: Initiation, Selection, Exploration, Formulation, Collection and Presentation. Ellis (et al.) [7–9] discussed a model with empirically supported categories, termed *features*: Starting, Chaining, Browsing, Differentiating, Monitoring, Extracting, Verifying and Ending. If the models' perspectives coincide, they even can be aggregated, c.f. Wilson [35]. Especially in a collaborative setting this cognitive perspective can be used to describe the current state of understanding and sensemaking within the team.

Information seeking can also be studied from a perspective related to conducted information activities, i.e., interactions with the information system and its components, such as result information acquisition, comparison or planning, are addressed. To consider these activities for collaboration is essential as well, since the individual information needs and the resulting individual information seeking behaviour of the professionals need to be coordinated to contribute to the team's goal to solve a complex task. An established model for search activities was proposed by Marchionini [21] based on the concept of *exploratory search*. Exploratory search is usually motivated from the uncertainty of a user in his information need or lack of knowledge of how to tackle it. It combines a standard lookup-search with the activities learning and investigation. Lookup-search can be understood as a standard fact-finding search, with a specified query request, that is related to Kuhlthau's selection stage and contains activities like navigation, verification and question answering. Learning and investigation are both iterative processes, that involve different search strategies and contain activities like comparison, interpretation, synthesis and planning.

Collaborative search can be defined as a special case of a social search [10], in which all participants have the same information need and actively conduct a specific search together in order to achieve a common search goal [13]. While in [12] different roles and dimensions of collaboration are discussed, such as intent (explicit and implicit), depth of mediation, concurrency and location, Shah provides in [30] a more general introduction and definition of *collaborative information seeking*. Poltrock's et al. [25] definition of collaborative information seeking as "the activities that a group or team of people undertakes to identify and resolve a shared information need" (p. 239) nicely agrees with the activity related perspective as discussed above. Reddy and Jansen [26] study the collaborative information seeking behaviour of two healthcare teams in a business setting. They found that collaborative information behaviour differs from individual information behaviour on several dimensions and present a model in which they contrast the context (individual vs. collaborative information behaviour) with the actual behaviour (information seeking vs. searching). Capra et al. [5] study search strategies in a collaborative search task. Their results show that collaboration in a search task occurs at various stages. They present three higher-level search strategies how collaborative information seeking is carried out: Participants acted on their own, unaware of their collaborators (independent strategy), they also used their collaborators' previous work to do additional work in the same space (parallel strategy), and used knowledge of what their collaborators have done to take new directions (divergent strategy). In her early assessment Morris [22] advocates four aspects (coverage, confidence, exposure, and productivity) in which dedicated collaborative search systems can influence a user's search experience in an exploratory search task. A collaborative search system has been proposed by Morris et al. [24]. They study how personalization of web search can be achieved based on a membership in a group that works on the same task. They show how three techniques (groupization, smart splitting, and group hit-highlighting) can enhance the individual search experience in a collaborative context.

3 Information Seeking for Professionals

Powerful (web) search technologies have made a lot of business-relevant information available for domain experts of a company to explore, collect, and use in their problem-solving tasks. These experts satisfy most of the characteristics described by Knight and Spink [17]. The experts are not necessarily information professionals, i. e., are "unlikely to have any formal training in developing appropriate search queries or retrieval strategies", "likely to use a wider variety of search strategies, with more inconsistent results", and "more likely to be the'information user' of the information they are seeking." However, they often have (a lot of) domain expertise which influences individual search strategies and often leads to more successful findings than having little expertise [15,33].

Professionals often perform a complex, exploratory search task, to gather domain-related information for an underlying problem-solving task [21]. This search task is usually open-ended and has an uncertain process and outcome. Furthermore, problem-solving often requires collaboration in exploring the information space together, collecting domain-related information, making sense of it and using it. Professionals within an organization are often part of communities and typically know each other personally. Therefore, in addition to the exploratory nature of this task, there are further characteristics which can be attributed to the business setting in which a search is performed. The domain-related problems that need to be solved by the community often exist over a longer period of time which results in a continuous information need. That is, the search topics need to be updated, which leads to repeatedly executed search tasks dealing with similar or overlapping contents. In the following, we discuss crucial aspects of collaborative information seeking for professionals in more detail and provide a model that links essential components for search systems.

3.1 Aspects of Collaborative Information Seeking

Problem-Solving Context: The type of professional search we want to address is often part of a so-called *known genuine decision task* (c.f. Byström and Järvelin's [4] categorization in which they distinguish between five task categories based on a priori determinability of the tasks). In our case, the structure of the result is often known a priori but the procedures for performing the task, i. e., the needed information and the process are unknown. This kind of task often goes along with a complex information need. There has been some debate about what constitutes a complex information need or, more generally, a complex search task especially in contrast to an exploratory search task. Aula and Russell [2] present an interpretation that fits to our professional search scenario. Among other criteria they argue that complex search often requires exploration and more directed information finding activities, where the searcher often uses multiple sources of information. Additionally, a complex search often requires note-taking because of the searcher's limited ability to hold all gathered information in memory. Besides, relevant information is typically spread across lots of resources in the information space. This makes the information space sparse

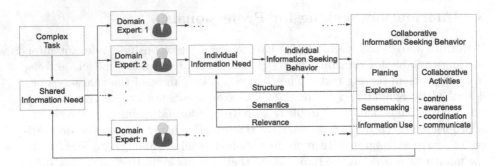

Fig. 2. Illustration of collaborative information seeking with an emphasis on a group of domain experts

with facts, as opposed to a dense information space where a single resource may contain all relevant information to sufficiently answer the information need.

Collaboration: Professional search often concerns a community of experts that face similar problems and thus have similar, overlapping information needs. A professional search tool, therefore, should allow these experts to work together in these tasks. Most experts within such a community know each other personally, which distinguishes it from other scenarios where collaborative search is analyzed. The collaboration is explicit, active, remote (mostly), and asynchronous. In the context of a collaborative exploratory search, it is important to note that it may not be known beforehand, who will take part in the search task. It may happen that some experts join the team while others have already started gathering and using information. Based on Reddy and Jansen [26], reasons why users engage in collaboration are (1) the complexity of information need, (2) fragmented information resources (sources reside in multiple and dispersed systems), (3) the lack of domain expertise and (4) the lack of immediately accessible information.

Updates: Professionals are often required to update their knowledge about the domains they are responsible for which is why they have to repeatedly perform search tasks about various, sometimes overlapping search topics. Professional search requires the ability to investigate, update and extend previous search tasks. In Kotov et al. [18] such tasks are considered cross-session tasks which often evolve over time. The information need in a cross-session task is typically complex and progressively refined with each new update.

The diagram in Fig. 2 is based on Wilson's information behaviour model [34] (c.f. Fig. 1) and provides an extension regarding collaborative information seeking with an emphasis on a group of domain experts. After the emergence of a complex task, the group of professionals has to discuss about and define the corresponding, shared information need. Even if the need cannot be specified precisely (due to the exploratory character of the task), the group has to divide it in sub-needs that can be (at least initially) processed by an individual. As a result each domain expert can start to satisfy their resulting individual information need by performing individual information seeking. Since this information seeking occurs in the context of a collaborative task the collaborative information seeking behaviour component emphasises that search-related and collaborative activities have to be taken into account when the experts reveal new information. Here, it is important that the group can organize the seeking process and that they can follow and participate in understanding the revealed information. The organization can be enabled by the collaborative activities illustrated on the right. The tracing and the cognitive phases of the seeking process are supported by planning, exploration, sensemaking and summarization (as depicted on the left). By exploration, the team reveals structural information that can influence the individual information need or the information seeking behaviour directly. Sensemaking and information use allow to reveal new insights and key aspects that influence the information need on a semantic level and to perform a relevance evaluation. In the end, the gathered and combined information discovered by the collaborative seeking may influence the initial shared information need.

3.2 Traceability and Creative Sensemaking

When it comes to search-related activities that are performed by the whole group of collaborating searchers exploring an information space, making sense of collected information and using this information in a problem solving situation should be *traceable* for each individual, so that he or she understands how the various contributions of the searchers relate to each other. Every team member needs to be able to understand their joint search strategy in order to make better or more relevant contributions and benefit from each others' domain knowledge and search expertise. The second challenge in professional search is *sensemaking* in context of the underlying genuine decision task in which the search process is embedded in. Sensemaking can be understood as the "process of searching for a representation and encoding data in that representation to answer task-specific questions" [27]. It is an integral part of many information seeking models because it describes how a searcher (mentally) models, interprets, disambiguates, and interacts with the information that is gathered during search. The requirements on traceability and sensemaking can be defined as follows:

Traceable Collaboration: Traceability in collaborative search describes the team's ability to understand the structure, semantics, and relevance of their collaborative information seeking behaviour. Traceability concerns especially the search-related activities exploration, sensemaking, and information use. Co-searchers should be able to understand how they explore the information space as a team, what information they collect in the resources they discover, and how they synthesise/interpret this information with respect to their search goal.

Creative Sensemaking: Creative sensemaking can be defined as satisfying (complex) information needs in a problem solving context to "form a coherent functional whole" and reorganize "elements into a new pattern or structure through generating, planning, or producing" (c.f. Anderson and Krathwohl's [1] taxonomy of learning). The core task is to make sense of the gathered information of a search task and create solutions to the underlying domain problem. Therefore, creative sensemaking inherits some properties of information use as well. Since professional search is often embedded in a problem-solving task creatively using the collected information and generating new ideas, concepts, or solutions to solve the problems is very important. Creative sensemaking is central to search tasks with complex information needs where solutions in an application domain have to be generated based on the collected information.

Traceability and creative sensemaking are still rarely addressed in (collaborative) search settings. They are, however, particularly important in order to support experts engaged in a professional search task. Since the type of professional search we outlined above refers to an explicit collaboration between experts, one approach of supporting them is to design specially-tailored user interfaces that provide new types of visualizations and interaction methods. Before we outline an example of a tool that is designed with traceability and creative sensemaking in mind, we briefly discuss current shortcomings of collaborative search tools and our general approach in the next section.

3.3   Challenges of Collaborative Search User Interfaces

There already exist some interesting approaches towards supporting explicit collaboration in a search task with the help of special collaborative search user interfaces. Some of them are mentioned in Sect. 2. However, there are reasons why collaborative search tools have not become widely accepted (yet). Hearst [14] argues that in order for users to move from a solitary to a collaborative search tool there "must be enough additional value as yet in the tools offered." In particular, Shah [29] mentions cost factors that one should keep in mind when designing collaborative search tools, e.g., the *cost of learning* a new system, *adaption/adoption costs* when using a collaborative system, and the *collaborative costs* when being part of group task. Capra et al. [6] study how searchers perform ongoing, exploratory searches on the web and share their findings with others. Their results show that searchers employ a variety of tools and techniques that go "beyond the functionalities offered by today's search engines and web browsers", e. g., note-taking, information management, and exchange. The study by Kelly and Payne [16] confirms these results. They also find that (collaborative) searchers want to "repurpose" their search results at the end of the task to arrange them into a more meaningful way. Shah [28] proposed guidelines for the design of a collaborative search tool that focus on behavioural aspects of collaboration. These include that a tool should allow for effective communication, encourage individual searchers to make contributions, coordinate the individual actions and needs, and provide means to explore and negotiate individual differences. When it comes to concrete features that a collaborative search tool should support, various authors have contributed their ideas:

– *Awareness:* "knowing what other people are doing" during collaborative information behaviour activities [23, 26].
– *Communication:* share information with other members of the collaboration team bilaterally or in conference [26].

- *Division of Labour:* reduce individual effort by avoiding redundant actions and allow for effective "divide-and-conquer" techniques [14,23].
- *Feedback:* with respect to collaborative search includes a "feeling of accomplishment"; Co-searchers should be able to step back and get an understanding of what actions are required next and by whom [14].
- *Overview:* refers to a visualization of the "land-scape" that the team has covered in their collaborative search task that also allows them to depict what they still have to do [14]. "Users must have access to a visualization of not only their search process, but also of their collaborators. ... [This] will allow users to discuss each other's searches and provide feedback on how to improve them." [26]
- *Persistence:* makes the context, content, and task of a search session available for future access and for others in a collaboration; In particular, it is the precondition for remote and asynchronous collaborative search [23].
- *Personalization:* means to provide "structure to let individuals define what their personal constraints or preferences are" when they engage in collaborative search [14].

There are still many features missing in today's collaborative search tool stack [14]. Therefore, two design decisions are central to our approach presented in the following. First, we create an independent collaborative layer that can be used in conjunction with any (standard) solitary web-search tool. This additional layer should integrate seamlessly and effortless into the user's web-search infrastructure. The idea is to be as little intrusive to the user's search environment as possible. The layer adds custom collaborative features to enhance the individual's collaborative search experience while maintaining most of the solitary appearance. Second, searchers should be able to personalize the outcome of a collaborative search task given they often have individual needs within the collaboration. This is achieved by allowing searchers to create personalized views with which they can interpret the outcome of the collaborative search task in their own individual context.

4   Traceable Collaborative Search

Most of the current collaborative search systems are designed to "allow participants to find, save, and share documents, and see the activities of others in the collaboration group" (Hearst [14]). These tools are used, e. g., to increase awareness, communication, control, and coordination of the collaboration. In our attempt to make a collaborative information seeking more traceable within a group we focus more on the search-related activities of the task. In particular, we seek to make individual exploratory and sensemaking activities of each participant more transparent and understandable for the others.

Our general approach is to treat exploratory search like an orienteering hike where participants use maps and other tools to navigate in previously unfamiliar terrain to find special points of interest (control points) within a given time. In exploratory search points of interest are resources that contain information that

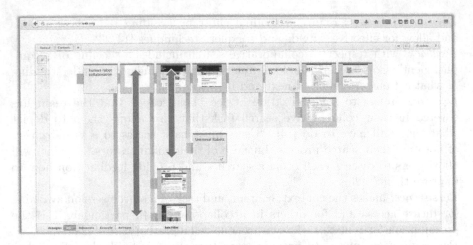

Fig. 3. UI: Search map.

(partially) answer an information need. One of the main differences between orienteering and exploratory search is that in orienteering the maps of the terrain are provided upfront to help navigation, whereas maps of the information space typically do not exist in exploratory search. In contrary, even the "terrain" of the information space is unknown beforehand and unveils itself dynamically in the course of the exploration. Moreover, in our case exploration is carried out as a team endeavour. Members need to be able to trace what part of the information space they have covered as a team, i.e., what directions they took, where they found relevant information, and how they arrived there. Similar to the idea of a land-scape that provides a visual overview of search activity our approach is to create a map of the explored information space during (collaborative) search on-the-fly. This map displays relevant exploratory actions of each searcher and sets them into context with those of the others. The idea is to visualize how their individual information seeking behaviours complement each other so that they are able to see the outcome of their joint exploration graphically.

A concrete implementation of such a map, which we call a Search Map [31], is shown in Fig. 3. A Search Map lays out exploratory activities (of a team of searchers) as tiles in 2-dimensional space. The tiles are organized as a horizontal tree where the root is left, so that exploration paths can be read from left to right. We have chosen a tree visualization because it provides a definite start (root) and end (leaf) for each path. We considered using a more general graph-like visualization instead to emphasise that exploratory search allows cycles but choose not to in favour of readability. A user study is still needed to confirm our decision. There are a couple of interaction features we have implemented into the Search Map. For example, it is possible to zoom in and out of the map so that searchers can either receive a general idea of what paths have been taken in general or look into details of a path and examine the actual actions. Since such a map can become large quickly, especially in a collaborative context, it is also possible to fold/unfold or hide exploration paths on demand, e.g., by filtering classes of actions like queries, documents, or snippets, or by issuing meta search queries that highlight parts of the map that match these queries. Additional interactions with the map encompass annotations, like comments or symbols, that can be pinned on the map to communicate (meta) information concerning the exploration. Such meta information can be, for instance, a hint on a dead-end in a search path or the need for future updates. Also, while moving the Search Map (up and down or left and right), a special layout algorithm automatically adjusts the placement of the tiles so that the tiles of a search path are moved up and down such that the path remains visible. Green arrows in Fig. 3 illustrate the movement of two tiles that belong to the topmost search path. If the map is moved downwards the tiles move down, too, and upwards respectively. Some of the tiles represent visited resources (like websites). Other tiles show search queries that a user issued to a search engine[1]. Again other tiles show extracted snippets from websites. These snippets often contain information that helps to answer the shared information need. We distinguish two types of snippets. Searchers can extract sentences or images from resources which, for them, contain useful facts. They can also extract keywords from these resources that are often concepts or entities that relate to the search topic. By displaying these keywords, facts, or images as tiles on the map, we seek to make it easier for the team to understand the outcome of a search path. The keywords are also used as input to the creative sensemaking interface, which is part of the collaboration layer described in the next section.

Since the overall idea is to interfere as little with solitary information search tools as possible the Search Map interface can be faded over any active website in a browser window using a hotkey or a button on a browser toolbar, but remains invisible otherwise. So, whenever individual searchers want to know what the current progress of the collaborative search is, they can investigate the Search Map. In order to personalize the collaboration, searchers can create individual views of the Search Map by organizing tiles or whole paths according to their needs. These views can be considered as "sub-versions" of a Search Map that automatically merge new tiles or paths according to the changes that have been made. By visualizing the joint search strategy of a team with the help of a Search Map we enable individuals to trace and be more aware of how they explore the information space together. Considering that search tasks need to be extended at a later time, this is aimed to quickly access the resources that have been particularly helpful when answering the information need and understanding how the team arrived at these resources. They can also be used to pick up loose ends and drill into topics for which no answers were available before.

5 Creativity-Focused Sensemaking

As outlined in Sect. 3.1 sensemaking in professional search often goes along with generating solutions to a given (domain-related) problem within a group of experts. There are some major challenges that arise when designing a search

---

[1] The actual search engine being used does not affect the Search Map, so searchers are able to use any search engine they want, even Intranet search engines of companies.

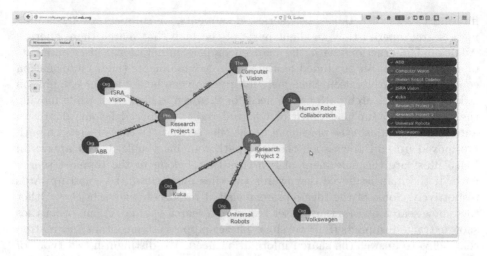

Fig. 4. UI: topic graph.

user interface to support this creative process: The interface should provide inter-action capabilities so that the group can express and discuss their (individual) concepts and merge these into a coherent whole; the interface should be based on a visualization that allows each individual searcher to (1) contribute their view, and (2) draw their own conclusions when the task is completed. Our general idea is to augment the collaborative layer created by the first interface by supporting the creative sensemaking and use of gathered information of the search task.

For the design of our creative sensemaking interface we lend some ideas from collaborative learning research. In collaborative learning mind maps, also called concept maps, have been reported to show good results when learners work together in a meaning-making and meaning-negotiation task (e. g., [3]). There-fore, the interface is designed like a mind mapping interface that we integrate into the collaboration layer. This interface can be used by searchers to organize and share their understanding of the search topic graphically and iteratively refine their individual and group's view during search. This is particularly help-ful in an exploratory setting where this understanding develops over time and is seldom very elaborate at the beginning. A simple example of such an interface is shown in Fig. 4. We call this example a Topic Graph because it is a graph-based representation of the group's view about the search topic [32]. Nodes of the topic graph represent domain entities of a search topic and edges represent rela-tionships between these entities. The entities are either extracted during explo-ration (see Sect. 4) or added manually. Typically, mind maps do not possess any limitation concerning the use of entity classes or relationship types. The topic graph, however, is based on a flexible schema that provides (some) structure and semantics. Although, this schema is originally derived from a domain ontol-ogy which was developed together with domain experts, the central idea of the schema is to remain open towards changes along the search process and, thus, be more flexible in the creative process it is used in. This degree of flexibility is often not possible when using ontologies, especially when they become large/complex. The schema restricts the use of entity classes in the interface and the available relationships that can be added between them. The Topic Graph also makes the sensemaking results of the group traceable by allowing each member of the team to (formally) express their thoughts on the topic. Since experts sometimes have different backgrounds they are able to provide additional knowledge and context of their domain. Similarly to our Search Maps (Sect. 4), experts are able to express (contradictory) interpretations by creating their own Topic Graphs as tabs in the interface, so that they are visible for the rest of the group.

In practice, when working with the two interfaces presented above, Search Maps and Topic Graphs are aimed to complement each other. Topic graphs help to gain an overall understanding of the search topic by looking at the mind map-like representation of domain-related information. When a member of a team identifies an entity or a relation of interest they can use the Search Map to investigate the exploratory activities that led to its discovery. In a professional setting we believe this makes it easier to address complex search tasks more completely and synergies can be leveraged more effectively. For example, sparse information spaces can be explored more systematically even if new information becomes available at a fast pace. Especially in situations where new information may nullify previously collected data, working with Search Maps and Topic Graphs may help to understand and interpret these changes across search tasks.

6   Summary

Domain experts often perform professional information seeking tasks as part of their daily work. Designing adequate computer support is challenging, especially due to the often collaborative nature of these tasks, which demands for specialized interaction features. Experts typically have to solve an underlying domain problem using the information they gather together as a group. Solving these problems requires extensive exploratory search, collaborative sensemaking and repeated updates as new information becomes available. In order to tackle these challenges we highlighted two aspects of a collaborative search task that are still rarely addressed: traceability and creative sensemaking. Traceability describes a group's ability to understand the structure, semantics, and relevance of their collaborative information seeking behaviour. Creative sensemaking describes the group's ability to solve a shared domain problem together by reorganizing newly acquired information into a coherent whole that satisfies their underlying information need. We outlined how these aspects blend into the collaborative search process with the help of an extended model of collaborative information seeking that we built based on Wilson's earlier model. Although, we present user interface prototypes that support traceability and creative sensemaking in a collaborative search task, much of the challenges in professional information seeking still remain. Especially, for the design of future search systems it is important to investigate the dynamics and demands of the professional setting in more detail.

Search systems that allow a lean participation of group members and at the same time maintain much of their individual experience, will likely advance and may overthrow how we search together in a professional environment.

References

1. Anderson, L.W., Krathwohl, D.R., Airasian, P.W., Cruikshank, K.A., Mayer, R.E., Pintrich, P.R., Raths, J., Wittrock, M.C.: A taxonomy for learning, teaching, and assessing: a revision of bloom's taxonomy of educational objectives, 2nd edn. Allyn & Bacon, Boston (2001)
2. Aula, A., Russell, D.M.: Complex and exploratory web search. In: Information Seeking Support Systems (2008)
3. Basque, J., Pudelko, B.: Intersubjective meaning-making in dyads using object-typed concept mapping. In: Torres, P.L., Marriott, R.C.V. (eds.) Handbook of Research on Collaborative Learning Using Concept Mapping, Chapter 10, pp. 180–206. IGI Global, Pennsylvania (2010)
4. Byström, K., Järvelin, K.: Task complexity affects information seeking and use. Inf. Process. Manage. **31**(2), 191–213 (1995)
5. Capra, R., Chen, A.T., McArthur, E., Davis, N.: Searcher actions and strategies in asynchronous collaborative search. In: Proceedings of 76th ASIS&T Annual Meeting: Beyond the Cloud: Rethinking Information Boundaries, pp. 75:1–75:10 (2013)
6. Capra, R., Marchionini, G., Velasco-Martin, J., Muller, K.: Tools-at-hand and learning in multi-session, collaborative search. In: Proceedings of SIGCHI Conference on Human Factors in Computing Systems, pp. 951–960. ACM (2010)
7. Ellis, D.: A behavioral approach to information retrieval system design. J. Documentation **45**(3), 171–212 (1989)
8. Ellis, D., Cox, D., Hall, K.: A comparison of the information seeking patterns of researchers in the physical and social sciences. J. Documentation **49**(4), 356–369 (1993)
9. Ellis, D., Haugan, M.: Modelling the information seeking patterns of engineers and research scientists in an industrial environment. J. Documentation **53**(4), 384–403 (1997)
10. Evans, B.M., Chi, E.H.: Towards a model of understanding social search. In: Proceedings of ACM Conference on Computer Supported Cooperative Work, pp. 485–494. ACM (2008)
11. Gäde, M., Hall, M.M., Huurdeman, H., Kamps, J., Koolen, M., Skov, M., Toms, E., Walsh, D.: First workshop on supporting complex search tasks. In: Proceedings of the First International Workshop on Supporting Complex Search Tasks, part of ECIR (2015)
12. Golovchinsky, G., Qvarfordt, P., Pickens, J.: Collaborative information seeking. Computer **42**(3), 47–51 (2009)
13. Gossen, T., Bade, K., Nürnberger, A.: A comparative study of collaborative and individual web search for a social planning task. In: Proceedings of LWA Workshop (2011)
14. Hearst, M.A.: What's missing from collaborative search? Computer **47**(3), 58–61 (2014)
15. Hembrooke, H.A., Granka, L.A., Gay, G.K., Liddy, E.D.: The effects of expertise and feedback on search term selection and subsequent learning: research articles. J. Am. Soc. Inf. Sci. Technol. **56**(8), 861–871 (2005)

16. Kelly, R., Payne, S.J.: Collaborative web search in context: A study of tool use in everyday tasks. In: Proceedings of the 17th ACM Conference on Computer Supported Cooperative Work & #38; Social Computing, CSCW 2014, pp. 807–819. ACM, New York, NY, USA (2014)
17. Knight, S.A., Spink, A.: Toward a web search information behavior model. In: Spink, A., Zimmer, M. (eds.) Web Search. Information Science and Knowledge Management, vol. 14, pp. 209–234. Springer, Heidelberg (2008)
18. Kotov, A., Bennett, P.N., White, R.W., Dumais, S.T., Teevan, J.: Modeling and analysis of cross-session search tasks. In: Proceedings of the 34th International ACM SIGIR Conference on Research and Development in Information Retrieval, pp. 5–14. ACM (2011)
19. Kuhlthau, C.C.: Inside the search process: information seeking from the user's perspective. J. Am. Soc. Inf. Sci. 42(5), 361–371 (1991)
20. Kuhlthau, C.C.: Seeking Meaning: A Process Approach to Library and Information Services. Ablex Publishing, Norwood, NJ (1994)
21. Marchionini, G.: Exploratory search: from finding to understanding. Commun. ACM 49(4), 41–46 (2006)
22. Morris, M.R.: Interfaces for collaborative exploratory web search: motivations and directions for multi-user designs. In: CHI 2007 Workshop on Exploratory Search and HCI (2007)
23. Morris, M.R.: Collaborating alone and together: investigating persistent and multi-user web search activities, Technical report MSR-TR-2007-11, Microsoft Research (2007)
24. Morris, M.R., Teevan, J., Bush, S.: Enhancing collaborative web search with personalization: groupization, smart splitting, and group hit-highlighting. In: Proceedings of ACM Conference on Computer Supported Cooperative Work, pp. 481–484. ACM (2008)
25. Poltrock, S.E., Grudin, J., Dumais, S.T., Fidel, R., Bruce, H., Pejtersen, A.M.: Information seeking and sharing in design teams. In: Schmidt, K., Pendergast, M., Tremaine, M., Simone, C. (eds.) GROUP, pp. 239–247. ACM, New York (2003)
26. Reddy, M.C., Jansen, B.J.: A model for understanding collaborative information behavior in context: a study of two healthcare teams. Inf. Process. Manage. 44(1), 256–273 (2008)
27. Russell, D.M., Stefik, M.J., Pirolli, P., Card, S.K.: The cost structure of sensemaking. In: Proceedings of INTERACT 1993 and CHI 1993 Conference on Human Factors in Computing Systems, pp. 269–276. ACM (1993)
28. Shah, C.: Collaborative information seeking: a literature review. In: 2009 Workshop on Collaborative Information Behavior (2009)
29. Shah, C.: Collaborative Information Seeking - The Art and Science of Making the Whole Greater than the Sum of All, vol. 34. Springer, Heidelberg (2012)
30. Shah, C.: Collaborative information seeking. J. Assoc. Inf. Sci. Technol. 65(2), 215–236 (2014)
31. Stange, D., Nürnberger, A.: Search maps: enhancing traceability and overview in collaborative information seeking. In: de Rijke, M., Kenter, T., de Vries, A.P., Zhai, C.X., de Jong, F., Radinsky, K., Hofmann, K. (eds.) ECIR 2014. LNCS, vol. 8416, pp. 763–766. Springer, Heidelberg (2014)
32. Stange, D., Nürnberger, A.: When experts collaborate: sharing search and domain expertise within an organization. In: Proceedings of the 15th International Conference on Knowledge Technologies and Data-driven Business, ACM, New York, NY, USA (2015, to appear)

33. White, R.W., Dumais, S.T., Teevan, J.: Characterizing the influence of domain expertise on web search behavior. In: Proceedings of the Second ACM International Conference on Web Search and Data Mining, pp. 132–141. ACM (2009)
34. Wilson, T.D.: On user studies and information needs. J. Documentation **37**(1), 3–15 (1981)
35. Wilson, T.D.: Models in information behaviour research. J. Documentation **55**(3), 249–270 (1999)

Recommending Web Pages Using Item-Based Collaborative Filtering Approaches

Sara Cadegnani[1], Francesco Guerra[1(✉)], Sergio Ilarri[2],
María del Carmen Rodríguez-Hernández[2], Raquel Trillo-Lado[2],
and Yannis Velegrakis[3]

[1] Università di Modena e Reggio Emilia, Modena, Italy
71052@studenti.unimore.it, francesco.guerra@unimore.it
[2] University of Zaragoza, Zaragoza, Spain
{silarri,raqueltl}@unizar.es, mary0485@gmail.com
[3] University of Trento, Trento, Italy
velgias@disi.unitn.eu

Abstract. Predicting the next page a user wants to see in a large website has gained importance along the last decade due to the fact that the Web has become the main communication media between a wide set of entities and users. This is true in particular for institutional government and public organization websites, where for transparency reasons a lot of information has to be provided. The "long tail" phenomenon affects also this kind of websites and users need support for improving the effectiveness of their navigation. For this reason, complex models and approaches for recommending web pages that usually require to process personal user preferences have been proposed.

In this paper, we propose three different approaches to leverage information embedded in the structure of web sites and their logs to improve the effectiveness of web page recommendation by considering the context of the users, i.e., their current sessions when surfing a specific web site. This proposal does not require either information about the personal preferences of the users to be stored and processed or complex structures to be created and maintained. So, it can be easily incorporated to current large websites to facilitate the users' navigation experience. Experiments using a real-world website are described and analyzed to show the performance of the three approaches.

1 Introduction

A great amount of web sites, in particular the official web sites of Public Administrations and other Public Institution Bodies, are composed of a large number of web pages with a lot of information. These institutions are usually the creators of most of the content offered in their web pages (i.e., they are not simple information aggregators, but they are the providers of authoritative information). Therefore, a huge amount of visitors is interested in exploring and analyzing the information published on them. As an example, the ec.europa.eu and europa.eu

© Springer International Publishing Switzerland 2015
J. Cardoso et al. (Eds.): KEYWORD 2015, LNCS 9398, pp. 17–29, 2015.
DOI: 10.1007/978-3-319-27932-9_2

websites, managed by the European Commission, have been visited by more than $520M$ people in the last year[1].

The websites of Governments and Public Institutions typically offer large amounts of data which are usually organized in thematic categories and nested sections that generally form large trees with high height. In particular, the way in which the information is organized (i.e., the conceptualization of the website) can differ from what users are expecting when they navigate the website. Some techniques and best practices have been proposed and experimented for the design of a website. In some websites, for example, the information is grouped according to the topic. In other websites, the users are explicitly asked to declare their roles with respect to the website (e.g., in a university website the users can be asked to declare if they are students, faculty members, or companies, and according to this and the information provided when they enter in sections of the website, the information is structured in different ways). Nevertheless, due to the different conceptualizations and perspectives of users and publishers, visitors can spend a long time looking for information in which they are interested. Moreover, the "long tail" phenomenon[2] affects also the task of searching information in this kind of websites, where there are thousands of pages that can be accessed any time, independently of their publication date.

A number of approaches and techniques have dealt with the problem of designing websites to improve the users' experience. One of the solutions typically adopted is to include a search form in the header of the web pages to allow users to submit keyword queries representing their information needs. Another expedient to support users is to provide the pages with a little frame or a special web page with a list of "suggested links". The main disadvantage of the first approach is that it requires to maintain updated a complex indexed structure which must change when the web pages are modified (additions, removals, updates of content, etc.). With respect to the second approach, two trends have been identified: (1) showing the same content to all the users visiting the website at a specific moment, and (2) considering the profile of each user to offer him/her a personalized list of suggested links. Showing all users the same recommendations cannot be appropriate, as this type of web sites are oriented to a wide heterogeneous public, and what is interesting for a visitor can be useless for another. On the other hand, maintaining profiles of users implies that the users should be registered in the website, which also leads to the need to take into account complex and reliable procedures in order to securely maintain their personal information while respecting their privacy and legal issues.

In this paper, we propose to address the issue by introducing a recommender system for web pages to create a dynamic "suggested links" page which shows the possible interesting pages. Our recommender system takes into account:

– *The web pages that the user is visiting in the current session.* That is, the recommendation system works in real time and dynamically updates the links

---

[1] http://ec.europa.eu/ipg/services/statistics/performance_en.htm, statistics computed on June 1st, 2015.

[2] http://archive.wired.com/wired/archive/12.10/tail.html.

to propose to the user by taking into account the pages he/she is navigating. Moreover, the suggested links are updated after new pages are visited in a specific session.

- *Navigational paths (routes) of previous users.* By analyzing the website logs, we can discover the next pages visited by other users when they were in the same page as the current user. In particular, we consider that the users' navigation "sessions" extracted from the logs are sets of pages related to each other that satisfy the same information need. In fact, we assume that in a session the user is looking for something to satisfy a specific information need and that the session contains all the pages required for satisfying that need. In this way, the historical sessions can play the role of "suggestion spaces", as they include pages considered relevant in the same "context".
- *The website structure.* The structure of a web site follows a conceptual taxonomy that is exploited for the recommendation, by suggesting more specific or more general web pages than the current one.
- *Lexical and semantic knowledge about the pages.* The content of the pages is used in order to suggest pages with a similar content. The extraction of keywords/topics representing the content can be a huge and complex task for some websites. For this reason, we tried to exploit the URL as a means for approximating the content of the pages. This idea is based on the observation that in some particular web sites the URLs are highly explicative in the sense that they contain a lot of textual information about the pages and the categories the pages belong to. If this is the case for the website under analysis, we can exploit this information in order to make suggestions. It should be noted that the use of descriptive URLs is a usual recommendation for SEO (Search Engine Optimization); moreover, thanks to the use of descriptive URLs, end users can anticipate what they can expect from a web page.

In this paper, we propose three methods to make the recommendations: (1) No History method (NoHi), (2) My Own History method (MOHi), and (3) Collective History method (CoHi). The first method only considers the website structure and lexical and semantic knowledge of the pages. The second method additionally considers the information related to the pages that the user is visiting in the current session. Finally, the Collective History Method considers the same information as the two previous methods as well as navigational paths (routes) followed by previous visitors of the web site. Besides, the performance of the different methods is analyzed under different contexts by means of a wide set of experiments and considering the website of the Comune di Modena in Italy (http://www.comune.modena.it).

The rest of this paper is structured as follows. Firstly, some related work is studied and analyzed in Sect. 2. Secondly, the different proposals to recommend web pages in large web sites are presented in Sect. 3. After that, in Sect. 4 the results of a set of experiments to evaluate our proposals are presented. Finally, some conclusions and future work lines are depicted in Sect. 5.

2   Related Work

Some works tackle the problem of web page recommendation in a general context, aiming at providing the user with interesting web pages that could fit his/her interests (e.g., [1,2,11]). For example, [1,2] propose the use of a multiagent system to search interesting articles in the Web in order to compose a personalized newspaper. In [11,14], the idea is to estimate the suitability of a web page for a user based on its relevance according to the tags provided by similar users to annotate that page. The previous works do not explicitly consider the notion of user session, as their goal is just to recommend web pages to a user independently of his/her current navigation behavior within a specific web site, i.e., the current context of the user.

Other approaches, such as [3,5,6,13], explicitly exploit user sessions and therefore are more close in spirit to our proposal. The SurfLen system [5] suggests interesting web pages to users based on the sets of URLs that are read together by many users and on the similarity between users (users that read a significant number of similar pages). The proposal described in [6] tackles the recommendation problem within a single e-commerce website and proposes an approach to recommend product pages (corresponding to product records in the website database) as well as other web pages (news about the company, product reviews, advises, etc.); although the recommendation is based only on the web page that the user is currently visiting and not directly on the previous web pages visited by that user, user historical sessions are also exploited to extract information regarding the pages which are visited together (in one session). The approach presented in [3] is based on clustering user sessions and computing a similarity between user sessions in order to recommend three different pages that the user has not visited (a hit is considered if any of the three recommended pages is the next request of the user); the similarity between two user sessions is computed by considering the order of pages, the distance between identical pages, and the time spent on the pages. Another interesting proposal is introduced in [10], where the recommendation system is based on an ad-hoc ontology describing the website and on web usage information. The recommendation model PIGEON (PersonalIzed web paGe rEcommendatiON) [13] exploits collaborative filtering and a topic-aware Markov model to personalize web page recommendations: the recommendations are not just based on the sequence of pages visited but also on the interests of the users and the topics of the web pages.

There are also some proposals that generalize the problem of web page recommendation to that of web personalization (e.g., see [4,9]). The goal of web personalization is rather to compute a collection of relevant objects of different types to recommend [9], such as URLs, ads, texts, and products, and compose customized web pages. So, a website can be personalized by adapting its content and/or structure: adding new links, highlighting existing links, or creating new pages [4]. Interesting surveys on web mining for web personalization are also presented in [4] and in [7]. However, this kind of approaches require users to be registered in the web site and they need to create and maintain profiles for the different users.

As compared to the previous works, we aim at solving the problem of next URL recommendation within a single website and exploiting only a limited amount of information available in previous historical user logs. For example, we do not assume that information about the times spent by the users at each URL is available, which may be important to determine the actual interest of a web page (e.g., see [8,12]). Similarly, we do not assume that users can be identified (i.e., they are anonymous), and so it is not possible to extract user profiles. Instead, we propose several methods that require a minimum amount of information and evaluate and compare them in a real context. The methods proposed are also lightweight in the sense that they do not require a heavy (pre-)processing such as semantic extraction from the contents of web pages or the creation and maintenance of indexed structures such as inverted indexes on the content of the web pages.

3   Three Approaches for Recommending Web Pages

The goal of the different web page recommendation methods proposed in this paper is to provide a user with a suggested URL (available within a potentially-large website) by considering the context of the user (e.g., the URL that is currently visiting), information about the web site, and/or information available on the logs of the web servers where the web site is located. The content of the suggested URLs should be similar/related to the content offered by the web page that he/she is viewing at a specific moment, as it is assumed that the user behaves rationally and that the exploration performed by the user has a purpose (i.e., he/she is looking for information on a specific topic).

In this section, firstly, models and structures to represent the context of the user, and the content and structure of the web site, are presented. After that, three proposed methods (No History Method – NoHi, My Own History Method – MOHi, and Collective History Method – CoHi) to perform the recommendation are described in detail.

3.1   Representation of the User Context and the Web Site

By taking as inspiration different classic Information Retrieval (IR) models, a matrix where the rows represent the different URLs of the website being explored and the columns the vocabulary of those URLs (i.e., all the words that appear in the set of URLs) is used to model the content and the structure of the web site (see Fig 1). For example, if we consider the URL http://europa. eu/youreurope/citizens/travel/passenger-rights/index_en.htm of the official web site of the European Union, then the terms "your europe", "citizens", "travel", "passenger rights", "index" and "en" are part of the vocabulary of the URLs of the web site. In this way, the semantic and the lexical content of the web pages is indirectly considered, as it is supposed that the name of the web pages is not random and that the developers follow some kind of convention. Moreover, the structure of the web site is also taken into account, as the categories and nested

	F_1	F_2	F_3	...	F_m
P_1	W_{11}	W_{12}	W_{13}	...	W_{1m}
P_2	W_{21}	W_{22}	W_{23}	...	W_{2m}
P_3	W_{31}	W_{32}	W_{33}	...	W_{3m}
...	...	...	...	...	...
P_n	W_{n1}	W_{n2}	W_{n3}	...	W_{nm}

Fig. 1. Matrix representing a website.

sections used to organized the web site are usually reflected in the paths of the web pages.

The user's context is represented by the vector that represents the web page that he/she is currently visualizing, thus this vector is equal to the row corresponding to the URL of the web page in the matrix representing the web site (see Fig. 2).

$$\begin{bmatrix} W_{21} & W_{22} & W_{23} & ... & W_{2m} \end{bmatrix}$$

Fig. 2. User's context when he/she is visualizing the web page corresponding to the path P_2 of the web site, according to the matrix represented in Fig. 1.

To give a value to the different components of the vector representing the user context and the matrix representing the web site, classic Information Retrieval (IR) models are considered again as inspiration and the following configurations were analyzed:

- Binary configuration. This configuration is inspired by the Boolean IR model. Thus, each element in the matrix (or vector) indicates whether the URL considered (the row of the matrix or the vector representing the user context) contains (value 1) or does not contain (value 0) the keyword (the term) corresponding to the column of the matrix.
- Absolute-frequency configuration. This configuration is inspired by the earlier Vector Space IR models. Thus, each element in the matrix (or vector) indicates how many times the keyword corresponding to the column of the matrix appears in the URL considered (the row of the matrix or the vector representing the user context), i.e., the absolute frequency (or raw frequency) of the term in the URL. For example, if we consider the URL http://www.keystone-cost. eu/meeting/spring-wg-meeting-2015/ and the keyword "meeting" then the value of the element corresponding to the column of the term "meeting" is 2.

The absolute frequency of a term i in a URL j is usually represented by $f_{i,\,j}$. So, in this case $f_{meeting,\,www.keystone-cost.eu/meeting/spring-wg-meeting-2015/} = 2$.

- TF_IDF matrix. This configuration is inspired by more modern Vector Space IR models, where the length of the documents and the content of the corpus analyzed are considered. Thus, in this case, the length of the URLs and the vocabulary of the set of URLs of the website are considered to define the value of each element of the matrix. In more detail, each element in the matrix (or in each vector) is the product of the relative *Term Frequency* (*TF*) of the keyword corresponding to the column of the matrix in the URL considered (the row of the matrix) and the corresponding *Inverse Document Frequency* (*IDF*), i.e., the number of URLs in which that keyword appears. In more detail, $w_{ij} = TF_{ij} * IDF_i$ where

$$TF_{ij} = \frac{f_{i,\,j}}{maximum(f_{i,\,j})} \tag{1}$$

$$IDF_i = \log N/n_i \tag{2}$$

where N is the number of URLs of the website and n_i is the number of URLs where the term i appears.

Notice that the different models and structures proposed here can be used by the different methods described in the following.

3.2 Methods

Three different methods proposed to perform web page recommendation in large web sites are described and compared in the following:

- *No History method (NoHi).* In this method, only the current user context is considered, i.e., this method takes into account the information of the web page that the user is currently visualizing to make the recommendation but it does not consider the previous pages that the user has already visited in his/her current session. Thus, the pages recommended to the user are selected by computing the similarity between his/her current state represented by the vector of the URL of the web page visualized (see Fig. 2) and the remaining URLs of the website (the rows of the matrix representing the website in Fig. 1). The most similar URLs to the current user's state are recommended by using as measurement the cosine similarity. According to the literature, this method can be classified as a "content-based recommender system".

$$
\begin{aligned}
S_{k_{history}} = &\; P_1 \left[w_{11} \quad w_{12} \quad w_{13} \quad ... \quad w_{1m} \right] \oplus \\
&\; P_2 \left[w_{21} \quad w_{22} \quad w_{23} \quad ... \quad w_{2m} \right] \oplus \\
&\; ... \qquad\qquad\qquad\qquad\qquad\qquad \oplus \\
&\; P_k \left[w_{k1} \quad w_{k2} \quad w_{k3} \quad ... \quad w_{km} \right]
\end{aligned}
$$

Fig. 3. User historical context.

– *My Own History method (MOHi)*. In this method, the current web page visited by the user and also the web pages visited in his/her current session (i.e., his/her history) are considered to make the recommendation. Moreover, the number of pages previously visited taken into account can be limited to a certain number $K_{history}$, which is a configuration parameter of the system. In this case, the user context is modeled as the result of an aggregate function of the already-visited web pages. In this proposal, the sum of the vectors representing the web pages visited has been used. Nevertheless, any other aggregate function could be used, as for example a weighted sum (see Fig. 3). The recommendation is performed in an analogous way to the previous method (NoHi). Thus, the aggregated vector is compared with the URLs of the website (the rows of the matrix representing the web site in Fig. 1) and the most similar URLs are recommended. This method can also be classified as a "content-based recommender system".

– *Collective History method (CoHi)*. In this method, the history of the user in the current session is also considered. The history is modeled as a list where the items are the different URLs corresponding to the pages that the user has visited. Moreover, this method uses the previous sessions of other users to recommend the pages. The sessions of the other users are built by extracting information from the logs of the web server of the website and by considering the following rules:

• A session lasts at most 30 min.
• A session has to have at least 5 items (i.e., the user has to have visited at least 5 web pages of the website in a session).

In more detail, matrixes where rows represent the different sessions of the previous users of the website and columns the vocabulary of the URLs of the website are built in an analogous way to the previous methods (NoHi method and MOHi method). Aggregated vectors containing all the keywords of the URLs visited during the sessions of the users are built. Those aggregated vectors are built by a simple addition of all the weights of the vectors corresponding to the URLs of the resources visited during the session. Nevertheless, a weighted sum where for example, the URSLs visited initially have less importance than the URLs visited ate the end of the session could be applied. After that, the list that models the current session of the user is compared with the sessions of previous users and the top-k similar sessions are retrieved according to the cosine distance. Now, for suggesting the web pages from the top-k sessions we adopt a voting system based on a simple heuristic rule. In particular, we extract all the pages from the sessions and we weigh them according to the position of the session. The rule we follow is that the pages extracted from the top-1 session are weighted k times more than the ones in the k-th session retrieved. The weights in the web pages are then added up, thus generating their rank. Since it exploits the knowledge provided by the navigation of other users, this method can be classified as an "item-based collaborative filtering" recommendation system.

4   Experimental Evaluation

In this section, we present the experimental evaluation performed to evaluate the proposed methods for web page recommendation. First, in Sect. 4.1 we focus on the dataset used. Then, in Sect. 4.2 we describe the experimental settings. Finally, the results of the experimental evaluation are presented and analyzed in Sect. 4.3.

4.1   Dataset

The "Comune di Modena" Town Hall website[3] has been used in our experiments. This is the official website of an Italian city, having a population of 200000 citizens. The website visitors are mainly citizens looking for information about institutional services (schools, healthcare, labour and free time), local companies that want to know details about local regulations, and tourists interested in information about monuments, cultural events, accommodations and food. To understand the main features of the dataset, we performed two complementary analysis: firstly, we analyzed the website structure to evaluate the main features of the dataset independently of its actual exploitation by the users; then, we evaluated the users' behaviors in 2014 by analyzing the logs of the accesses. For achieving the first task, a crawler has been built and adapted for extracting some specific metadata (URL, outgoing links, creation date, etc.) describing the pages. A graph where the web pages are nodes and the links between them are direct edges has been built. The graph representation allowed us to apply a number of simple statistical and network analysis to obtain some details about the website. The results we obtained show that this is a large website composed of more than 13000 pages, classified into more than 30 thematic areas. The average in-degree and out-degree of the pages (i.e., the average number of incoming and outgoing links) is around 13. This value shows that pages are largely interconnected with each other. As a consequence, despite the large number of pages, the diameter of the website is small: in the worst case one page can reach another page following a path that crosses 8 other pages. Nevertheless, the average path length is 4.57.

This analysis was complemented by the analysis of the logs showing the real website usage by the users. In 2014, the number of sessions[4] computed was more than 2.5 millions. The average length of the session is 2.95 pages. Around 10000 pages (72.29 % of the overall number of pages) have been visited by at least one visitor in 2014. Only 2809 sessions (0.11 % of the overall number of sessions) include in their page the "search engine page" or do not follow the direct links provided in their pages. This demonstrates the quality of the structural design of the website.

---

[3] http://www.comune.modena.it.

[4] As described in Sect. 3.2, a session includes the pages which are visited by the same user, i.e., the same IP address and User-Agent, in 30 min.

4.2   Experimental Settings

In our experiments, we considered the logs from the website limiting our focus on sessions composed of at least 5 pages. The sessions satisfying this requirement are 303693, 11 % of the overall amount. The average length of these sessions is 7.5 pages. The vocabulary of terms used in our experiments is built by stemming the words (we adopted the usual Porter stemming algorithm) extracted from the URLs. The vocabulary is composed of 5437 terms representing single words. For improving the accuracy, we added 23555 terms to the previous set, by joining each two consecutive words in the URLs.

For evaluating the predictions, we divided the pages in a session in two parts: we considered the first 2/3 web pages in a session as representing the current user's navigation path (we called these pages as the *set of navigation history*), and the remaining 1/3 contains pages which we evaluated as good predictions (the *set of correct results*). Therefore, our approaches take for each session the set of navigation history as input and provide a recommended page. Only if the page is in set of correct results the result is considered as good.

The following configurations are also considered to decide the types of web pages that can be recommended:

- **No_Exclusion**. This is the general case where URLs that the user has already visited in the current session can also be suggested. Notice that, in this case, the URL where the user is in a specific moment can be also suggested, i.e., the suggestion in this case would be to stay in the same page and not to navigate to another one.
- **Exclusion**. URLs that the user has already visited in the current session cannot be suggested. In this way, the recommendation of staying in the same page is avoided. Moreover, with this configuration, navigating to a previously visited page or the home page of the website is never recommended, despite the fact that coming back to a specific web page already visited during a session is a typical pattern of the behavior of web users.
- **Sub_No_Exclusion**. The difference between this configuration and the one called Exclusion is that we consider only the sessions with no repeated web pages in the set of navigation history. This reduces the number of sessions used in the experiments to 107000. In this configuration, we aim at comparing the performance of our proposal with the one of a typical recommending system. These systems usually do not to recommend items already known/owned by the users. Nevertheless, in the context of websites it is normal that people navigate the same pages multiple times. For this reason in this configuration we consider only cases where in the navigation history there are no pages visited several times in the same sessions. The same constraint is not applied in the set of correct results where we can find pages which are also part of the navigation history (pages already visited).
- **Sub_With_Exclusion**. The difference between this configuration and the one called Sub_No_Exclusion is that here we remove sessions containing repeated web pages independently of their position in the session. In this case, we aim at perfectly simulating the behavior of a typical recommending system.

Note that, for the creation of the matrixes we did not exploited all the logs provided by the web server. Actually, logs are split into two groups (2/3 are used as training set, i.e., they are used to create the matrixes, and 1/3 is used as test set, i.e., they provide the sessions used to evaluate the performance of the method). In our experiments, the logs of the 20 first days of each month are considered as training sets while the logs of the last 10 days of each month are considered as test sets.

4.3   Results of the Experiments

Table 1 shows the accuracy of our three approaches computed according to the experimental setting defined in the previous section. In particular, Table 1(a) shows the accuracy obtained by the NoHi method, Table 1(b) the accuracy of the MOHi method and finally Table 1(b) the accuracy of CoHi method. Each column of the tables represents one of the configurations introduced in Sect. 3.1 for weighting the matrix that represents the pages visited by the users. In particular, the results applying absolute-frequency, binary, and TF_IDF configurations are shown, in the first, second and third column, respectively.

The experiments show that the accuracy of the methods NoHi and MOHi is only partially satisfactory. Moreover, considering the user history in MOHi introduces some noise except in the *No_Exclusion* configuration. Conversely, the accuracy obtained by the application of the CoHi method is good enough for a real application and in line with most of the existing recommender systems. In particular, all the experiments show that users typically need to visit the same pages several times, thus the better results obtained with the No_Exclusion settings. Moreover, considering only the sessions with no repeated web pages does not improve the results.

Finally, let us observe that evaluating a recommender system against logs is unfair. Doing it, we assume that the interesting pages for the users are only

Table 1. Accuracy achieved in the experiments.

(a) Accuracy on the NoHi method

Configuration	Abs. Freq	Binary	tf_idf
No_Exclusion	0.204	0.21	0.218
Exclusion	0.125	0.130	0.133
Sub_No_Exclusion	0.235	0.243	0.256
Sub_With_Exclusion	0.242	0.252	0.264

(b) Accuracy on the MOHi method

Configuration	Abs. Freq	Binary	tf_idf
No_Exclusion	0.397	0.417	0.467
Exclusion	0.095	0.101	0.101
Sub_No_Exclusion	0.178	0.186	0.194
Sub_With_Exclusion	0.172	0.186	0.188

(c) Accuracy on the CoHi method

Configuration	Abs. Freq	Binary	tf_idf
No_Exclusion	0.584	0.587	0.595
Exclusion	0.192	0.194	0.203
Sub_No_Exclusion	0.310	0.314	0.332
Sub_With_Exclusion	0.360	0.363	0.384

the ones that they have really visited. It would be similar to evaluating a recommender system that suggests products in an e-commerce system based only
on the actual purchases made by the users. Other products (web pages in our
case) can also be interesting for the users (and potentially suggested by our
approaches), even if they did not generate a real purchase (a visit in our case)
in the historical data available. Therefore, the results shown in Table 1 represent
the evaluation in the worst possible scenario.

5   Conclusions and Future Work

In this work, we have introduced two content-based recommendation systems
(the NoHi and MOHi methods) to suggest web pages to users in large web sites.
These methods base their recommendations on the structure of the URLs of
the website. In particular, they take into account the keywords included in the
website's URLs. Moreover, we have also presented the CoHi method, that we can
consider as a hybrid approach between two types of recommendation systems:
content-based recommendation and item-based collaborative filtering. This last
approach does not only consider the structure of the URLs, but it also considers
information provided by previous users (in particular, the sessions of previous
users).

The evaluation of the accuracy of the methods in a real scenario provided
by the analysis of the logs of the "Comune di Modena" website shows that the
approaches, in particular the last one, achieve a good performance level. Along
this work, we have assumed that if a user visits a page, he/she is interested in
the content of that page in the web site. However, it is possible that a user visits
a page for other reasons (the pages have been provided by a search engine but
they do not satisfy the user information need, the user has clicked on a wrong
link, etc.). So, analysis taking into account the amount of time the users spend
in the pages will be considered to filter data from the logs used to train and
valid the proposed methods.

Acknowledgement. The authors would like to acknowledge networking support by
the ICT COST Action IC1302 KEYSTONE - Semantic keyword-based search on structured data sources (www.keystone-cost.eu). We also thank the support of the CICYT
project TIN2013-46238-C4-4-R and DGA-FSE.

The authors would also thank the Rete Civica Mo-Net from the Comune di Modena
for having provided the data exploited in this research.

References

1. Balabanović, M.: Learning to surf: multiagent systems for adaptive web page recommendation. Ph.D. thesis, Stanford University, May 1998
2. Balabanović, M., Shoham, Y.: Fab: content-based, collaborative recommendation.
   Commun. ACM **40**(3), 66–72 (1997)

3. Gündüz, Ş., Özsu, M.T.: A web page prediction model based on click-stream tree representation of user behavior. In: Ninth ACM SIGKDD International Conference on Knowledge Discovery and Data Mining (KDD 2003), pp. 535–540. ACM (2003)
4. Eirinaki, M., Vazirgiannis, M.: Web mining for web personalization. ACM Trans. Internet Technol. **3**(1), 1–27 (2003)
5. Fu, X., Budzik, J., Hammond, K.J.: Mining navigation history for recommendation. In: Fifth International Conference on Intelligent User Interfaces (IUI 2000), pp. 106–112. ACM (2000)
6. Kazienko, P., Kiewra, M.: Integration of relational databases and web site content for product and page recommendation. In: International Database Engineering and Applications Symposium (IDEAS 2004), pp. 111–116, July 2004
7. Kosala, R., Blockeel, H.: Web mining research: a survey. SIGKDD Explor. **2**(1), 1–15 (2000)
8. Lieberman, H.: Letizia: an agent that assists web browsing. In: 14th International Joint Conference on Artificial Intelligence (IJCAI 1995), vol. 1, pp. 924–929. Morgan Kaufmann (1995)
9. Mobasher, B., Cooley, R., Srivastava, J.: Automatic personalization based on web usage mining. Commun. ACM **43**(8), 142–151 (2000)
10. Nguyen, T.T.S., Lu, H., Lu, J.: Web-page recommendation based on web usage and domain knowledge. IEEE Trans. Knowl. Data Eng. **26**(10), 2574–2587 (2014)
11. Peng, J., Zeng, D.: Topic-based web page recommendation using tags. In: IEEE International Conference on Intelligence and Security Informatics (ISI 2009), pp. 269–271, June 2009
12. Shahabi, C., Zarkesh, A.M., Adibi, J., Shah, V.: Knowledge discovery from users web-page navigation. In: Seventh International Workshop on Research Issues in Data Engineering (RIDE 1997), pp. 20–29. IEEE Computer Society, April 1997
13. Yang, Q., Fan, J., Wang, J., Zhou, L.: Personalizing web page recommendation via collaborative filtering and topic-aware markov model. In: 10th International Conference on Data Mining (ICDM 2010), pp. 1145–1150, December 2010
14. Zeng, D., Li, H.: How useful are tags? — An empirical analysis of collaborative tagging for web page recommendation. In: Yang, C.C., et al. (eds.) ISI Workshops 2008. LNCS, vol. 5075, pp. 320–330. Springer, Heidelberg (2008)

Processing Keyword Queries Under Access Limitations

Andrea Calì[1,4]([⊠]), Thomas W. Lynch[1,5,6], Davide Martinenghi[2],
and Riccardo Torlone[3]

[1] University of London, Birkbeck, UK
andrea@dcs.bbk.ac.uk
[2] Politecnico di Milano, Milano, Italy
davide.martinenghi@polimi.it
[3] Università Roma Tre, Rome, Italy
torlone@dia.uniroma3.it
[4] Oxford-Man Institute of Quantitative Finance,
University of Oxford, Oxford, UK
[5] Reasoning Technology Ltd, London, UK
thomas.lynch@reasoningtechnology.com
[6] Birkbeck University of London, London, UK

Abstract. The Deep Web is constituted by data accessible through web pages, but not readily indexable by search engines, as they are returned in dynamic pages. In this paper we propose a framework for accessing Deep Web sources, represented as relational tables with so-called access limitations, with keyword-based queries. We formalize the notion of optimal answer and investigate methods for query processing. We also outline the main ideas of our implementation of a prototype system for Deep Web keyword search.

1 Introduction

It is reasonable to assume that a user might want or need to query relational data with keywords – for instance, if he is accessing data whose structure he ignores; in this setting, the user is also free from having to know the query language. This idea has been around for over a decade [2] Since then, a vast corpus of research has been carried out in this field from the point of view of applications (see e.g. [7] for a survey). The problem has been recently formalized in [1], where a formal approach is provided, which is independent of the organization of data in tables.

In this paper we propose an approach to keyword search on so-called Deep Web sources. The Deep Web is constituted by data that are accessible only if queried through a web page, usually by filling in an HTML form. We represent

A preliminary version of this paper was published in the 9th Alberto Mendelzon Workshop on Foundations of Data Management, 2015, http://ceur-ws.org/Vol-1378.

J. Cardoso et al. (Eds.): KEYWORD 2015, LNCS 9398, pp. 30–35, 2015.
DOI: 10.1007/978-3-319-27932-9_3

Deep Web sources as relational tables; the necessity of filling in the aforementioned form with values forces one to access the relations with suitable selections; these restrictions are referred to as *access limitations*. It is well known that answering relational queries under access limitations requires the execution of a recursive query plan [3, 4]. This is also true in our setting, where a recursive extraction of tuples (or facts) is performed, according to the access limitations, so as to search for the keywords in the data.

Our main contributions are the following.

- We formally define the notion of keyword queries under access limitations, and the notion of answer (Sect. 2).
- We propose an algorithm for processing keyword queries under access limitations (Sect. 3).
- We discuss the computational complexity of our algorithm, showing that the problem of computing answers to keyword queries in our setting is tractable (Sect. 3).
- We outline the main features of a prototype system that processes keyword queries in the Deep Web (Sect. 4).

2   Problem Definition

Basics. We model data sources as relations of a relational database and we assume that, albeit autonomous, they have "compatible" attributes. For this, we assume that the attributes of relations are defined over a set of *abstract domains* $\mathbf{D} = \{D_1, \ldots, D_m\}$, which, rather than denoting concrete value types (such as string or integer), represent data types at a higher level of abstraction (for instance, *car* or *country*). The set of all values is denoted by $\mathcal{D} = \bigcup_{i=1}^{n} D_i$.

In the following, we shall denote by $R(A_1, \ldots, A_k)$ a (relation) schema, by $dom(A) \in \mathbf{D}$ the domain of an attribute A, by r a relation over R, and by $r = \{r_1, \ldots, r_n\}$ a (database) instance of a database schema $\mathbf{R} = \{R_1, \ldots, R_n\}$.

Access Limitations. An *access pattern* Π for a schema $R(A_1, \ldots, A_k)$ is a mapping sending each attribute A_i into an *access mode*, which can be either input or output; A_i is correspondingly called an *input* (resp., *output*) *attribute* for R wrt. Π. For ease of notation, we shall mark input attributes with an 'i' superscript to distinguish them from the output ones. Let $A'_1, \ldots, A'_l$ be all the input attributes for R wrt. Π; any tuple $\langle c_1, \ldots, c_l \rangle$ such that $c_i \in dom(A'_i)$ for $1 \leq i \leq l$ is called a *binding* for R wrt. Π. An *access* α consists of an access pattern Π for a schema R and a binding for R wrt. Π; the *output* of such an access α on an instance r is the set $\mathcal{T} = \sigma_{A_1=c_1,\ldots,A_l=c_l}(r)$. Intuitively, we can only access a relation if we can provide a value for every input attribute. Given an instance r for a database schema $\mathbf{R}$, a set of access patterns Π for the relations in $\mathbf{R}$, and a set of values $\mathcal{C} \subseteq \mathcal{D}$, an *access path* (for $\mathbf{R}$, Π and $\mathcal{C}$) is a sequence of accesses $\alpha_1, \ldots, \alpha_n$ on r such that each value in the binding of α_i, $1 \leq i \leq n$, either occurs in the output of an access α_j with $j < i$ or is a value in $\mathcal{C}$. A tuple t in r is said to be *reachable* if there exists an access path P such that t is in the output of some

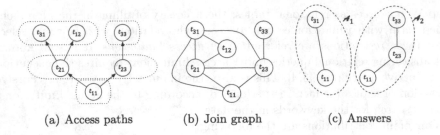

(a) Access paths   (b) Join graph   (c) Answers

Fig. 1. Example 1: Reachable portion, corresponding join graph, and answers.

access in P; the *reachable portion* $reach(r, \Pi, \mathcal{C})$ of r is the set of all reachable tuples in r given the values in $\mathcal{C}$.

Keyword Queries. A *keyword query* is a set of values in $\mathcal{D}$ called *keywords*.

Example 1. Consider a query $q = \{k_1, k_2\}$, a schema (with access patterns Π) $\mathbf{R} = \{R_1(A_1^i, A_2), R_2(A_2^i, A_1), R_3(A_1^i, A_2, A_3)\}$, and an instance r such that

$$r_1 = \begin{array}{|cc|c} A_1^i & A_2 & \\ \hline k_1 & c_1 & t_{11} \\ c_2 & c_3 & t_{12} \end{array} \quad r_2 = \begin{array}{|cc|c} A_2^i & A_1 & \\ \hline c_1 & c_2 & t_{21} \\ c_4 & c_2 & t_{22} \\ c_1 & c_6 & t_{23} \end{array} \quad r_3 = \begin{array}{|ccc|c} A_1^i & A_2 & A_3 & \\ \hline c_2 & c_1 & k_2 & t_{31} \\ c_5 & c_4 & k_2 & t_{32} \\ c_6 & c_7 & k_2 & t_{33} \end{array}$$

Figure 1(a) shows the reachable portion of r given the values in q along with the access paths used to extract it, with dotted lines enclosing outputs of accesses. ∎

Given a set $\mathcal{T}$ of tuples, the *join graph* of $\mathcal{T}$ is a node-labelled undirected graph $\mathcal{T} = \langle N, E \rangle$ constructed as follows: *(i)* the nodes N are labelled with tuples of $\mathcal{T}$, and *(ii)* there is an arc between two nodes n_1 and n_2 if the tuples labelling n_1 and n_2 have at least one value in common.

Example 2 (cont.). The join graph of $reach(r, \Pi, q)$ is shown in Fig. 1(b). ∎

Definition 1 (Answer). *An answer to a keyword query q against a database instance r over a schema $\mathbf{R}$ with access patterns Π is a set of tuples $\mathcal{A}$ in $reach(r, \Pi, q)$ such that: (1) each $c \in q$ occurs in at least one tuple t in $\mathcal{A}$; (2) the join graph of $\mathcal{A}$ is connected; (3) for every subset $\mathcal{A}' \subseteq \mathcal{A}$ such that $\mathcal{A}'$ enjoys Condition 1 above, the join graph of $\mathcal{A}'$ is not connected.*

It is straightforward to see that there could be several answers to a keyword query; below we give a widely accepted criterium for ranking such answers [7].

Definition 2. *Let $\mathcal{A}_1, \mathcal{A}_2$ be two answers of a keyword query q on an instance r of size $|\mathcal{A}_1|$ and $|\mathcal{A}_2|$ respectively; we say that $\mathcal{A}_1$ is better than $\mathcal{A}_2$, denoted $\mathcal{A}_1 \preceq \mathcal{A}_2$, if $|\mathcal{A}_1| \leq |\mathcal{A}_2|$. The* optimal *answers are those of minimum size.*

Example 3 (cont.). The sets $\mathcal{A}_1 = \{t_{11}, t_{31}\}$ and $\mathcal{A}_2 = \{t_{11}, t_{23}, t_{33}\}$ are answers to q; $\mathcal{A}_1$ is better than $\mathcal{A}_2$ and is the optimal answer to q. ∎

3   Keyword-Based Answering in the Deep Web

We now present a vanilla algorithm to discuss the computational complexity of answering a keyword query q in the deep Web modeled as an instance r of a schema $\mathbf{R}$ with access patterns Π. Example 1 shows that, in the worst case, we need to extract the whole reachable portion to obtain the tuples involved in an optimal answer. In fact, $s = reach(r, \Pi, q)$ is actually a connected join graph, since every tuple in it is in some output of some access path starting from the values in the query (see for example Fig. 1a), but further paths may exist between tuples in s (see Fig. 1b). Therefore, query answering requires in general two main steps, described in Algorithm 1: *(i)* item extract the reachable portion s of r; *(ii)* if possible, remove tuples from s so that the obtained set satisfies the conditions of Definition 1, while minimizing its size.

Algorithm 1. Computing an optimal answer ($Answer(q, \Pi, r)$)

Input: *Keyword query q, access patterns Π, instance r over $\mathbf{R}$*
Output: *Answer $\mathcal{A}$*
  1. $\mathcal{A} := reachablePortion(r, \Pi, q)$; // see Algorithm 2
  2. **if** $\mathcal{A}$ does not contain all values in q **then return** nil;
  3. **else** $prune(\mathcal{A}, q)$; // see Algorithm 3
  4. **return** $\mathcal{A}$;

A simple way of extracting the reachable portion, inspired by the procedure described in [3], is shown in Algorithm 2. This algorithm may be allowed to terminate early if the answer is not required to be optimal (flag ω set to *false*), and thus can stop as soon as the reachable portion contains all the keywords in the query. This is coherent with the *distinct root-based semantics* of keyword search in relational databases, which provides a tradeoff between quality of the result and efficiency of the method to evaluate it [7].

Algorithm 2. Reachable portion ($reachablePortion(r, \Pi, q)$)

Input: *Instance r over $\mathbf{R}$, access patterns Π, initial values q*
Flag: *boolean ω // if $\omega = true$ the answer is guaranteed to be optimal*
Output: *Reachable portion RP*
  1. $RP := \emptyset; \mathcal{C} := \emptyset$;
  2. **while** an access can be made with a new binding b for some $R \in \mathbf{R}$ wrt. Π using values in $\mathcal{C} \cup q$
  3. $\quad \mathcal{O} :=$ output of access to r over R with binding b;
  4. $\quad RP := RP \cup \mathcal{O}$; // cumulating all the obtained tuples into RP
  5. $\quad \mathcal{C} := \mathcal{C} \cup \bigcup_{A \in R, t \in \mathcal{O}} \{t(A)\}$; // cumulating all the obtained values into $\mathcal{C}$
  6. $\quad$ **if** $\mathcal{C} \supseteq q \wedge \neg\omega$ **then break**;
  7. **return** RP;

Basically, determining an optimal answer from the reachable portion corresponds to finding a Steiner tree of its join graph [7], i.e., a minimal-weight subtree of this graph involving a subset of its nodes. An efficient method for solving this problem in the context of keyword search over structured data is presented in [5], where a *q-fragment* can model our notion of answer. Yet, when optimality is not required, a simple technique (quadratic in the size of r) to obtain an answer (steps 2–6 of Algorithm 3) consists in trying to remove any tuple from the set as long as it contains all the keywords and remains connected.

Algorithm 3. Pruning $(prune(\mathcal{T}, q))$

Input: *Set of tuples $\mathcal{T}$, keyword query q*
Flag: *boolean ω // if ω = true the answer is guaranteed to be optimal*
Output: *Minimal set of tuples $\mathcal{T}$*
  1. **if** ω **then return** a minimal subtree of the join graph of $\mathcal{T}$ that contains q;
  2. $\mathcal{T}' := \mathcal{T}; \mathcal{T}'' := \emptyset$;
  3. **while** $\mathcal{T}'' \neq \mathcal{T}'$
  4. $\mathcal{T}'' := \mathcal{T}'$;
  5.   **for each** $t \in \mathcal{T}''$ **if** $\mathcal{T}' \setminus \{t\}$ is connected and $\mathcal{T}' \setminus \{t\} \supseteq q$ **then** $\mathcal{T}' := \mathcal{T}' \setminus \{t\}$;
  6. **return** $\mathcal{T}'$;

The extraction of the reachable portion of an instance r with access limitations can be implemented by a Datalog program over r [3], which can be evaluated in polynomial time in the size of the input [6]. In addition, in [5] it is shown that the optimal q-fragments of r can be enumerated in ranked-order with polynomial delay, i.e., the time for printing the next optimal answer is again polynomial in the size of r. Hence, we can state the following preliminary result.

Theorem 1. *An optimal answer to a keyword query against a database instance with access limitations can be efficiently computed under data complexity.*

4 Implementation

We have implemented a prototype version of a system for processing keyword queries over a set of Deep Web sources. Given the nature of the search, we extract data on-the-fly and store them in main memory, conveniently represented in graph format. The keyword search algorithms are run on the extracted data in main memory rather than in a DBMS; the nature of keyword query processing in this setting suggests that relying on a relational DBMS does not provide any significant advantage.

The system is based on an underlying relational layer of Deep Web data called *Dataplex*[1]. The Dataplex framework was developed in Racket, a language of the Lisp/Scheme family. In Dataplex, the only field type is text (string), and tables are seen as containers with interface methods. The main idea behind Dataplex is that facts can have *lists* as arguments; facts belong to *shapes*, that are the equivalent of single-relation schemata. A shape is created with the call

---

[1] http://thomaswlynch.com/liquid/liquid-doc/liquid/doc/liquid/index.html.

`(dataplex:create-shape `*`name length`*`)`

and a tuple can be placed into the created container by

`(shape:insert `*`name value_list`*`).`

Notice that in Dataplex data are stored, logically speaking, in two structures: one that holds the values, and the other that bridges references to these values; indices are used to improve performances in the accesses to data in Dataplex.

We are currently running experiments on keyword search by using the Dataplex framework, which we will publish soon. As it is natural to predict, the bottleneck in the efficiency of query processing is the extraction of data from the sources.

5   Discussion and Future Work

In this paper we provided preliminary insights on keyword search in the Deep Web. As future work on the problem, we plan to:

- devise optimization strategies for query answering; in particular, identify conditions under which an optimal answer can be derived without extracting the whole reachable instance;
- leverage known values (besides the keywords), modeled as relations with only one (output) attribute, to speed up the search for an optimal answer;
- study the problem in a scenario in which the domains of the keywords are known in advance: in this case schema-based techniques can be used;
- consider the case in which nodes and arcs of the join graph are weighed to model source availability and proximity, respectively.

Acknowledgments. Andrea Calì and Thomas Lynch acknowledge support by the EPSRC grant "Logic-based Integration and Querying of Unindexed Data" (EP/E010865/1).

References

1. Torlone, R.: Towards a new foundation for keyword search in relational databases. In: AMW (2014)
2. Hristidis, V., Papakonstantinou, Y.: DISCOVER: keyword search in relational databases. In: VLDB, pp. 670–681 (2002)
3. Calì, A., Martinenghi, D.: Querying data under access limitations. In: ICDE, pp. 50–59 (2008)
4. Li, C., Chang, E.Y.: Answering queries with useful bindings. ACM Trans. Database Syst. **26**(3), 313–343 (2001)
5. Kimelfeld, B., Sagiv, Y.: Finding and approximating top-k answers in keyword proximity search. In: PODS, pp. 173–182 (2006)
6. Vardi, M.: The complexity of relational query languages. In: STOC, pp. 137–146 (1982)
7. Xu Yu, J., Qin, L., Chang, L.: Search in relational databases: a survey. IEEE Data Eng. Bull. **33**(1), 67–78 (2010)

Balanced Large Scale Knowledge Matching Using LSH Forest

Michael Cochez[1]([⊠]), Vagan Terziyan[1], and Vadim Ermolayev[2]

[1] Department of Mathematical Information Technology, University of Jyväskylä,
P.O. Box 35(Agora), 40014 University of Jyväskylä, Finland
{michael.cochez,vagan.terziyan}@jyu.fi
[2] Department of IT, Zaporozhye National University, 66, Zhukovskogo Street,
Zaporozhye 69063, Ukraine
vadim@ermolayev.com

Abstract. Evolving Knowledge Ecosystems were proposed recently to approach the Big Data challenge, following the hypothesis that knowledge evolves in a way similar to biological systems. Therefore, the inner working of the knowledge ecosystem can be spotted from natural evolution. An evolving knowledge ecosystem consists of Knowledge Organisms, which form a representation of the knowledge, and the environment in which they reside. The environment consists of contexts, which are composed of so-called knowledge tokens. These tokens are ontological fragments extracted from information tokens, in turn, which originate from the streams of information flowing into the ecosystem. In this article we investigate the use of LSH Forest (a self-tuning indexing schema based on locality-sensitive hashing) for solving the problem of placing new knowledge tokens in the right contexts of the environment. We argue and show experimentally that LSH Forest possesses required properties and could be used for large distributed set-ups.

Keywords: Evolving knowledge ecosystems · Locality-sensitive hashing · LSH forest · Big data

1 Introduction

Perhaps, one of the biggest problems in making the Semantic Web a reality is that knowledge it represents is not evolving in line with the world it describes. This problem becomes even more challenging given the explosion in the volumes, complexity, variety of the information available about the world, and the velocity of its change. Recently a conceptual approach to attack this challenging problem has been proposed [1]. The core of that proposal is the understanding that the mechanisms of knowledge evolution could be spotted from evolutionary biology. These mechanisms are enabled in an *Evolving Knowledge Ecosystem* (EKE) populated with *Knowledge Organisms* (KO). Individual KOs carry their fragments of knowledge — similarly to different people having their individual and potentially dissimilar perceptions and understanding of their environment.

© Springer International Publishing Switzerland 2015
J. Cardoso et al. (Eds.): KEYWORD 2015, LNCS 9398, pp. 36–50, 2015.
DOI: 10.1007/978-3-319-27932-9_4

The population of KOs, like a human society, possesses the entire knowledge representation of the world, or more realistically — a subject domain. Information tokens flow into such an ecosystem, are further transformed into the knowledge tokens, and finally sown there. The KOs collect the available knowledge tokens and consume these as nutrition. Remarkably, the constitution of an EKE, allows natural scaling in a straightforward way. Indeed, the fragment of knowledge owned by an individual KO and the knowledge tokens consumed by KOs are small. Therefore, a well scalable method of sowing the knowledge tokens is under demand to complete a scalable knowledge feeding pipeline into the ecosystem. This paper reports on the implementation and evaluation of our knowledge token sowing solution based on the use of LSH Forest [2]. We demonstrate that: (i) the method scales very well for the volumes characteristic to big data processing scenarios; and (ii) yields results with sufficiently good precision and recall. The rest of the paper is structured as follows. Section 2 sketches out the concept of EKE and also explains how knowledge tokens are sown in the environments. Section 3 presents the basic formalism of Locality Sensitive hashing (LSH) and LSH Forest. Finally, it outlines our arguments for using LSH Forest as an appropriate method. Section 4 describes the settings for our computational experiments whose results are presented in Sect. 5. The paper is concluded and plans for future work are outlined in Sect. 6.

2   Big Knowledge — Evolving Knowledge Ecosystems

Humans make different decisions in similar situations, thus taking different courses in their lives. This is largely due to the differences in their knowledge. So, the evolution of conscious beings noticeably depends on the knowledge they possess. On the other hand, making a choice triggers the emergence of new knowledge. Therefore, it is natural to assume that knowledge evolves because of the evolution of humans, their decision-making needs, their value systems, and the decisions made. Hence, knowledge evolves to support the intellectual activity of its owners, e.g., to interpret the information generated in event observations — handling the diversity and complexity of such information. Consequently, Ermolayev et al. [1] hypothesize that the mechanisms of knowledge evolution are very similar to (and could be spotted from) the mechanisms of the evolution of humans. Apart from the societal aspects, these are appropriately described using the metaphor of biological evolution.

A biological habitat is in fact an ecosystem that frames out and enables the evolution of individual organisms, including humans. Similarly, a knowledge ecosystem has to be introduced for enabling and managing the evolution of knowledge. As proposed in [1], such EKE should scale adequately to cope with realistic and increasing characteristics of data/information to be processed and balance the efficiency and effectiveness while extracting knowledge from information and triggering the changes in the available knowledge.

2.1   Efficiency Versus Effectiveness

Effectiveness and efficiency are the important keys for big data processing and for the big knowledge extraction. Extracting knowledge out of big data would be effective only if: (i) not a single important fact is left unattended (completeness); and (ii) these facts are faceted adequately for further inference (expressiveness and granularity). Efficiency in this context may be interpreted as the ratio of the utility of the result to the effort spent.

In big knowledge extraction, efficiency could be naturally mapped to timeliness. If a result is not timely the utility of the resulting knowledge will drop. Further, it is apparent that increasing effectiveness means incrementing the effort spent on extracting knowledge, which negatively affects efficiency. In other words, if we would like to make a deeper analysis of the data we will have a less efficient system.

Finding a solution, which is balanced regarding these clashes, is challenging. In this paper we use a highly scalable method to collect the increments of incoming knowledge using a 3F+3Co approach, which stand for Focusing, Filtering, and Forgetting + Contextualizing, Compressing, and Connecting (c.f. [1] and Sect. 3.2).

2.2   Evolving Knowledge Ecosystems

An environmental context for a KO could be thought of as its habitat. Such a context needs to provide nutrition that is "healthy" for particular KO species — i.e. matching their genome noticeably. The nutrition is provided by Knowledge Extraction and Contextualization functionality of the ecosystem [1] in a form of *knowledge tokens*. Hence, several and possibly overlapping environmental contexts need to be regarded in a hierarchy which corresponds to several subject domains of interest and a foundational knowledge layer. Environmental contexts are sowed with knowledge tokens that correspond to their subject domains. It is useful to limit the lifetime of a knowledge token in an environment – those which are not consumed dissolve finally when their lifetime ends. KOs use their perceptive ability to find and consume knowledge tokens for nutrition. Knowledge tokens that only partially match KOs' genome may cause both KO body and genome changes and are thought of as mutagens. Mutagens in fact deliver the information about the changes in the world to the environment. Knowledge tokens are extracted from the information tokens either in a stream window, or from the updates of the persistent data storage and further sown in the appropriate environmental context. The context for placing a newly coming knowledge token is chosen by the contextualization functionality. In this paper we present a scalable solution for sowing these knowledge tokens in the appropriate environmental contexts.

3   Locality-Sensitive Hashing

The algorithms for finding nearest neighbors in a dataset were advanced in the work by Indyk and Motwani, who presented the seminal work on Locality-sensitive hashing (LSH) [3]. They relaxed the notion of a nearest neighbor to that of an approximate one, allowing for a manageable error in the found neighbors. Thanks to this relaxation, they were able to design a method which can handle queries in sub-linear time. To use LSH, one has to create a database containing outcomes of specific hash functions. These hash functions have to be independent and likely to give the same outcome when hashed objects are similar and likely to give different outcomes when they are dissimilar. Once this database is built one can query for nearest neighbors of a given query point by hashing it with the same hash functions. The points returned as approximate near neighbors are the objects in the database which got hashed to the same buckets as the query point. [4] If false positives are not acceptable, one can still filter these points.

Formally, to apply LSH we construct a family $\mathcal{H}$ of hash functions which map from a space $\mathcal{D}$ to a universe $\mathcal{U}$.

Let $d_1 < d_2$ be distances according to a distance measure d on a space $\mathcal{D}$. The family $\mathcal{H}$ is (d_1, d_2, p_1, p_2)-sensitive if for any two points $p, q \in \mathcal{D}$ and $h \in \mathcal{H}$:

- if $d(p, q) \leq d_1$ then $\Pr[h(p) = h(q)] \geq p_1$
- if $d(p, q) \geq d_2$ then $\Pr[h(p) = h(q)] \leq p_2$

where $p1 > p2$.

The probabilities p_1 and p_2 might be close to each other and hence only one function from $\mathcal{H}$ giving an equal result for two pints might not be sufficient to trust that these points are similar. Amplification is used to remedy this problem. This is achieved by creating b functions g_j, each consisting of r hash functions chosen uniformly at random from $\mathcal{H}$. The function g_j is the concatenation of r independent basic hash functions. The symbols b and r stand for *bands* and *rows*. These terms come from the representation of data. One could collect all outcomes of the hash functions in a two-dimensional table. This table can be divided in b bands containing r rows each. (See also [5].) The concatenated hash function g_j maps points p and q to the same bucket if all hash functions it is constructed from hashes the points to the same buckets. If for any j, the function g_j maps p and q to the same bucket, p and q are considered close. The amplification creates a new locality sensitive family which is $\left(d_1, d_2, 1 - (1 - p_1{}^r)^b, 1 - (1 - p_2{}^r)^b\right)$ sensitive.

3.1 LSH Forest

The standard LSH algorithm is somewhat wasteful with regards to the amount of memory is uses. Objects always get hashed to a fixed length band, even if that is not strictly needed to decide whether points are approximate near neighbors. LSH Forest (introduced by Bawa et al. [2]) introduces variable length bands and stores the outcomes of the hashing in a prefix tree data structure.

The length of the band is reduced by only computing the hash functions if there is more than one point which is hashed to the same values. Put another way, in LSH the function g_j maps two points to the same bucket if all functions it is constructed from do so as well. LSH Forest potentially reduces the number of evaluations by only computing that much of g_j as needed to distinct between the different objects. Alternatively, one can view this as assigning a unique label with a dynamic length to each point. In the prefix tree the labels on the edges are the values of the sub-hash functions of g_j.

Hashing and quantization techniques have a limitation when considering very close points. If points are arbitrarily close to each other, then there is no number of hash functions which can tell them apart. This limitation applies to both traditional LSH and the Forest variant. Therefore, LSH assumes a minimum distance between any two points and LSH Forest defines a maximum label length equal to the maximum height of the tree (indicated as k_m).

3.2   Sowing Knowledge Tokens Using LSH Forest

The first requirement for knowledge token sowing is that similar tokens get sown close to each other. This is achieved by adding knowledge tokens to the forest. Similar ones will get placed such that they are more likely to show up when the trees are queried for such tokens. Further requirements come from the 3F+3Co [1] aspects. When using LSH Forest:

Focusing is achieved by avoiding deep analysis when there are no similar elements added to the trees.

Filtering is done by just not adding certain data to the tree.

Forgetting is achieved by removing data from the tree. Removal is supported by the Forest and is an efficient operation.

Contextualizing happens when different parts of the token are spread over the trees. A token may therefore belong to several contexts simultaneously.

Compressing the tree compresses data in two different ways. Firstly, it only stores the hashes computed from the original data and, secondly, common prefixes are not duplicated but re-used. Note that it is possible to store the actual data on a secondary storage and keep only the index in memory.

Connecting the Forest is a body which grows incrementally. Since representations of different tokens can reside together in disparate parts of the trees, they can be considered connected. However, the real connection of these parts will be the task of the KOs which will consume the knowledge tokens which are sown in a tree.

In the next section we will introduce our experiments. In the first experiment series we show that the Forest is able to fulfill the *focusing* requirement. The second one shows that the forest is able to aid the KO to *connect* concepts together. Finally, the last series shows that the data structure has desirable spacial and temporal properties, demonstrating that the tree is able to *compress* data meanwhile offering an appropriate efficiency — effectiveness trade-off.

4   Evaluation

The experiments are designed so that we start from a fairly simple set-up and more complexity is added in each following experiment. In the first series of experiments, we feed knowledge tokens created from three different data sources into an LSH tree and present measure how they are spread over the tree. In the following series, we use two and later three data sources and measure how the LSH Forest classifies the tokens and how it is capable of connecting the knowledge tokens. Finally, in the third series we add dynamism to the experiment by sampling the knowledge tokens in different ways and measure how the memory usage and processing time evolve.

Finding a suitable dataset for the experiment is not obvious. What we need are small pieces of information (i.e., the knowledge tokens) about which we know how they should be connected (i.e., a gold standard). Further, the dataset should be sufficiently large to conduct the experiments. We solved this issue by selecting three large ontologies for which a so-called alignment [6] has been created. These particular ontologies are large and have a fairly simple structure. Further,by using only the labels of the ontology a reasonable alignment can be found [7]. Therefore, we extract the labels from these ontologies and use them as knowledge tokens. This is a relaxation of the knowledge token concept. In the earlier work [1] a knowledge token has an internal structure. Finally, similar to the earlier work, we use the Jaccard distance for sets ($d\left(A,B\right) = 1 - sim\left(A,B\right)$) to measure the distance between sets of words created from the labels. The LSH function used is Minhash from Broder [8].

Datasets. The *Large Biomed Track* of the Ontology Alignment Evaluation initiative[1] is the source of the datasets used in our evaluation. The FMA ontology[2], which contains 78,989 classes is the first dataset. The FMA ontology only contains classes and non-hierarchical datatype properties, i.e., no object or datatype properties nor instances. Secondly, there is the NCI ontology[3] containing 66,724 classes, and finally a fragment of 122,464 classes of the SNOMED ontology[4]. The NCI ontology contains classes, non-hierarchical datatype and hierarchical object properties. The classes of all ontologies are structured in a tree using *owl:SubClassOf* relations. The UMLS-based reference alignments as prepared for OAEI[5] are used as a gold standard. From these reference alignments we only retain the equal correspondences, with the confidence levels set to one.

Preprocessing. We preprocess the ontologies by computing as many representations for each class as it has labels in the ontology. The preprocessing is very similar to the second strategy proposed in [7]. According to this strategy, for each label of each class, a set of strings is created as follows: the label is converted to lowercase and then split in strings using all the whitespace and punctuation marks as a delimiter. If this splitting created strings of 1 character, they are

---

[1] http://www.cs.ox.ac.uk/isg/projects/SEALS/oaei/2013/.

[2] http://sig.biostr.washington.edu/projects/fm/.

[3] http://www.obofoundry.org/cgi-bin/detail.cgi?id=ncithesaurus.

[4] http://www.ihtsdo.org/index.php?id=545.

[5] http://www.cs.ox.ac.uk/isg/projects/SEALS/oaei/2013/oaei2013_umls_reference.
html.

concatenated with the string that came before it. In addition to these steps, we also removed possessive suffixes from the substrings and removed the 20 most common English language words according to the Oxford English Dictionary[6]. This preprocessing results in 133628, 175698, and 122505 knowledge tokens, i.e., sets of strings for the FMA, NCI, and SNOMED ontology, respectively.

Implementation. The implementation of our evaluation code heavily uses parallelism to speed up the computation. From the description of the LSH algorithm, it can be noticed that the hashing of the objects happens independent of each other. Therefore they can be computed in parallel using a multi-core system.

Inspired by Rajaraman and Ullman [5], 'normal' uniform hashing was used several times to speed up computations or save storage space. One important saving is due to using random (non locality-sensitive) hash functions, which map each original index to a target index, instead of creating real permutations. This hashing is performed using Rabin fingerprints as described by Broder [9]. An improvement over the earlier work [7] where Rabin hashing was also used is due to the fact that we invert the bits of the input to the hashing function. We noticed that small inputs gave a fairly high number of collisions using the functions normally, while the inverted versions do hardly cause any. The experiments are performed on hardware with two Intel Xeon E5-2670 processors (totaling 16 hyper-threaded cores) and limited to use a maximum of 16 GB RAM.

4.1   Single Data Source — Single Tree

In this series of experiments, we use only one LSH tree and knowledge tokens from a single dataset. First, the ontology is parsed and all its concepts are tokenized as described above. The resulting knowledge tokens are then fed into the LSH tree. We then analyze the distribution of the knowledge tokens in the tree by looking at how deep they are located in the tree and how many siblings the leaves in the tree have. Further, we investigate chains of nodes which are only there because of a low number of tokens at the bottom of the tree.

4.2   Connecting Knowledge Tokens Using LSH Forest, i.e. Matching

The objective of our the first experiment in this second series is to show how the ontology matching using LSH Forest compares to standard LSH. Besides the change in data structure we use the experimental set-up similar to what was used for testing standard LSH in our earlier research work [7]. In that work the best result for matching the SNOMED and NCI ontologies was obtained using 1 band of 480 rows which corresponds to 1 tree of maximum height $k_m = 480$. To keep the results comparable, we also do not use the reduced collision effect from inverting before hashing (see **Implementation** above). It needs to be noted, however, that we use a slightly different approach for selecting near neighbors

---

[6] http://www.oxforddictionaries.com/words/the-oec-facts-about-the-language.

compared to the standard LSH Forest approximate nearest neighbor querying. Since we are not interested in neighbors if they are to far away, we only take the siblings of each leaf into account when searching for related concepts. Further, we ignore concepts if they their similarity is less than 0.8. Next to the traditional ontology matching measures of precision, recall, and F-measure, the potential memory and processing power savings are evaluated.

In the second part of this series we use our improved version, applying the inversion before hashing, and the knowledge from the previous experiments to test how LSH Forest can perform when connecting knowledge tokens using a shorter tree. We measure both runtime performance and quality metrics for different number of trees.

In the last part we use the fact that there is no reason to limit ourselves to only using two data sources. Hence, we demonstrate scalability of the system by feeding all knowledge tokens created for all three datasets. We also analyze the time saving compared to performing three separate alignment tasks when pairs of datasets are used.

4.3   Adding Dynamics

In the final series of experiments we observe how the tree reacts to dynamic insertion of concepts. In the basic case, we select 10^6 knowledge tokens (from the three sets) using a uniform distribution. These are then one by one inserted into the tree. After every 10^4 insertions we measure number of hash operations used to measure the time complexity. The cumulative memory consumption is measured as the number of edges used in the trees. We also measure the real elapsed time after the insertion of every 10^5 knowledge tokens.

On an average system some knowledge tokens will be added much more frequently than others. This is due to the fact that the information or queries which the system processes are somehow focused on a certain domain. This also means that the tokens would not arrive according to a uniform distribution. A more plausible scenario is that certain concepts are very likely to occur, while others do hardly occur at all. We model this phenomena by using a so-called Zipf distribution with exponent 1 which causes few concepts to be inserted frequently while most are inserted seldom. Using this set-up we perform the same measurements as made for the uniform distribution.

It has to be noted that we need to make a minor change to the way our trees process the tokens. When a token already exists at a node, the standard implementation would build a chain which can only end at k_m. This is related to our above remark about the minimal distance between any two points. To solve this problem, the lowest internal nodes check whether the newly added representation is already existing and if so, it will ignore the representation. We shortly analyzed the effect of this change using the same set-up as in the second experiment series and noticed that this check does hardly affect runtime performance. The main effect is visible in the number of edges and hash operations which both drop by about 30 %. Further, a marginal decrease of the precision and a marginal increase of the recall is observable.

5   Results

5.1   Single Data Source — Single Tree

After feeding the knowledge tokens of each set into a single LSH Tree with $k_m = 80$, we find clusters of leaves as shown in Fig. 1. The figure shows how often a group of n siblings occurs as a function of the depth in the tree.

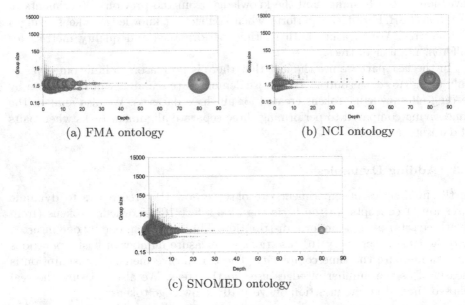

(a) FMA ontology   (b) NCI ontology

(c) SNOMED ontology

Fig. 1. Frequency of sibling groups of a given size at a given level in one LSH Tree. Note the logarithmic scale.

What we notice in the figures is that most of the concepts are fairly high up in the tree. After roughly 30 levels all the concepts, except these residing at the bottom of the tree, are placed. It is also visible that most knowledge tokens are located in the leaves which either have very few siblings or are located high up in the tree. This indicates that the tree is able to distinguish between the representations fairly fast. In both the FMA and NCI ontologies, we notice a high amount of knowledge tokens at the bottom of the tree, i.e., at level $k_m = 80$. We noticed that the same amount of concepts end up at the bottom of the tree even if k_m is chosen to be 1000, which indicates that hashing might be incapable to distinguish between the representations, i.e., they are so close that their hashes virtually always look the same. After further investigation, we found that the Jaccard similarities between the sibling concepts at the bottom of the tree are all equal to 1. This means that there are concepts in the ontology which have very similar labels, i.e., labels which (often because of our preprocessing steps) get reduced to exactly the same set of tokens. One problem with this phenomenon is that the tree contains long chains of nodes, which are created exclusively for these few siblings. We define an *exclusive chain* as the chain of nodes between an internal node at one level above the bottom of the tree, and another (higher) node which has more than one child. The lengths of these exclusive chains are illustrated in Fig. 2a.

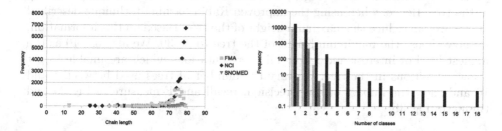

(a) Frequency of a given exclusive chain length for nodes at k_m

(b) Frequency of a given number of classes represented in a leaf at level k_m for each ontology. Note the log scale.

Fig. 2. Analysis for the leaf nodes

We notice that mainly the NCI ontology causes long exclusive chains. The most plausible cause for this is that NCI has a higher average number of representations per concept (2.6) than the other two ontologies (1.7 — FMA and 1.0 — SNOMED). To investigate this further, we plot the number of classes which the siblings at the lowest level represent. The result of analyzing the number of classes represented by the leaves in each sibling cluster can be found in Fig. 2b.

From the figure we notice that, indeed, very often there is a low number of classes represented by the siblings of the final nodes. We also notice that the NCI ontology has the most severe representation clashes.

5.2 Connecting Knowledge Tokens Using LSH Forest, i.e. Matching

When matching the SNOMED and NCI ontologies using a single tree of height 480, we obtain the precision of 0.838, recall of 0.547, and hence F-measure of 0.662. These results are similar to the results of the standard LSH algorithm which attained the precission of 0.842, recall of 0.535, and F-measure of 0.654.

The LSH Forest algorithm, however, uses only 30 % of the amount of hash function evaluations compared to the standard LSH algorithm. Furthermore, the Forest saves around 90 % of the memory used for storing the result of the hash evaluations. This is because the tree saves a lot of resources by only computing and storing the part of the label which is needed. Further, a result is stored only once if the same outcome is obtained from the evaluation of a given hash function for different representations. It should, however, be noted that using LSH Forest also implies a memory overhead for representing the tree structure, while the standard algorithm can place all hash function evaluations in an efficient two dimensional table.

The speed of the two algorithms with the same set-up is very similar. Using the Forest, the alignment is done in 20.6 s, while the standard algorithm completes in 21.5 s.

As can be seen in the distribution of the ontologies over the tree in our previous experiment series (Fig. 1) non-similar concepts remain fairly high up in the tree. Hence, when using the improved Rabin hashing technique described above, we can reduce the maximum height of the tree. Based on this information, we now choose the maximum height of the tree to be 30. We also use 10 as the highest level of interest and ignore all representations which are unable to get a lower positions in the tree. We vary the number of trees used between 1 and 10 and show the impact on the precision, recall and F-measure in Fig. 3a and timing in Fig. 3b.

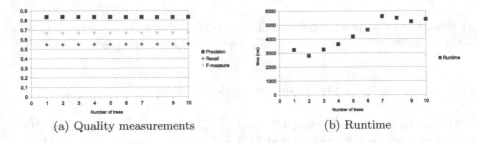

(a) Quality measurements   (b) Runtime

Fig. 3. Quality measurements and runtime behavior for an ontology matching task using different number of trees.

From the quality measurements, we see that the number of trees has little effect. It is hard to see from the figure, but the precision lowers ever so slightly when more trees are used. Concretely, it goes from 0.836947 when using one tree to 0.831957 with 10 trees. The recall has the opposite behavior growing from 0.546824 to 0.550616. The net effect of these two on the F-measure is a slight increase when more trees are used, namely from 0.661472 to 0.662662. It needs to be noted that also these results are in the same range as the measures in the previous experiment. Hence, we can conclude that constraining the height of a tree does not affect the quality much, if at all. However, as can be seen in the timing chart, the tree works much faster when its height is reduced. When only one tree is used, roughly 3 s are needed to obtain results. Increasing the number of trees to 10 only doubles the time, most likely because the system is better able to use multiple threads or the virtual machine might do a better just-in-time compilation. In any case, we note that using the forest and better hashing, we can create a system which is roughly 7 times faster and produces results of similar quality.

To try whether we can also use the tree for bigger datasets, we now feed all knowledge tokens created from all three ontologies into the system and present similar measurements in Fig. 4.

Now, we notice the effect on the precision and recall more profoundly. Also the runtime increases faster when the input is larger. We do however see only

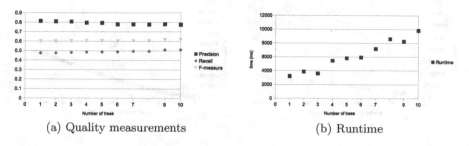

(a) Quality measurements   (b) Runtime

Fig. 4. Quality measurements and runtime behavior for a three way ontology matching task using different number of trees.

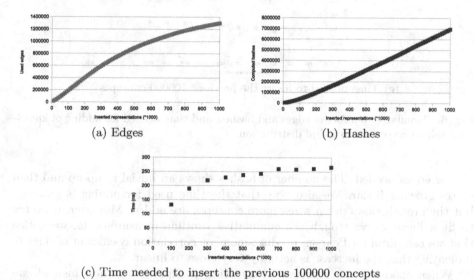

(a) Edges   (b) Hashes

(c) Time needed to insert the previous 100000 concepts

Fig. 5. Cumulative number of edges and hashes; and time needed for uniform adding of knowledge tokens

a three-fold increase when the number of trees is ten-folded. When comparing these results to our earlier work [7] we can see the speed-up of using LSH Forest and performing multiple alignments at once. In our previous work we used 45.5 s for doing three 2-way alignment tasks. Using the LSH Forest we can perform the 3-way alignment in less than 10 s. When using a single tree, we measured a time of 3.2 s yielding roughly a ten-fold speed-up.

5.3 Adding Dynamics

The results of adding knowledge tokens according to a uniform distribution are in Fig. 5. From the figures we note that the number of edges needed grows sub-linear. This is as expected since both the fact that certain knowledge tokens will be selected more than once and the reuse of edges decreases the number

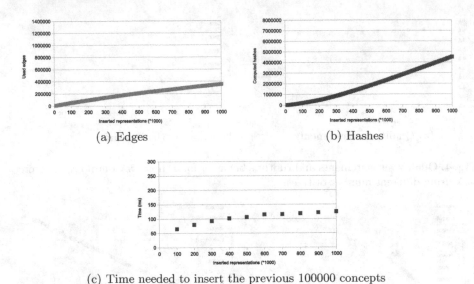

(a) Edges

(b) Hashes

(c) Time needed to insert the previous 100000 concepts

Fig. 6. Cumulative number of edges and hashes; and time needed for adding of knowledge tokens according to a Zipf distribution

of new edges needed. The number of hashes shows an initial ramp-up and then starts growing linear. We also note that the time used for adding is growing, but the growth slows down when more concepts are added. Moreover, if we try to fit a linear curve trough the cumulative runtime measurements, we notice that we can obtain a Pearson product-moment correlation coefficient of 0.9976, indicating that the increase is actually very close to linear.

When choosing the representations using a Zipf distribution instead, we obtain the results as depicted in Fig. 6. When comparing the charts for insertion using the normal and Zipf distribution, we notice that the later puts much less of a burden upon the system. This is a desirable effect since it means that the system is likely to work well with more organic loads. Also here, we can fit a linear curve trough the cumulative runtime measurements with a high correlation coefficient of 0.9968.

6 Conclusions and Outlook

When trying to understand and follow what is happening around us, we have to be able to connect different pieces of information together. Moreover, the amount of information which we perceive does not allow us to look at each detail, instead we need to focus on specific parts and ignore the rest. When we want to built a system capable of embodying evolution in knowledge, similar challenges have to be tackled. In this paper we investigated one of the first steps needed for this type of system, namely bringing related pieces of knowledge together.

The system we envision is an Evolving Knowledge Ecosystem in which Knowledge Organisms are able to consume Knowledge Tokens, i.e., pieces of knowledge, which have been sown in the environment. In this paper we looked at the application of LSH Forest to dynamically sow knowledge tokens in the environmental contexts.

We found out that LSH Forest is a suitable approach because it is able to balance well between efficiency and effectiveness. This can be observed from the fact that the method scales well, both from a space and runtime perspective; and from the fact that the quality measures are sufficiently high. Further, the Forest makes it possible to focus on these parts which need further investigation and it allows for connecting between the knowledge tokens.

There are still several aspects of using LSH Forest which could be further investigated. First, the problem caused by exclusive chains could be mitigated by measuring the distance between knowledge tokens when they reach a certain depth in the tree. Only when the concepts are different enough, there is a need to continue; this however requires to parametrize the inequality. Another option to reduce at least the amount of used memory and pointer traversals is using PATRICIA trees as proposed by Bawa et al. [2].

Secondly, we noted that the LSH tree allows for removal of concepts and that this operation is efficient. Future research is needed to see how this would work in an evolving knowledge ecosystem. Besides, as described in [1], the knowledge tokens do not disappear at once from an environmental context. Instead, they might dissolve slowly, which could be thought of as a decreasing fuzzy membership in the context. One straightforward method for achieving this would be to use a sliding window which has an exponential decay, similar to what is proposed in [10]. Also more complex ideas could be investigated, perhaps even providing a bonus for concepts which are queried often or using hierarchical clustering techniques to remove tokens from areas which are densely populated [11]. This would mean that some tokens remain in the system even when other (less popular or more common) concepts with similar insertion characteristics get removed.

Lastly, it would be interesting to see how the Forest would react when the input data becomes that big that it is impossible to keep the tree in the physical memory available. Then, using a distributed setting, ways should be found to minimize the overhead when concepts are added and removed from the tree. One promising idea is the use of consistent hashing for the distribution of knowledge tokens as proposed in [12].

Acknowledgments. The authors would like to thank the department of Mathematical Information Technology of the University of Jyväskylä for financially supporting this research. This research is also in part financed by the N4S SHOK organized by Digile Oy and financially supported by TEKES. The authors would further like to thank Steeri Oy for supporting the research and the members of the Industrial Ontologies Group (IOG) of the University of Jyväskylä for their support in the research. Further, it has to be mentioned that the implementation of the software was greatly simplified by the Guava library by Google, the Apache Commons Math^{TM} library, and the Rabin hash library by Bill Dwyer and Ian Brandt.

References

1. Ermolayev, V., Akerkar, R., Terziyan, V., Cochez, M.: Towards evolving knowledge ecosystems for big data understanding. Big Data Computing, pp. 3–55. Taylor & Francis group - Chapman and Hall/CRC, New York (2014)
2. Bawa, M., Condie, T., Ganesan, P.: LSH forest: self-tuning indexes for similarity search. In: Proceedings of the 14th International Conference on World Wide Web, pp. 651–660. ACM (2005)
3. Indyk, P., Motwani, R.: Approximate nearest neighbors: towards removing the curse of dimensionality. In: Proceedings of the Thirtieth Annual ACM Symposium on Theory of Computing, pp. 604–613. ACM (1998)
4. Andoni, A., Indyk, P.: Near-optimal hashing algorithms for approximate nearest neighbor in high dimensions. Commun. ACM $51(1)$, 117–122 (2008)
5. Rajaraman, A., Ullman, J.D.: Finding similar items. Mining of Massive Datasets, pp. 71–128. Cambridge University Press, Cambridge (2012)
6. Ermolayev, V., Davidovsky, M.: Agent-based ontology alignment: basics, applications, theoretical foundations, and demonstration. In: Proceedings of the 2nd International Conference on Web Intelligence, Mining and Semantics, WIMS 2012, pp. 3:1–3:12. ACM, New York, NY, USA (2012)
7. Cochez, M.: Locality-sensitive hashing for massive string-based ontology matching. In: Proceedings of IEEE/WIC/ACM International Joint Conferences on Web Intelligence (WI) and Intelligent Agent Technologies (IAT) (2014) (accepted)
8. Broder, A.Z.: On the resemblance and containment of documents. In: Proceedings of the Compression and Complexity of Sequences 1997, pp. 21–29. IEEE (1997)
9. Broder, A.: Some applications of rabin's fingerprinting method. In: Capocelli, R., Santis, A., Vaccaro, U. (eds.) Sequences II, pp. 143–152. Springer, New York (1993)
10. Datar, M., Gionis, A., Indyk, P., Motwani, R.: Maintaining stream statistics over sliding windows. SIAM J. Comput. $31(6)$, 1794–1813 (2002)
11. Cochez, M., Mou, H.: Twister tries: approximate hierarchical agglomerative clustering for average distance in linear time. In: Proceedings of the 2015 ACM SIGMOD International Conference on Management of Data, pp. 505–517. ACM (2015)
12. Karger, D., Lehman, E., Leighton, T., Panigrahy, R., Levine, M., Lewin, D.: Consistent hashing and random trees: distributed caching protocols for relieving hot spots on the world wide web. In: Proceedings of the Twenty-ninth Annual ACM Symposium on Theory of Computing. STOC 1997, pp. 654–663. ACM, New York, NY, USA (1997)

Improving css-KNN Classification Performance by Shifts in Training Data

Karol Draszawka[1]([✉]), Julian Szymański[1], and Francesco Guerra[2]

[1] Gdańsk University of Technology, Gdańsk, Poland
{kadr,julian.szymanski}@eti.pg.da.pl
[2] Universita' di Modena e Reggio Emilia, Modena, Italy
francesco.guerra@unimore.it

Abstract. This paper presents a new approach to improve the performance of a css-k-NN classifier for categorization of text documents. The css-k-NN classifier (i.e., a threshold-based variation of a standard k-NN classifier we proposed in [1]) is a lazy-learning instance-based classifier. It does not have parameters associated with features and/or classes of objects, that would be optimized during off-line learning. In this paper we propose a training data preprocessing phase that tries to alleviate the lack of learning. The idea is to compute training data modifications, such that class representative instances are optimized before the actual k-NN algorithm is employed. The empirical text classification experiments using mid-size Wikipedia data sets show that carefully cross-validated settings of such preprocessing yields significant improvements in k-NN performance compared to classification without this step. The proposed approach can be useful for improving the effectivenes of other classifiers as well as it can find applications in domain of recommendation systems and keyword-based search.

Keywords: KNN classifier · Wikipedia · Documents classification · Missing data imputation

1 Introduction

Text classification finds many applications e.g., in the library systems where it aggregates thematically related resources into a one category, in e-commerce, where it serves for profiling users on the basis of their behaviours, and in the organization of the web, where categories of pages have been proposed (e.g., see the DMOZ directory).

Classification is a task that only for small repositories can be performed manually, in almost all the cases the size of the data requires the development and exploitation of the automatic techniques. The text classification problem is widely studied and approached using variety of methods such as: SVM [2], Bayesian [3] and others [4,5]. Due to their simplicity, k-Nearest Neighbours algorithms [6] have been frequently used for this task, achieving also good results as

© Springer International Publishing Switzerland 2015
J. Cardoso et al. (Eds.): KEYWORD 2015, LNCS 9398, pp. 51–63, 2015.
DOI: 10.1007/978-3-319-27932-9_5

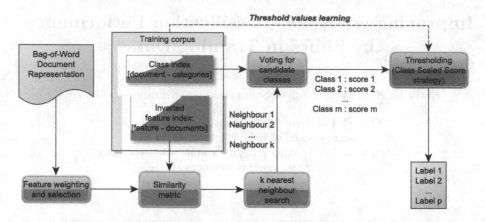

Fig. 1. The architecture of css-KNN-classifier used in experiments (details in [1]).

in [7,8]. Modifications in k-Nearest Neighbours algorithms also enables multi-label classification [9,10] that can be introduced with relatively low computational cost, in comparison to prominent SVM classifiers that are known to have troubles with scalability and multi-label tasks [11,12].

The main disadvantage of the typical k-NN approaches is that they do not provide ability for improving the results using the learning by the examples. Success and popularity of k-NN approach to multi-label large-scale text classification encouraged us to undertake research in this field. In [1], we proposed an approach based on k-NN to text classification that introduced class-specific parameters that can be cross-validated to generate best results. Figure 1 shows the architecture of our classifier: it is based on a typical k-NN classifier, with cosine metric, and k parameter set to 30. The nearest neighbors contribute to the calculation of each class's score, according to scoring formula described in [7]. Then, a thresholding phase using so called Class-specific Scaled Score strategy (CSS) determines the output of the classifier: if a score of class exceeds a threshold specific for this class it is added to the final prediction. The values of class-specific thresholds are tuned using training set subsampling and validation.

In this paper we propose a new approach for improving the results of k-NN classifier. Our idea is to introduce a training phase where we "modify the training dataset" to generate better results in terms of classification accuracy. In particular, in Sect. 3 we propose four methods in which training data examples are *translated* or *shifted* in the feature space, i.e. their feature values are modified, so that they become more similar to other examples. In geometrical interpretation, the points in the high dimensional feature space, representing training data examples, are translated towards other points. In particular, for attributes that a given example do not have any value, these approaches induce values, which relates the approaches to "missing value management" methods, largely studied in the literature. The k-NN classification on such enhanced training dataset shows better performance than without modifications. The results obtained by our experiments, computed with large and sparse datasets, as it is typical in text classification, encourage us to proceed in this direction.

Machine learning techniques have been widely used for supporting keyword search. k-NN classification techniques have been in particular adopted in the field of textual documents, images or videos retrieval, allowing users to "query by example" and obtaining items close to the ones given as input. Nevertheless, machine learning can support other tasks in keyword search: k-NN classification can be particularly useful in the keyword search field, in two areas: disambiguation and expansion of the users' keywords. Disambiguation task is necessary in solving queries, where the keywords have several meanings according to the reference context. To be able to select among the possible meanings the one suitable for the keywords, in the specific query, different techniques are typically applied. One of them is to make a reduction of the document search space, thus providing a large benefit in the accuracy of the results. The classification of the keyword query obtained by the exploitation of the k-NN classification on a feature vector representing the user's keyword query can be exploited for this purpose, by identifying the possible categories where the query belongs to, and in consequence the set of the interesting documents.

Query expansion is another approach that aims at improving the retrieved results accuracy. The typical approaches employ dictionaries of different but semantically related terms. Query expansion provides an additional number of keywords to be included in the original set formulated by the user. In this case, the technique for completing missing values introduced in the paper can be directly adopted for modification of the feature vector representing the user's keyword query. In particular, the technique can be used for changing the values of terms not provided in the original query (i.e., having a 0 value in the query feature vector), with new estimated values. This enhancement of the feature vector can subsequently be adopted for selection of similar documents or identification of the possible reference categories as described below.

The paper is constructed as follows: Sect. 2 introduces some Related Work with the emphasis on dealing with missing values, Sect. 3 describes our *shifting* methods, which are evaluated by the results of the experiments presented in Sect. 4. Finally in Sect. 5 we sketch out some conclusions and future work.

2   Related Work

Our proposal computes changes in the dataset for improving the k-NN classifier. Techniques for modifying values in the datasets have been developed in the literature as related to the management for missing values.

All the existing solutions can be usually classified in one of the following categories [13]: (1) Ignoring and discarding incomplete records and attributes; (2) Managing missing data as special values; and (3) Parameter estimation in the presence of missing data.

The elimination of all samples with missing values and the consequent reduction of the dataset is the simplest solution for managing the issue. Nevertheless, this solution is not always suitable due to the discard of significant fragments of the dataset with potentially useful informative power.

Approaches falling in the second category treat "unknown" itself as a new value to be treat in the same way as other values [14].

Finally, the problem of missing values can be handled by various imputation methods. Working with these approaches, we make the assumptions the "missingness mechanism" can be analyzed and patterns of missing values (if any) can be applied for imputation. As stated in [15], there are three different mechanisms for induction of missing values: 1. Missing completely at random (MCAR), when the distribution of an example having a missing value for an attribute does not depend on either the observed data or the missing values; 2. Missing at random (MAR), when the distribution of an example having a missing value for an attribute depends on the observed data, but does not depend on the missing values; and 3. Not missing at random (NMAR), when the distribution of an example having a missing value for an attribute depends on the missing values. Unfortunately missing values imputation methods are suitable only for missing values caused by MCAR and some of them for MAR mechanisms. If missing values are caused by NMAR, it must be handled by going back to the source of data and obtaining more information or the appropriate model for the missing data mechanism have to be taken into account [13]. Techniques in this category include: replacing missing value with mean, mean or median for the given class, most common attribute value, with values computed with machine learning techniques, association rules (see [13,14,16] for some surveys). Our approach can also be interpreted as a data smoothing technique, a preprocessing commonly used especially in connection with Bayes classifiers [17].

3   Shifting Methods of Training Examples

This section describes four types of training data modifications used in our experiments. A given training dataset D_{train} consists of N training pairs (examples):

$$D_{\text{train}} = \left\{ (x, \mathcal{Y}) : x \in \mathbf{R}^M, \mathcal{Y} \subseteq \mathcal{L} \right\},$$

where x is a M-dimensional feature vector and $\mathcal{Y}$ is a set of objects' labels, which is some subset of the set of all labels/classes $\mathcal{L}$ in the data. Each of the following methods can be treated as a function that modifies a training feature vector x according to its label set $\mathcal{Y}$ and its relation to the rest of training examples in D_{train}:

$$x' = shift\,(x, \mathcal{Y}, D_{\text{train}})\,.$$

The whole modified training data set D'_{train} is then composed of $(x', \mathcal{Y})$ pairs.

It is important to notice that such modifications of the training dataset should be applied to test examples, because label sets of test examples are assumed to be unknown. Therefore, transformations are employed only to training data, the modified training examples are given to a classifier, but during testing the classifier is fed with test examples not affected by any such transformation. The following approach then breaks the usual scheme, that the processing pipeline from an input data feature vector to an output prediction vector is the same in the training and testing phases.

The four proposed modifications of the training dataset have a common form, given by Eq. (1):

$$x'^{(i)} = x^{(i)} + \alpha \cdot \left(d^{(i)} - x^{(i)} \right) = (1 - \alpha) \cdot x^{(i)} + \alpha \cdot d^{(i)}. \tag{1}$$

They are vector translations (shifts) of an i-th data point $x^{(i)}$ towards some destination point $d^{(i)}$ by some *step size* $\alpha \in [0, 1]$. The knowledge of $\mathcal{Y}^{(i)}$ as well as the rest of D_{train} is necessary to compute $d^{(i)}$.

How exactly calculating the destination point of a given training dataset is the first differentiating factor of the following methods. $d^{(i)}$ can be determined by global or local feature space examination. The second differentiating factor specifies the way of multi-labeled training examples treatment. These two factors taken together generate the following four methods of shifts in training data.

3.1   Shifts Towards Globally Defined Destinations

In the first two methods the direction towards which a data point is pushed is determined by examining the data set globally. Particularly, the shift destination point is the center of the class to which an object belongs. In this paper, a class center is chosen to be an average of all examples in the class (i.e. a simple *centroid* of the class), although a medoid representation of a class center should also work. The centroid c_i of a class C_i is given by:

$$c_i = \frac{\sum_{x \in C_i} x}{|C_i|} \tag{2}$$

Because of multi-label character of the problem, the arising question is how to move objects that belong to more than one class. Moving a point towards all of its classes' centers sequentially, i.e. in the direction of a centroid of one class, then towards other centroid of an affiliated class and then towards another and so on, is not a correct strategy. In effect, this would place the point nearest to the last class and farthest from the first class to which it was pushed. Therefore the object's classes would not be treated equally and this is unjustified. Instead, there are two other ways of translating multi-labeled objects having known the centers of their affiliated classes.

Translation to Centroid of Centroids (T2CC). In this approach, we average the centroids of the classes to which object $x^{(i)}$ belongs:

$$cc^{(i)} = \frac{\sum_{j \in \mathcal{Y}^{(i)}} c_j}{|\mathcal{Y}^{(i)}|} \tag{3}$$

After obtaining such *centroid of centroids* for each object, the object can be shifted in accordance to Eq. (1), with $d^{(j)} = cc^{(j)}$.

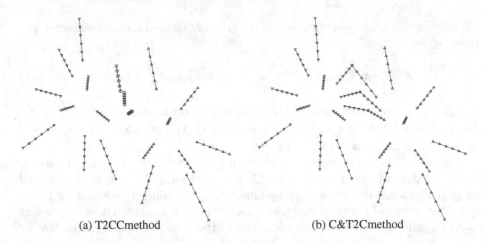

(a) T2CCmethod   (b) C&T2Cmethod

Fig. 2. Comparison of two methods using global dataset investigation to calculate destination points and then translate towards them using α values ranging from 0.1 to 0.5. The difference is visible in the way in which multi-labeled objects are treated. Examples in the middle, depicted as stars, are assigned to both upside and downside triangle labels. T2CC calculates the centroid out of both labels centroids and moves the objects towards that single point, whereas C&T2C splits the objects into two single-labeled ones and translates them to respective class centers.

Copy and Translate (C&T2C). Here, we begin by decomposing each multi-labeled object in the dataset into single-labeled copies of it. That is, an object associated with p classes (i.e. $|\mathcal{Y}^{(i)}| = p$) is replaced by p copies of itself and each of these copies is marked with a different class from the set of original object's labels:

$$(\boldsymbol{x}, \{l_1, l_2, \ldots, l_p\}) \implies (\boldsymbol{x}, \{l_1\}), (\boldsymbol{x}, \{l_2\}), \ldots, (\boldsymbol{x}, \{l_p\}) \tag{4}$$

After such operation, in C&T2C method each object is pushed according to (1), having $\boldsymbol{d}^{(j)}$ set to a suitable class centroid $\boldsymbol{c}$. Figure 2 illustrates the difference between T2CC and C&T2C translation methods in a simple 2D example.

It should be noticed that this dataset transformation, objects' *forking*, significantly increases the number of training objects. This may be a potential drawback for some applications, because much more memory space is needed to store the data. It also changes the character of the training data, which is not multi-labeled any more. In connection with the fact that the classification problem to solve is still multi-labeled, this means that the approach can be used only when working with classifiers capable of dealing with such situations.

3.2   Shifts Towards Locally Defined Destinations

In contrast to the above global methods, the local approach to calculate destination points for data shifts is presented here. The idea is that instead of choosing a class center as the point $(\boldsymbol{d}^{(i)})$ towards which executing a movement of a feature vector $\boldsymbol{x}^{(i)}$, it is determined by m closest examples to $\boldsymbol{x}^{(i)}$ (with respect to some distance metric, e.g. cosine) among those that belong to the same class as $\boldsymbol{x}^{(i)}$ does (assuming for a while that it is single labeled). Therefore, they can be called m nearest *in-class* neighbors (*nin*-s) of the example.

When m *nin*-s of an $\boldsymbol{x}^{(i)}$ are found, constituting a set $\mathcal{N}_{\boldsymbol{x}^{(i)}}$, then $\boldsymbol{d}^{(i)}$ is simply the average of these points, analogously to class centroid calculation:

$$\boldsymbol{d}^{(i)} = \frac{\sum_{\mathcal{N}_{\boldsymbol{x}^{(i)}}} \boldsymbol{n}}{|\mathcal{N}_{\boldsymbol{x}^{(i)}}|} = \frac{\sum_{\mathcal{N}_{\boldsymbol{x}^{(i)}}} \boldsymbol{n}}{m} \qquad (5)$$

For single-labeled datasets, the parameter m can be fixed to a constant value for all classes or it could be proportional to the size of the class to which $\boldsymbol{x}^{(i)}$ is assigned. For multi-labeled cases, the following two methods have been developed.

Translation to Centroid of Nearest In-Class Neighbors (T2CNIN). In this approach, the local destination point calculation given above is adapted to multi-labeled objects by changing the notion of an in-class object. Now, an example is considered as in-class with respect to some $\boldsymbol{x}^{(i)}$, if and only if *at least* one of this example's labels is in $\mathcal{Y}^{(i)}$ or, in other words, if the intersection between this example's $\mathcal{Y}$ and $\mathcal{Y}^{(i)}$ is not empty. With this adaptation, the rest of the procedure is the same as for a single-labeled case: the m nearest in-class neighbors have to be found, $\boldsymbol{d}^{(i)}$ is determined by applying Eq. 5, and the change of $\boldsymbol{x}^{(i)}$ by shift given in Eq. 1.

Of course, this method can have many other variants. For example, one can be more demanding in treating examples as an in-class *peers* to a given $\boldsymbol{x}^{(i)}$ by requiring the respective $\mathcal{Y}$ and $\mathcal{Y}^{(i)}$ to be the same (i.e. a label power set approach). Or, one can incorporate a weighted average, instead of Eq. 5, to vary the importance of m nearest neighbors, so that those with many common labels would pull stronger than those with, say, only one common label. In the experiments, these variants were not used.

Copy and Translate to Nearest In-Class Neighbors (C&T2NIN). The last proposed method is a result of applying local destination points calculation (Eq. 5) with previous multi- to single-label data transformation, presented by 4. After the object forking transformation, each example has exactly one label, so the notion of an in-class peer is not problematic, and Eq. 5 can be applied directly. Of course, all restrictions about the consequences of using the object forking transformation, described previously, apply here also.

The difference between the two local shift methods on a toy 2D example is shown in Fig. 3.

3.3   Pre- and Post-shift Data Pruning

For sparse data, the effect of points shifts in the feature space is the addition of many non-zero values, i.e. the sparseness of data is reduced. For example, the

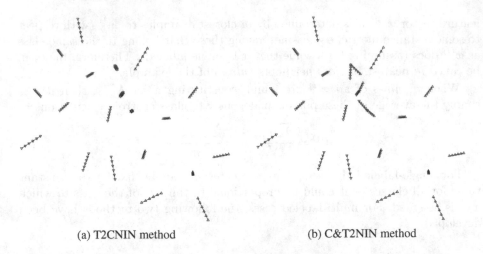

(a) T2CNIN method   (b) C&T2NIN method

Fig. 3. Comparison of two methods using local neighborhood investigation to calculate destination points and then translate towards them using α values ranging from 0.1 to 0.5, $m = 3$. Here also the difference lies in the way multi-labeled objects are treated. Objects in the middle, e.g., stars, are assigned to both upside and downside triangle labels. T2CNIN calculates centroids of in-class neighbors and moves the objects owards those points, whereas C&T2NIN splits the objects into two single-labeled ones and translates them to suitable in-class neighbors' centers.

average number of nonzero elements of a class centroid in our dataset (described in Sect. 4.1) is ca. 700, whereas the average number of nonzero elements of a single data example is 53. This means, that on average a shifted data example to a class centroid has over 1200 % nonzero elements of the original data example.

On the one hand, this is a massive data imputation, which was one of the aims of the methods and is beneficial for better classification. On the other hand, however, it significantly increases the space requirements for the transformed data which can cause memory problems. Therefore, in practice a deletion of small nonzero elements is needed to restrict the reduction of data sparsity. This is obtained in a process called *data pruning*. A pruning can be done by setting an *absolute threshold* value and zeroing feature values less than this threshold. The threshold can also be *relative*, in which case a feature is removed from the example, if its value *scaled* by example's highest feature value is below the threshold.

In the presented data shifts methods, pruning can be executed two times. First, after the calculation of the centroids (for global methods), the centroids can be immediately pruned, so that they contain only important features, that characterize classes. This can be called *pre-shift* pruning. For example, pruning the centroids of the above example with relative pruning $tr_{rel} = 0.05$, reduces their average number of nonzero elements from 700 to 311. After data movements, the obtained modified train dataset can also be pruned using the same technique. This process can be referenced to as *post-shift* pruning.

4 Experiments

4.1 The Dataset

The evaluation was performed using the dataset constructed from the corpus of articles from Simple English Wikipedia. It is a well known, frequently used dataset that has characteristic properties, such as: the data is highly multi-labeled (in some cases more than 5 labels), has many irregularities, contains noise and missing values, the articles are of different lengths, are not necessarily correctly assigned to categories (or not assigned to all categories to which they would fit well), and often have some less important content while missing crucial information. Simple English Wikipedia corpus is also suited well to test-bed experiments, because it is middle sized – big enough to exhibit most important properties of real problems, but computations upon it are relatively not much time consuming (all the data can fit at once into a typical computer memory).

The corpus was preprocessed using Matrix'u software [18] to obtain a bag-of-words representation of the articles. The *confidence weighting* scheme [19] was used, which gives slightly better classification accuracy than typical TF-IDF feature weighting. From the original corpus, the articles with less than 5 features as well as the categories with less than 5 articles were removed. After such filtering, the dataset has 55637 articles, connected in a multi-label fashion with 5679 categories.

The dataset was divided into train and test sets in proportion 3:1, so that at least one article from every category is included in the test set. The problem of stratified partitioning a multi-labeled dataset is NP-hard, therefore a version of simulated annealing was used to obtain a satisfactory partition.

4.2 Results

Figures 5 and 4 presents the quality of the test set examples classification using two KNN-based classifiers under train data examples shift. For comparison, the baseline (classification performance on raw training data) is also presented. For each method, the results were obtained by computation of destination points first and then gradually moving training data examples towards them (changing α in Eq.(1) from 0 to 1 by 0.1) each time checking the performance of classifiers on the same test set examples. The performance is expressed by a popular macro-averaged F1-score (abbrev. *maF*) [20]. Because Wikipedia category structure has a pseudo-hierarchical structure, besides typical "flat" maF, the measurements using a hierarchical version of it, abbreviated as *hMaF*, introduced in [21], are also presented (Fig. 5b and 4b).

It can be seen that all four methods can improve the training set leading to better classification performance. However, having chosen a method, it is very important to find a proper step size (α) value. The optimal α has to be large enough to reduce variance in the training data associated with noise, but small enough to maintain the variance resulting from class distribution in the feature space. Too small α may not increase the performance significantly and too big

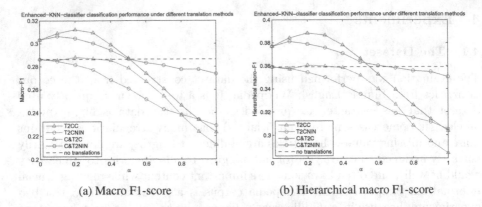

(a) Macro F1-score   (b) Hierarchical macro F1-score

Fig. 4. The results of Enhanced-KNN classifier [7] performance on a held out test set under train data translations using proposed methods. Simple English Wikipedia dataset, centroid pruning $th_{rel} = 0.05$, shifted data pruning $th_{rel} = 0.05$, neighborhood size for local methods: $m = 3$.

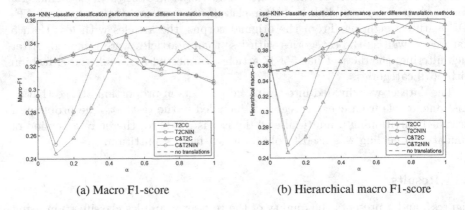

(a) Macro F1-score   (b) Hierarchical macro F1-score

Fig. 5. The results of css-KNN classifier performance on a held out test set under train data translations using proposed methods. Simple English Wikipedia dataset, centroid pruning $th_{rel} = 0.05$, shifted data pruning $th_{rel} = 0.05$, neighborhood size for local methods: $m = 3$.

value may even cause the performance to be worse than the baseline. Indeed, for methods with globally calculated destination points, shifting too much towards class centroids makes KNN to behave similarly to centroids-based classifiers (like nearest centroid / Rocchio classifier), which is known to be inferior than KNN in most cases.

The degree of data smoothing in methods incorporating nearest in-class neighbors (nin) is controlled not only by the step size, but also by the number of $nins$ involved in destination points calculation, i.e. the m parameter. The presented results were obtained with m set arbitrarily to 3 for all classes, without attempts to optimize it. Figure 5 shows that, css-KNN classifier is vulnerable to multi-label examples forking (red lines, performance even without shifts, i.e. for $\alpha = 0$) and therefore initially exhibits worse quality than the baseline. However, it becomes better after increasing the step size to 0.4–0.5. Interestingly, for enhanced-KNN classifier, the multi-label examples splitting instantly improves the outcome quality. The methods' usefulness is then closely connected with a chosen classifier.

It should also be noted, that the presented results are obtained using pre- and post-shift data pruning. In both the relative thresholds were used with set to 0.05. For selected α values, we also tested the classification performance on less pruned data (and even without pre-translation pruning), but the obtained results were almost identical. However, there is much difference in memory space requirements, which is presented in Table 1. With our simple, *all-data-in-memory* implementation, some data pruning was needed to avoid out of memory problems.

Table 1. The impact of pre- and post-translation data pruning on the size of the modified training dataset (in MB). Simple English Wikipedia train data. Original train data size is 25.

	post-shift pruning				
	no pruning	relative 0.01	absolute 0.01	relative 0.05	absolute 0.05
no pruning	-	-	-	-	34
relative 0.01	1060	149	78	40	34
absolute 0.01	430	143	78	40	34
relative 0.05	304	127	75	40	34
absolute 0.05	90	74	60	40	34

(left label: pre-shift)

5   Conclusions and Future Work

In our paper we present an approach for shifts in the training data for text classification based on KNN that allowed us to improve generalization of the categorization process. We proposed four variants of train data points shifts and shown that all of them can improve classification quality. The modifications perform a data smoothing, and, especially, can be seen as a type of missing data imputation.

The proposed modification lies before main classification phase and as a general approach can be used with other classification tools, thus improve their effectiveness. In future we plan to investigate the impact of training data modifications on results of the SVM and neural network models. For these models however, it may be necessary to *learn* a function that will perform a similar transformation, but in an unsupervised manner, i.e. without the knowledge of class labels, so that the transformations could be performed also on the test examples.

Besides this, future work will also be oriented in two main directions. Firstly we will investigate whether the approach for dealing with missing data can be applied to keyword search over databases that do not offer direct access to their instances (e.g. deep web databases, which can be typically accessed by query forms). In this case, the proposed technique can be used for estimating the assignment of a keyword to a particular database schema element, thus completing and extending our previous work [22]. Then we will adopt the technique in a recommender system, where we have to discover the users' preference rates for unrated items. In this case, unrated preference rates have to be thought of as missing value. We plan to perform this experimentation in the field of recommendation of web pages, where new pages can be proposed to a user on the basis of the analysis of the pages visited in the current session.

Acknowledgement. The authors would like to acknowledge networking support by the ICT COST Action IC1302 KEYSTONE - Semantic keyword-based search on structured data sources (www.keystone-cost.eu).

References

1. Draszawka, K., Szymanski, J.: Thresholding strategies for large scale multi-label text classifier. In: The 6th International Conference on Human System Interaction (HSI), 2013, pp. 350–355. IEEE (2013)
2. Joachims, T.: Transductive inference for text classification using support vector machines. In: ICML, vol. 99, pp. 200–209 (1999)
3. McCallum, A., Nigam, K., et al.: A comparison of event models for naive bayes text classification. In: AAAI-98 Workshop on Learning for Text Categorization, vol. 752, pp. 41–48. Citeseer (1998)
4. Sebastiani, F.: Machine learning in automated text categorization. ACM Comput. Surv. (CSUR) **34**, 1–47 (2002)
5. Westa, M., Szymański, J., Krawczyk, H.: Text classifiers for automatic articles categorization. In: Rutkowski, L., Korytkowski, M., Scherer, R., Tadeusiewicz, R., Zadeh, L.A., Zurada, J.M. (eds.) ICAISC 2012, Part II. LNCS, vol. 7268, pp. 196–204. Springer, Heidelberg (2012)
6. Tan, S.: Neighbor-weighted k-nearest neighbor for unbalanced text corpus. Expert Syst. Appl. **28**, 667–671 (2005)
7. Wang, X., Zhao, H., Lu, B.: Enhanced k-nearest neighbour algorithm for largescale hierarchical multi-label classification. In: Proceedings of the Joint ECML/PKDD PASCAL Workshop on Large-Scale Hierarchical Classification, Athens, Greece, vol. 5 (2011)
8. Zhou, Y., Li, Y., Xia, S.: An improved knn text classification algorithm based on clustering. J. Comput. **4**, 230–237 (2009)
9. Zhang, M.L., Zhou, Z.H.: Ml-knn: a lazy learning approach to multi-label learning. Pattern Recogn. **40**, 2038–2048 (2007)
10. Read, J.: Scalable multi-label classification. Ph.D. thesis, University of Waikato (2010)
11. Yu, H., Yang, J., Han, J., Li, X.: Making svms scalable to large data sets using hierarchical cluster indexing. Data Min. Knowl. Disc. **11**, 295–321 (2005)

12. Tang, L., Rajan, S., Narayanan, V.K.: Large scale multi-label classification via metalabeler. In: Proceedings of the 18th International Conference on World Wide Web, pp. 211–220. ACM (2009)
13. Kaiser, J.: Dealing with missing values in data. J. Syst. Integr. **5**, 42–51 (2014)
14. Grzymała-Busse, J.W., Hu, M.: A comparison of several approaches to missing attribute values in data mining. In: Ziarko, W.P., Yao, Y. (eds.) RSCTC 2000. LNCS (LNAI), vol. 2005, p. 378. Springer, Heidelberg (2001)
15. Little, R.J.A., Rubin, D.B.: Statistical Analysis with Missing Data, 2nd edn. Wiley, New York (2002)
16. Farhangfar, A., Kurgan, L.A., Dy, J.G.: Impact of imputation of missing values on classification error for discrete data. Pattern Recogn. **41**, 3692–3705 (2008)
17. Juan, A., Ney, H.: Reversing and smoothing the multinomial naive bayes text classifier. In: PRIS, pp. 200–212. Citeseer (2002)
18. Szymanski, J.: Comparative analysis of text representation methods using classification. Cybern. Syst. **45**, 180–199 (2014)
19. Soucy, P., Mineau, G.W.: Beyond tfidf weighting for text categorization in the vector space model. IJCAI. **5**, 1130–1135 (2005)
20. Tsoumakas, G., Vlahavas, I.P.: Random k-Labelsets: an ensemble method for multilabel classification. In: Kok, J.N., Koronacki, J., Lopez de Mantaras, R., Matwin, S., Mladenič, D., Skowron, A. (eds.) ECML 2007. LNCS (LNAI), vol. 4701, pp. 406–417. Springer, Heidelberg (2007)
21. Kiritchenko, S., Matwin, S., Nock, R., Famili, A.F.: Learning and evaluation in the presence of class hierarchies: application to text categorization. In: Lamontagne, L., Marchand, M. (eds.) Canadian AI 2006. LNCS (LNAI), vol. 4013, pp. 395–406. Springer, Heidelberg (2006)
22. Bergamaschi, S., Domnori, E., Guerra, F., Trillo-Lado, R., Velegrakis, Y.: Keyword search over relational databases: a metadata approach. In: SIGMOD, pp. 565–576. ACM (2011)

Classification Using Various Machine Learning Methods and Combinations of Key-Phrases and Visual Features

Yaakov HaCohen-Kerner[1(✉)], Asaf Sabag[1], Dimitris Liparas[2],
Anastasia Moumtzidou[2], Stefanos Vrochidis[2],
and Ioannis Kompatsiaris[2]

[1] Department of Computer Science, Jerusalem College of Technology - Lev
Academic Center, 9116001 Jerusalem, Israel
kerner@jct.ac.il, sabag.asaf.1@gmail.com
[2] Centre for Research and Technology Hellas, Information Technologies
Institute, Thermi, Thessaloniki, Greece
{dliparas,moumtzid,stefanos,ikom}@iti.gr

Abstract. In this paper, we present a comparative study of news documents classification using various supervised machine learning methods and different combinations of key-phrases (word N-grams extracted from text) and visual features (extracted from a representative image from each document). The application domain is news documents written in English that belong to four categories: Health, Lifestyle-Leisure, Nature-Environment and Politics. The use of the N-gram textual feature set alone led to an accuracy result of 81.0 %, which is much better than the corresponding accuracy result (58.4 %) obtained through the use of the visual feature set alone. A competition between three classification methods, a feature selection method, and parameter tuning led to improved accuracy (86.7 %), achieved by the Random Forests method.

Keywords: Document classification · Feature selection · Key-phrases · N-gram features · Supervised learning · Visual features

1 Introduction

During the last years, news agencies and newspapers face the challenge of automatically classifying news documents into a set of categories. This challenge becomes even more attractive when the documents contain not only text but also images. One such typical news document is depicted in Fig. 1. Moreover, in light of the explosion in the number of available news documents, the issue of fast and error-free classification of such documents is becoming more critical.

Classification using supervised learning is a task that is supervised by a set of examples with class assignments and the goal is to assign documents to one or more predefined categories [1]. Many supervised machine learning (ML) methods have been applied to document classification. The classification models are automatically built from annotated corpora. Comprehensive overviews of classification are given by [2–4].

© Springer International Publishing Switzerland 2015
J. Cardoso et al. (Eds.): KEYWORD 2015, LNCS 9398, pp. 64–75, 2015.
DOI: 10.1007/978-3-319-27932-9_6

Although many news documents include images in addition to text, most of the classification approaches make use of only textual data, in order to build the models. Therefore, it is interesting to perform a comparative study of news documents classification using different ML methods and different combinations of textual and visual feature sets, in order to see whether the addition of the visual features can improve the classification performance.

Fig. 1. Web-based news document from the guardian entitled: the man in the digital mask (http://www.theguardian.com/technology/2015/sep/10/the-man-in-the-digital-mask-bill-shannon)

In this paper, we explore domain-based classification of news documents using three general types of features: textual N-gram features, visual features and a combination of the above. The classification experiments are performed using three different supervised ML methods, namely J48, Random Forests (RF) and Sequential Minimal Optimization (SMO).

The rest of the paper is structured as follows: Sect. 2 provides the relevant background concerning document classification. Section 3 describes the textual and visual feature extraction procedures. Section 4 presents the involved classification methods, the experimental results and their analysis. Finally, Sect. 5 summarizes the main findings, concludes and suggests future directions.

2 Document Classification

Current-day document classification presents challenges due to the large number of training documents, the large number of available features and their dependencies. The document classification task is one of the most fundamental tasks in data mining and ML literature [5]. Document classification has been successfully applied to many fields such as document filtering, information extraction and text mining [6–8].

Document classification can be divided into two main types: according to categories (e.g., fields and topics) and according to stylistic classification. Document classification according to categories is usually based on content word or character N-grams. Some examples of document classification according to categories are the following: detection of author profiles for authorship attribution [8], detection of virus programs [9] and phrase and topic discovery [10].

In contrast, stylistic classification utilizes various linguistic features, e.g., function words, orthographic features, parts of speech (PoS) features, topographic features and vocabulary richness features. Examples of document classification according to stylistic classification are: blog classification [11], computer science conference classification [12], ethnicity/time/place classification [13, 14], and sentiment classification [15].

The majority of document classification-related studies consider only textual features. For instance, [16] focus on political news by tracking blogs and the articles they cite, tagging each article with the number of blogs citing it. They use a maximum entropy classifier based on unigram features. Reference [17] develop various criteria to predict the popularity of news on Twitter and indicate that traditionally prominent news sources differ from news sources that are popular in social media platforms. Moreover, [18] present an approach for identifying and classifying contents of interest related to geographic communities from news articles streams. Their approach contains two stages: (1) Filtering out contents irrelevant to communities, and (2) Classifying the remaining relevant news articles by means of a Bayesian text classifier. Finally, [19] present learning of sentiment-specific word embedding for twitter sentiment classification. They learn embedding for unigrams, bigrams and trigrams separately using three developed neural networks.

Some examples of document classification studies that use only visual features are the following: [20] classify document pages using various visual features that express "visual similarity" of layout structure, e.g. percentages of text and non-text (graphics, images, tables, and rulings) content regions, column structures, relative point sizes of fonts, density of content area and statistics of features from connected components. They implement their classification scheme using decision tree classifiers and self-organizing maps. [21] explore image clustering as a basis for constructing visual words for representing documents. They apply the bag-of-words representation and standard classification methods to train an image-based classifier. Their main contribution is the exploration of a new space of features, based purely on the clustering of subfigures for document classification.

The task of classifying documents that contain both textual and visual features is a relatively new and interesting challenge. In this context, [22] explore the classification of news articles using both textual and visual features. By using only N-gram textual features they achieve a much better accuracy result than using only visual features. The use of both N-gram textual features and visual features leads to slightly improved accuracy results. Furthermore, [23] classify document images by combining 1000 textual features extracted with the Bag of Words (BoW) technique and 1000 visual features extracted with the Bag of Visual Words (BoVW) technique. Experiments conducted on an industrial document image database reveal that the proposed late fusion scheme significantly improves the classification performance.

3   Feature Extraction from News Documents

In this study, we assume that each news document has two main components: (a) the textual information, and (b) the image(s). Firstly, we extract continuous word N-grams (excluding stopwords) from the textual description of the given document. Secondly, we extract low-level visual features from the biggest image of the document, which is assumed to be the representative one.

3.1   Extraction of Key-Phrases

For the extraction of the textual features from a corpus of news web documents, the following procedure is applied:

1. All appearances of 421 stopwords for general texts in English are deleted [24].
2. All possible continuous N-gram words (N = 1, 2, 3, 4) from the examined corpus are created, provided that the all the words in a certain N-gram are in the same sentence.
3. The frequency of each N-gram feature in the corpus is counted.
4. The frequencies of the unigram, bigram, trigram and fourgram (each group alone) features are sorted in descending order.
5. To avoid unnecessarily large number of N-grams, only a subset of the most frequent features from each group is selected. More specifically, in our study, 624 of the most frequent N-gram features are selected as follows: (a) 500 most frequent unigrams; (b) 100 most frequent bigrams; (c) 20 most frequent trigrams and (d) 4 most frequent fourgrams. The motivation for these numbers is as follows: The larger the value of N is, the smaller the number of relatively frequent N-grams in the corpus is. According to the abovementioned frequencies of the N-grams, the reduction factor was determined to be 5.

3.2   Extraction of Visual Features

The low-level visual feature that was used for capturing the characteristics of images is the RGB-SIFT visual descriptor [25], which is an extension of SIFT. In general, SIFT descriptors belong to the category of local descriptors that represent local salient points and thus capture the characteristics of the interest points (or keypoint) of images. For each keypoint only the pixel intensity of it is considered, while the color information is dropped. On the other hand, RGB-SIFT considers not only the pixel intensity, but also the color itself in the three channels Red, Green, Blue for each interest point. Thus, it captures more information and is able to better represent the image, compared to SIFT. However, when local descriptors are employed and given that the whole procedure is arduous, a visual word assignment step is applied after the feature extraction step. Specifically, k-means clustering is applied to the produced features vectors, in order to acquire the visual vocabulary. Finally, VLAD encoding is realized for representing images [26].

As a result, a descriptor is produced that gives an overall impression of the visual data. In this case, the dimensionality of the visual feature set is 4000.

4 Application of ML Methods for Classification of News Documents

Three supervised ML methods have been selected for the experiments in this study: J48, Random Forests (RF) and Sequential Minimal Optimization (SMO). Below, a short description of the methods is provided.

J48 is an improved variant of the C4.5 decision tree ML method [27], which is implemented in the WEKA ML platform [28]. J48 generates pruned or unpruned C4.5 decision trees. At each step, the most predictive attribute is determined and a node is split based on this attribute. J48 attempts to account for noise and missing data. It also deals with numeric attributes by determining where thresholds for decision splits should be placed.

Random Forests (RF) is an ensemble learning method for classification and regression [29]. The basic concept of RF is the construction of a set of decision trees. Moreover, two sources of randomness are employed in the operational procedures of RF: (1) Each decision tree is grown on a different bootstrap sample drawn randomly from the training data. (2) At each node split during the construction of a decision tree, a random subset of m variables is selected from the original variable set and the best split based on these m variables is used.

Sequential Minimal Optimization (SMO) [30, 31] is an algorithm for solving the optimization problem that occurs during the training of Support Vector Machines (SVM) [32]. SMO divides this problem into a series of smallest possible sub-problems, which are then resolved analytically.

5 Examined Corpus, Experimental Setup and Results

5.1 Examined Corpus

The application domain is news documents written in English that belong to four categories: Health, Lifestyle-Leisure, Nature-Environment and Politics. The news documents were downloaded from a large number of news web-sites (http://www.washingtonpost.com/, http://www.huffingtonpost.com/, etc.) and were annotated manually. The 1237 documents of the corpus contain around one million words and around 6.2 million characters. Table 1 presents some general information about the dataset and its domains including number of documents, number of words, number of characters, average number of words per document and average number of characters per document.

5.2 Experimental Setup

The three supervised ML methods were applied using the WEKA platform, along with their default parameter values, which are described below:

Table 1. General information about the dataset

Domain	# of documents	# of words	# of characters	Avg. # of words per document	Avg. # of characters per document
Health	187	130,157	795,435	696	4253.7
Lifestyle-Leisure	326	297,492	1,712,799	912.6	5254
Nature-Environment	447	250,859	1,543,137	561.2	3452.2
Politics	277	352,177	2,145,257	1271.4	7744.6
Total	1237	1,030,685	6,196,628	833.2	5009.4

- J48: minNumObj = 2 (the minimum number of instances per leaf), confidenceFactor = 0.25 (the confidence factor used for pruning) and seed = 1 (the value used for randomizing the data when reduced-error pruning is used).
- RF: numTrees = 100 (the number of trees to be generated), maxDepth = 0 (unlimited maximum depth of the trees) and seed = 1 (the random number seed to be used).
- SMO: The kernel to use is the polynomial kernel (exponent = 1.0 and cachSize = 250007), c = 1.0 (the complexity parameter), toleranceParameter = 0.001 and randomSeed = 1 (the random number seed for the cross-validation).

It should be noted that for all classification experiments, a 10-fold cross-validation scheme was adopted. The measures used for evaluating the performance of the methods are the following: accuracy (test set), precision, recall and F-score for each category.

After determining the two ML methods that gave the best results, we performed additional experiments using only these methods. Non-relevant features were filtered out by means of a filter method for feature selection in WEKA called CfsSubsetEval (Correlation-based Feature Subset Selection) [33]. CfsSubsetEval evaluates a subset of features by considering the individual predictive ability of each feature along with the degree of redundancy between them. Subsets of features that are highly correlated with the class, while having low inter-correlation are preferred. All the optimized parameter values were obtained as follows: each parameter was tuned in a hill climbing fashion, changing one parameter at a time (manually) until the best value was obtained.

5.3 Results

Table 2 presents the accuracy results (%) for various combinations of feature sets using 3 ML methods (J48, RF and SMO) with their default parameter values. We relate to the accuracy that were achieved by all 624 N-gram features (81.0 %) using the RF method with default parameter values (the number of trees was set to 100) as the baseline, with which to compare the other results. The performance of the N-gram feature set is superior to that of the visual feature set (58.4 %) not only in this study, but in a previous related study as well [22].

Table 2. Accuracy results (%) for various combinations of feature sets using 3 ML methods

Combinations of features	J48	RF	SMO
624 textual features	69.6	81.0	80.8
4000 visual features	55.1	58.4	57.3
59 textual features (Best First – 565 were filtered)	72.9	82.3	79.8
31 visual features (Best First – 3969 were filtered)	54.2	59.4	52.1
624 textual & 4000 visual features	69.7	68.5	81.2
59 textual & 4000 visual features	69.5	68.5	80.8
624 textual & 31 visual features	68.4	85.2	83.9
59 textual & 31 visual features	72.7	**85.9**	82.9

Some general conclusions that can be drawn from Table 2 are the following:

- The results presented in the first two rows of the table show that the basic textual feature set is superior to the corresponding visual feature set for all three ML methods. A possible explanation for this is the following: the textual features describe widespread information about the whole text, while the visual features describe information about only one representative image.
- The best accuracy result (85.9 %) is achieved by RF using two reduced feature sets: 59 textual features and 31 visual features. On the other hand, SMO achieves only 82.9 % for the same combination of features. Finally, the J48 method obtains the worst accuracy results for almost all the conducted experiments.
- There are two interesting opposing phenomena: SMO beats RF when using 4000 visual features and any set of textual features, while RF is better than SMO for all the other experiments. A possible explanation for this could be the fact that SVM (SMO in our case) is known to perform well in high-dimensional feature spaces [34].
- The improvement rate from the best unique set (59 textual features – 82.3 %) to the best combination of feature sets (59 textual features & 31 visual features – 85.9 %) is 3.6 %.

As previously mentioned, we decided to perform further experiments using only the two best ML methods according to Table 2: RF and SMO. Tables 3 and 4 provide the optimized accuracy results for all combinations of feature sets using RF and SMO, respectively. In both Tables we also present the precision, recall and F-score results for each category and for all feature set combinations presented in Table 2.

The optimized results in Table 3 for the RF model have been achieved with 800 trees (experiments were conducted for various numbers of trees between 100 and 1200) and seed = 3. On the other hand, the optimized results in Table 4 for the SMO model have been achieved with Normalized Polynomial Kernel, toleranceParameter = 0.003, c = 9 and randomSeed = 1. For both ML methods, parameters that are not mentioned here are kept with their default values. Any change in their values did not improve the classification performance results.

Table 3. Classification results (%) for different combinations of feature sets (RF with the best parameter values)

Combinations of features	Acc	Health			Lifestyle-Leisure			Nature-Environment			Politics		
		Pre	Rec	F-s	Pre	Rec	F-s	Pre	Rec	F-s	Pre	Rec	F-s
624 textual	83.1	93.3	59.4	72.5	79.2	92.0	85.1	81.3	91.7	86.2	88.1	74.7	80.8
4000 visual	58.3	61.1	57.2	59.1	53.6	66.9	59.5	58.3	63.5	60.8	66.7	40.4	50.3
59 textual	82.5	83.1	71.1	76.7	79.4	85.0	82.1	83.1	88.8	85.8	85.2	76.9	80.8
31 visual	59.7	59.8	57.2	58.5	57.1	67.8	62.0	59.2	66.0	62.4	30.2	66.5	41.5
624 textual & 4000 visual	67.8	77.4	56.7	65.4	60.2	77.0	67.6	68.5	75.8	72.0	76.1	51.6	61.5
59 textual & 4000 visual	69.0	83.2	61.0	70.4	58.4	81.3	67.9	72.5	75.4	73.9	76.2	49.8	60.2
624 textual & 31 visual	84.9	87.7	65.1	74.7	82.0	91.1	86.3	83.2	93.1	87.9	91.1	77.6	83.8
59 textual & 31 visual	86.7	89.2	75.4	81.7	85.7	90.2	87.9	85.8	91.7	88.6	88.0	81.9	84.8

Below we provide some general conclusions that can be drawn from Table 3:

- The best combination of features (59 textual features and 31 visual features) achieves an accuracy value of 86.7 % and F-score values between 81.7 % and 88.6 % for the four categories.
- The precision values for the textual feature sets (624 and 59 textual features) are significantly higher than the corresponding recall values for the categories "Health" and "Politics". Higher precision values indicate less false positives, which means that the RF method with the use of the textual features has a high ability to present relevant "Health" and "Politics" documents. Similar observations can be made for the feature combinations that include both textual and visual features, probably due to the decisive impact of the textual features.
- On the other hand, the recall values are significantly higher than the corresponding precision values for the categories "Lifestyle-Leisure" and "Nature-Environment", Higher recall values indicate less false negatives. This means that the RF method has a high ability to classify "Lifestyle-Leisure" and "Nature-Environment" documents accurately.
- The worst results for all types of feature combinations are obtained for the categories "Health" and "Politics". A possible explanation is that these categories contain a widespread variety of topics and therefore, their features vary strongly.

Table 4. Classification results (%) for different combinations of feature sets (SMO with the best parameter values)

Combinations of features	Acc	Health			Lifestyle-Leisure			Nature-Environment			Politics		
		Pre	Rec	F-s	Pre	Rec	F-s	Pre	Rec	F-s	Pre	Rec	F-s
624 textual	82.3	89.9	66.8	76.6	79.0	86.5	82.6	81.1	90.2	85.4	85.2	75.1	79.8
4000 visual	57.9	59.2	55.1	57.1	55.5	65.3	60.0	57.9	61.3	59.6	61.2	45.5	52.2
59 textual	76.6	72.8	71.7	72.2	71.0	75.8	73.3	80.5	79.4	80.0	79.9	76.2	78.0
31 visual	55.8	52.2	50.3	51.2	52.2	58.6	55.2	57.9	65.1	61.3	60.6	41.2	49.0
624 textual & 4000 visual	71.2	72.4	60.4	65.9	68.9	77.6	73.0	70.9	78.5	74.5	74.9	59.2	66.1
59 textual & 4000 visual	54.7	51.9	42.8	46.9	50.8	65.0	57.0	54.6	64.0	58.9	69.7	35.7	47.2
624 textual & 31 visual	**85.2**	87.9	78.0	82.6	85.3	87.1	86.2	83.5	88.4	85.9	86.4	82.7	84.5
59 textual & 31 visual	83.9	86.5	75.4	80.6	81.4	88.7	84.9	86.3	85.7	86.0	81.8	81.2	81.5

Below we provide some general conclusions that can be drawn from Table 4:

- In contrast to the best RF combination of features (59 textual features and 31 visual features), the best feature combination for SMO uses 31 visual and all 624 textual features. This combination achieves an accuracy value of 85.2 % and F-score values between 82.6 % and 86.2 % for the four categories.
- Similar to the RF results, the SMO precision values regarding the best unique textual feature set (624 textual) are significantly higher than the corresponding recall values for the categories "Health" and "Politics". On the other hand, for the majority of the feature sets, the recall values are significantly higher than the corresponding precision values for the categories "Lifestyle-Leisure" and "Nature-Environment". Finally, just like in the case of the RF model, the SMO worst results are obtained for the "Health" and "Politics" categories for almost all types of feature combinations.

6 Summary, Conclusions and Future Work

In this study, we present a comparative classification study of news documents using three popular ML methods (J48, RF, and SMO), and different combinations of key-phrases (word n-grams excluding stopwords) and visual features. This comparative study is in contrast to two previous studies [22, 23] that also perform classification with both textual and visual features but using only one ML method, one combination of textual and visual features and no feature selection.

Using the N-gram textual feature set containing 624 features led to an accuracy result of 81.0 %. This result was much better than the accuracy result (58.4 %) obtained for the visual feature set containing 4000 low-level features. A possible explanation for this finding is that the textual features describe widespread information about the whole text, while the visual features describe information about only one representative image. The use of the best combination of feature sets (59 textual features and 31 visual features) and the best parameter values for the RF model (800 trees) resulted in an accuracy result of 86.7 %. Regarding SMO, the use of the best combination of feature sets (624 textual features and 31 visual features) and the best parameter values led to a small accuracy improvement of 1.3 % (from 83.9 % to 85.2 %).

Suggestions for future research are: (1) Define and implement additional types of features, such as function words, morphological features (e.g. nouns, verbs and adjectives), quantitative features (e.g. average number of letters per word, average number of words per sentence) and web-oriented features, (2) Define and implement high-level visual concepts, in order to employ them in the classification tasks and (3) Apply additional ML methods to larger datasets in the news documents area, as well as in other areas, using various combinations of textual and visual features.

Acknowledgments. This work was supported by MULTISENSOR project, partially funded by the European Commission, under the contract number FP7-610411. The authors would also like to thank Avi Rosenfeld, Maor Tzidkani and Daniel Nissim Cohen from the Jerusalem College of Technology, Lev Academic Center, for their assistance to the authors in providing the software tool to generate the textual features used in this research. The authors would also like to acknowledge the networking support by the COST Action IC1302: semantic KEYword-based Search on sTructured data sOurcEs (KEYSTONE) and the COST Action IC1307: The European Network on Integrating Vision and Language (iV&L Net).

References

1. Sebastiani, F.: Machine learning in automated text categorization. ACM Comput. Surv. **34**(1), 1–47 (2002)
2. Ozgür, A.: Supervised and unsupervised machine learning techniques for text document categorization. Doctoral dissertation, Bogaziçi University (2004)
3. Kotsiantis, S.B., Zaharakis, I., Pintelas, P.: Supervised machine learning: a review of classification techniques. Informatica **31**, 249–268 (2007)
4. Aggarwal, C.C., Zhai, C · Mining Text Data. Springer, Heidelberg (2012)
5. Pazienza, M.T.: Information Extraction A Multidisciplinary Approach to an Emerging Information Technology. LNCS, vol. 1299. Springer, Heidelberg (1997)
6. Sebastiani, F.: Text categorization. In: Zanasi, A. (ed.) Text Mining and its Applications to Intelligence. CRM and Knowledge Management, pp. 109–129. WIT Press, Southampton (2005)
7. Kim, S.M., Hovy, E.: Automatic identification of pro and con reasons in online reviews. In: Proceedings of the COLING/ACL on Main Conference Poster Sessions, pp. 483–490. Association for Computational Linguistics (2006)

8. Kešelj, V., Peng, F., Cercone, N., Thomas, C.: N-gram-based author profiles for authorship attribution. In: Proceedings of the Conference Pacific Association for Computational Linguistics, PACLING, vol. 3, pp. 255–264 (2003)

9. Reddy, D.K.S., Pujari, A.K.: N-gram analysis for computer virus detection. J. Comput. Virol. 2(3), 231–239 (2006)

10. Wang, X., McCallum, A., Wei, X.: Topical N-grams: phrase and topic discovery, with an application to information retrieval. In: Seventh IEEE International Conference on ICDM, pp. 697–702 (2007)

11. Ikeda, D., Takamura, H., Okumura, M.: Semi-supervised learning for blog classification. In: AAAI, pp. 1156–1161 (2008)

12. HaCohen-Kerner, Y., Rosenfeld, A., Tzidkani, M., Cohen, D.N.: Classifying papers from different computer science conferences. In: Motoda, H., Wu, Z., Cao, L., Zaiane, O., Yao, M., Wang, W. (eds.) ADMA 2013, Part I. LNCS, vol. 8346, pp. 529–541. Springer, Heidelberg (2013)

13. HaCohen-Kerner, Y., Beck, H., Yehudai, E., Mughaz, D.: Stylistic feature sets as classifiers of documents according to their historical period and ethnic origin. Appl. Artif. Intell. 24(9), 847–862 (2010)

14. HaCohen-Kerner, Y., Beck, H., Yehudai, E., Rosenstein, M., Mughaz, D.: Cuisine: classification using stylistic feature sets and/or name-based feature sets. J. Am. Soc. Inf. Sci. Technol. 61(8), 1644–1657 (2010)

15. Kennedy, A., Inkpen, D.: Sentiment classification of movie reviews using contextual valence shifters. Comput. Intell. 22(2), 110–125 (2006)

16. Gamon, M., Basu, S., Belenko, D., Fisher, D., Hurst, M., König, A.C.: BLEWS: using blogs to provide context for news articles. In: Proceedings of the Second International AAAI Conference on Weblogs and Social Media (ICWSM), Seattle, Washington, 30 March–2 April 2008

17. Bandari, R., Asur, S., Huberman, B.A.: The pulse of news in social media: forecasting popularity. In: Proceedings of the Sixth International AAAI Conference on Weblogs and Social Media (ICWSM) (Arxiv preprint arXiv), Dublin, vol. 1202, pp. 26–33, 4–7 June 2012

18. Swezey, R.M.E., Sano, H., Shiramatsu, S., Ozono, T., Shintani, T.: Automatic detection of news articles of interest to regional communities. Int. J. Comput. Sci. Netw. Secur. (IJCSNS) 12(6), 99–106 (2012)

19. Tang, D., Wei, F., Yang, N., Zhou, M., Liu, T., Qin, B.: Learning sentiment-specific word embedding for twitter sentiment classification. In: Proceedings of the 52nd Annual Meeting of the Association for Computational Linguistics, vol. 1, pp. 1555–1565 (2014)

20. Shin, C., Doermann, D., Rosenfeld, A.: Classification of document pages using structure-based features. Int. J. Doc. Anal. Recogn. 3(4), 232–247 (2001)

21. Chen, N., Shatkay, H., Blostein, D.: Exploring a new space of features for document classification: figure clustering. In: Proceedings of the 2006 Conference of the Center for Advanced Studies on Collaborative research, p. 35. IBM Corp (2006)

22. Liparas, D., HaCohen-Kerner, Y., Moumtzidou, A., Vrochidis, S., Kompatsiaris, I.: News articles classification using random forests and weighted multimodal features. In: Lamas, D., Buitelaar, P. (eds.) IRFC 2014. LNCS, vol. 8849, pp. 63–75. Springer, Heidelberg (2014)

23. Augereau, O., Journet, N., Vialard, A., Domenger, J.P.: Improving classification of an industrial document image database by combining visual and textual features. In: In Proceedings of the 11th IAPR International Workshop on Document Analysis Systems (DAS), pp. 314–318. IEEE (2014)

24. Fox, C.: A stop list for general text. ACM SIGIR Forum 24(1–2), 19–35 (1989)

25. Van De Sande, K.E., Gevers, T., Snoek, C.G.: Evaluating color descriptors for object and scene recognition. IEEE Trans. Pattern Anal. Mach. Intell. 32(9), 1582–1596 (2010)

26. Jégou, H., Douze, M., Schmid, C., Pérez, P.: Aggregating local descriptors into a compact image representation. In: Proceedings of the IEEE Conference on Computer Vision and Pattern Recognition, pp. 3304–3311 (2010)
27. Quinlan, J.R.: C4.5: Programs for Machine Learning. Morgan Kaufmann, San Mateo (1993)
28. Hall, M., Frank, E., Holmes, G., Pfahringer, B., Reutemann, P., Witten, I.H.: The WEKA data mining software: an update. ACM SIGKDD Explor. Newslett. **11**(1), 10–18 (2009)
29. Breiman, L.: Random forests. Mach. Learn. **45**(1), 5–32 (2001)
30. Platt, J.: Fast training of support vector machines using sequential minimal optimization. In: Schoelkopf, B., Burges, C., Smola, A. (eds.) Advances in Kernel Methods – Support Vector Learning, pp. 185–208. MIT Press, Cambridge (1998)
31. Keerthi, S.S., Shevade, S.K., Bhattacharyya, C., Murthy, K.R.K.: Improvements to platt's SMO algorithm for SVM classifier design. Neural Comput. **13**(3), 637–649 (2001)
32. Cortes, C., Vapnik, V.: Support-vector networks. Mach. Learn. **20**, 273–297 (1995)
33. Hall, M.A.: Correlation-based Feature Subset Selection for Machine Learning. Hamilton, New Zealand (1998)
34. Forman, G.: An extensive empirical study of feature selection metrics for text classification. J. Mach. Learn. Res. **3**, 1289–1305 (2003)

Mining Workflow Repositories for Improving Fragments Reuse

Mariem Harmassi, Daniela Grigori, and Khalid Belhajjame[✉]

LAMSADE, Paris Dauphine University, Paris, France
Khalid.Belhajjame@dauphine.fr

Abstract. Public repositories of scientific and business workflows are gaining growing attention as a means to enable understanding, reuse and ultimately the reproducibility of the processes such workflows incarnate. However, as the number of workflows hosted by such repositories grows, their users face difficulties when it come to exploring and querying workflows. In this paper, we explore a functionality that can help repository administrators to index their workflows, and users to identify the workflows that are of interest to them. In particular, we investigate the problem of finding frequent and similar fragments in workflows using graph mining techniques. Our objective is not to come up with yet another graph mining or similarity technique. Instead, we explore different representations that can be used for encoding workflows before assessing their similarity taking into consideration the effectiveness and efficiency of the mining algorithm.

1 Introduction

In many experimental scientific domains, scientific workflows have been used to encode in-silico experiments in the form of flow of data consuming and producing programs or services, thereby allowing scientists to gain better understanding of the phenomenon or hypothesis they are investigating. The design of scientific workflows can however be a difficult task as it requires a deep knowledge of the domain as well as awareness of the programs and services available for implementing the workflow steps. To overcome this obstacle and facilitate the design of workflows, many scientific workflows repositories have emerged, e.g., myExperiment [1], Crowdlabs [2] and Galaxy [3] to share, publish and enable reuse of workflows. For example, De Roure et al. [1] pointed out the advantages of sharing and reusing workflows as a solution to face the difficulty and cost of design.

Sharing and publishing workflows is however not sufficient to enable their reuse. Over the past several years, an important number of workflows has been shared by scientists in several domains on the myExperiment workflow repository. As the number of workflows hosted by such repositories grows, their users face difficulties when it come to exploring and querying workflows. Indeed, users will still have to go through published workflows to identify those that are relevant for their purposes. The situation is exacerbated by the fact that the number of workflows hosted by workflow repositories in rapidly increasing. To overcome

© Springer International Publishing Switzerland 2015
J. Cardoso et al. (Eds.): KEYWORD 2015, LNCS 9398, pp. 76–87, 2015.
DOI: 10.1007/978-3-319-27932-9_7

this problem, mining techniques can be utilized to automatically analyze the workflows in the repository with the objective to provide templates that assist users in the design of their own workflows, thereby allowing them to take advantage of a knowledge-asset gained and verified by their peers.

Several works have been proposed in the literature for mining workflows (see, e.g. [4–6]). Unlike these proposals, our objective is not to propose yet another mining algorithm. Instead, we investigate the graph representations that can be used to encode workflow specifications into graphs before they are examined by existing graph mining algorithms. (We are particularly interested in sub-graph mining techniques that find commonalities among fragments of workflows that may correspond to important functions.) In doing so, we take into consideration the cost in terms of time that the graph mining algorithm spends given a workflow representation, and the impact of the representation on the effectiveness of the mining algorithm results. Specifically, we make the following contributions:

- We systematically compare different representation models for encoding a workflow in a graph format. The models were compared in terms of efficiency and qualitative aspects of the mining algorithm.
- The workflows uploaded within a repository are specified by different scientists. Therefore, they are likely to use different (geneous) names for workflows and activities in the workflows. We advance the state of the art by taking into consideration such heterogeneity. Specifically, we augment the mining task with a pre-processing phase that homogenizes the names used for the activities and parameters of the workflows before running the mining algorithm.
- We elaborated a method that reuse the knowledge encoded in frequent workflow fragments for facilitating workflow design by recommending such fragments to the designer during workflow specification.

The paper is structured as follows. We start by analyzing related works in Sect. 2. We present our solution for mining frequent workflow fragments in Sect. 3, some preliminary experimental results in Sect. 4 and conclude the paper in Sect. 5.

2   Related Work

There are two lines of work that are close to our proposals which we analyze in this section and compare to our work: workflow similarity and mining, and semantic enrichment as a means for improving workflow discovery.

Workflow Similarity and Workflow Mining. The literature of business and scientific workflows is rich with proposals that seek to mine existing workflows and/or identify similarities between workflows. Existing work on workflow mining, focused mainly on deriving a workflow specification (usually as a petri-net) from logs of executions of the workflows. There are however some proposals that focused on examining workflow specification using clustering [7] and case-based reasoning [8], among other techniques. For example, in the case of clustering-based techniques, several similarity measures were employed to estimate the distance between workflows. For example, Bae *et al.* [4] proposed a metric that uses tree structures to take into account flow blocks such as parallel branching and conditional choice. Wang *et al.* estimate the similarity between workflows based on the representation of workflows as Event Condition Action rules (ECA) that encode the workflows [9]. Other authors apply sub-graph isomorphism techniques, e.g. [5,6].

The above methods assess the similarity between entire workflows. In our work, we are interested in identifying the similarity between fragments of workflows. In this respect, our work is more related to the proposal by Diamantini *et al.* [10] who applied hierarchical graph clustering method in order to extract common fragments of workflows. We focus on fragment as opposed to entire workflows since there are more (realistic) opportunities for reuse at the level of the fragment as opposed to the entire workflow. In other words, the chances that the user find a workflow that match her needs are slim. On the other hand, the chances that she find workflows that contains one of more fragments that may help her composing her workflow are more substantial.

Improving Similarity using Semantic Enrichment. A comparative study of different methods for scientific workflow matching confirms that inclusion of external knowledge improves both computational complexity and often improves result quality [11]. While the application of semantic enrichment has received notable attention in the literature as a means to enhance the quality of workflow matching, enhancing the quality of fragments matching has received less attention and is by and large unexplored.

One of the main issue that benefit from semantic enrichment is that of heterogeneity in naming labelling of the parameters of the workflows and their constituent activities. To do so, taxonomies are used to infer relationships between activities and their parameters [12,13]. We use a different strategy by augmenting existing sub-graph mining techniques [12–15] by using a semantic filter that prune the database from unneeded workflows (i.e. noise) and delimit the search space. Trying to make a naive clustering of workflows in a repository would lead us to inefficient and limited method, given workflow repository size. Moreover, a striking distinction is that the previous works [13,14,16] propose the most reused fragments among the dataset as templates. Instead our work consists on assisting designer, i.e. on demand, we derive the mining process to choose the most probable component thta could help him. Due to the large collection of available data on-line, the number of templates increases, which leads the designer to a heavy activity of browsing and analysis the pool of templates in order to understand what could be useful to him.

The potential of the graph representation model of workflows to enhance not only the temporal complexity but also the effectiveness of the clustering method has been addressed only recently. This problem was tackled by Diamantini *et al.* [10] and to the best of our knowledge it's the only proposal that is partially related to ours. We expand the comparative study of Diamantini *et al.* using an additional representation alternative.

3 Methodology for Recommending Relevant Workflow Fragments

We present in this section a methodology that combines semantics-based techniques and workflow encoding techniques to support effective and efficient scientific workflow mining. Our goal is to use the mined workflow fragments in a recommendation system for workflow modelling. Figure 1 illustrates the overall approach. While specifying her workflow (see the life cycle of workflow design on the left hand side of the figure), the user can submit a fragment of her workflow to our system to identify similar fragments within the workflow repository. The user may do so for several reasons. For example, she may have an idea of how the steps within the fragment she submits are related to each other but does not know what programs (services) can be used to implement them. In this case, our system will return to the user candidate fragments from the repository where the steps are bound to actual programs (web services). The user can then choose one of the fragments returned by the system to replace the (abstract) fragment she has in her workflow. The user can also submit a fragment to mine existing similar fragments to examine how her colleagues or other third party users designed them. This may help the user improve the design of the fragment within her own workflow, for example.

Once the workflow fragment is submitted to our system (right hand side of Fig. 1), it is transformed into a graph representation that can be processed by the mining algorithm, in this case the SUBDUE algorithm [17]. Before mining the repository, a filtering operation is performed to rule out workflows that are unlikely to contain true positive fragments. The mining algorithm is then applied, and the corresponding fragments in the workflow repository are extracted and returned to the user.

The challenges to be addressed are the following:

- How to find frequent patterns in the repository?
- Which graph representation is best suited for formatting workflows for mining frequent fragments?
- How to deal with the heterogeneity of the labels used by different users to model the activities of their workflows within the repository?.

A. Workflow Encoding. In the following we explain how we address the above challenges. In order to extract frequent patterns, we use an existing graph mining algorithm, SUBDUE [17]. SUBDUE is a heuristic approach that uses a measure-theoretic information, the minimum description length, to find important subgraphs. Thus, the workflow model must be translated to a graph format. To this end, we studied some of state-of art representation models and proposed one that can enhance the running time, the memory space required, and also the significance of the patterns extracted. In fact, the impact of representation model is of major importance. In addition, we proposed to semantically filter the input data before running the mining algorithm in order to prune the database.

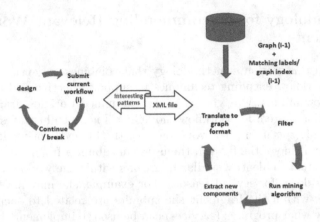

Fig. 1. An overview of the recommendation system

The pretreatments proposed improve the results as shown in the evaluation section. Instead of translating the whole workflow into a graph format in the pretreatment phase, we just take into account the fragment specified by the user. The preprocessing phase consists of transforming a rich workflow fragment into a compact graph representation. Indeed, the level of compactness depends on the representation model selected. As demonstrated by Diamantini *et al.* [10] and supported by our empirical results which we report on in the evaluation section, the choice of the encoding model affects not only the time required for mining fragment, but also the relevance of the fragments returned. Indeed, compact representations would require less processing time by the mining algorithm. On the other hand, they lead to a loss of information that may impact the quality of the results returned. Therefore, there is a trade-off to be made between the compactness of the graph representation and the loss of information. As the ability to handle large repositories is crucial, this trade-off became more difficult for large repositories.

A workflow consists of a set of activity and control flow nodes. Typical control flow operators are sequence, parallel execution of branches (AND-split, AND-join), exclusive choice of branches (XOR-split, XOR-join), and loops. To describe a sequence of activities the operator (SEQ) is used, for a parallelism the operator used is (split) and for a merging of activities the join operator (join). The operator (AND-join) means that an activity starts when all the previous activities are terminated; while a XOR-join means that an activity only begins when at least one of the previous activities has finish. The operator (AND-split) means that the end of an activity triggers the beginning of all the linked activities; while a (XOR-split) means the end of an activity triggers the beginning of a single activity from the linked activities.

In the experiment conducted by Diamantini and coauthors, they considered three representation models A, B and C (see Fig. 3). In all these models, the activities are mapped to the so called activity nodes, while the representation of operators differs from one model to another. Specifically, in model A, each operator is represented by two nodes one node called control node which is labelled "operator" and a second one which is used to specify the type of operator called control node. The labels that can be assigned to the latter one are: sequence, AND or XOR. The model A does not explicitly mention the difference between JOIN and SPLIT which can be deduced from the number of ingoing and outgoing arcs. On the other hand, Model B assigns a control node to each operator, i.e., AND-split, XOR-split, AND-join, XOR-join. The operator SEQ is not explicitly represented by a node, instead it is translated into an edge connecting the activity nodes in question.

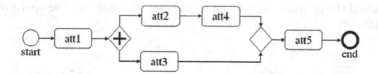

Fig. 2. An example of BPMN process (Figure extracted from [9]).

According to the experiments conducted by Diamantini *et al.*, model A is the most costly in terms of execution time and also the less effective as it generates the least significant patterns. Indeed, when using representation model A the majority of nodes are control nodes. On the other hand, the model C contains no control node. The advantage of the model C is that the edges conveys information about the nodes attached to and the nature of the operator connecting them, which resulted in a gain in terms of storage space and execution time required. However, the disadvantage of model C lies in the mapping of the "XOR" operator; a graph is generated for each alternative which makes spatio-temporal complexity grow exponentially with the size of input data. Indeed, let consider the case, where during the parsing of the original business process to convert into graph format the next node type is XOR-split with at least two incidents arcs, the number of graphs generated is doubled. In addition, if we consider an example repository where one of its most common substructures includes an operator XOR, this knowledge will not be discovered. Each path of the XOR operator will be extracted separately but the fragment of business processes which contains all of these alternatives will not be considered as a whole. However, the model C is suitable for the discovery of typical pathways, which can be useful depending on the applicative domain.

Compared to model A and C, the model B has the higher level of compactness without a loss of information. In fact, representation model B reflects most closely the initial business process scheme. Therefore, patterns discovered based on this latter model are more interesting than those extracted by model A and C for searching and indexing cases.

We suggest a new representation model for workflows. We tried to take advantage of the previous models A, B and C and come up with a new model D that alleviates the disadvantages of such representation models. Specifically, we use the same strategy as the model C in the sense that no control node is used.

The arc connecting the activity nodes will be directly labelled with a label indicating the kind of the control operator connecting the nodes. The XOR-join and XOR-split operators will not be treated in the same way as in the Model C. The difference between a JOIN and SPLIT will be implicitly deduced from the number of ingoing and outgoing arcs, as in the model A. Moreover, the model D will assume three types of labels: SEQ, AND, XOR. Do we have to follow the strategy used in model C or model B; In addition to mention the operator connecting the nodes directly on edges, shall the edges conveys information about the nodes attached to? These problematic, haven?t been resolved yet, so we propose an experimental study where testing two version of Model D, referring the activities and the operator nature namely D and referring just the operator node namely D1.

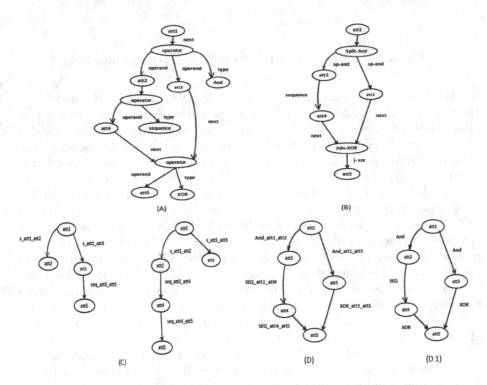

Fig. 3. Graphic of Different representation models A, B, C and D.

B. Semantic Filter. The major challenge we deal with is to propose an efficient and effective identification of similar fragments in a heterogeneous collection of scientific workflows. To improve the quality of results, we filter out irrelevant workflows by selecting only those that meets some criteria specified by the user. Specifically, we only consider workflows the activities of which are tagged with labels that are similar to keywords that are entered by the user. Such keywords may be for instances the tags that are used to label the activities in the workflow fragment submitted by the user.

To identify relevant workflows, we use semantic similarity that considers the terms (words) used to label the activities within the workflow. Let consider set1 a set of words employed by the user, set2 a set of distinct words existing in the repository. We calculate the degree of similarity between all the pairs of words used from the fist set (set1) and the second set associated to the repository (set2). If the degree of similarity is significant the concerned workflow will be selected for the mining step. To calculate the degree of similarity between two given words we used semantic similarity measure based on list of synsets returned by Wordnet. Let consider W a set of words, $Syn(w)$ a set of Synsets related to a given word w. A similarity relation that matches two words w_1 and w_2 returns true if the intersection of the synsets of the two words is not empty, i.e., $Syn(w_1) \wedge Syn(w_2) \neq \emptyset$. It returns false, otherwise.

A workflow is considered similar if it contains at least one label semantically related to one of the labels entered by the user (which may simply consist of the labels used to identify the activities in the fragment she submits to the system). Then, the subset of Workflows/business process selected will be homogenized; similar labels are replaced by the synonym given by the user. This second phase is aimed to delimit the search space and eliminate the unneeded workflows that may decrease the quality of results. In fact, running the mining phase on the whole base will lead us to propose the most common fragments in a general way but not necessarily those interesting for the user. Once the data preprocessing performed, the system applies the SUBDUE algorithm to extract the recurrent motifs. Then the list of common fragments is displayed to the user.

4   Empirical Evaluation

The methodology we have just described raises the following two questions: *Is the representation model that we propose suitable for mining frequent workflow fragments?* And, *does the semantic filter improve the results of the matching algorithm?* In this section we report on empirical evaluations that we conducted to answer the above questions.

Experimental Setting. We conducted two experiments. The first aims to validate our proposed representation models, D and D1. The second experiment assesses the impact of the semantic filter. The two experiments were carried on a DELL machine with an Intel Core i7-2670QM processor with a 2.20 GH frequency. In each experiment, we used the SUBDUE 5.5.2 tool for implementing the sub-workflow mining algorithm phase. In the following experiment we configured SUBDUE by choosing the MDL as a selection criterion with beam width equal to 4 and the number of top substructures returned is set to 10. To implement our solution, we used the Java API for WordNet Searching (JAWS) [18] to retrieve the synsets of a given label from WordNet [19].

In our case, we evaluate a recommender system that seeks to predict the interest 'preference' of the user. As the user target is known ahead, the effectiveness of the returned patterns can be reduced to a calculation of precision and recall for the first experiment and to a calculation of accuracy (less informative but sufficient) for the second one. In order to avoid giving the same weight to an activity node and any element proper to the representation model (e.g. control node) we will re-translate the top substructures returned by SUBDUE to a BPMN business process model notation. On an efficiency level, we aim to compare execution time and memory-space performances.

In the first experiment, we compared the representation models, namely A, B, C, D and D1. On an effectiveness level, our goal is to particularly show the drawback of the representation model C when it comes to deal with databases containing a quite significant number of XOR operators. To this end, we generated three datasets composed by 30, 42 and 72 workflows. The datasets are composed of a mixture of some synthetic workflows (extensions of Fig. 2) and some real ones selected from the Taverna 1 repository, with preserving the goal that the most recurrent sub-structure containing a XOR link.

In the second experiment we used real world workflows, namely the Taverna 1 workflows, which represent the largest subset of the workflows published on the well-known myExperiment repository[1]. The dataset consists of 498 public workflows. In the experiment we imagined the case where a user wants to use the tell service but she does not know how it should be properly used. She only knows that it may contain a local processor named tell. Our objective is to evaluate the impact of the semantic filter. For this purpose, we repeated the experiment twice, i.e., with and without preprocessing the input data by the semantic filter, to assess the difference.

4.1 Evaluation Results for the Fist Experiment

Figures 4 and 5 illustrate the size of the graphs created using the different representation models. It shows that model A is the most expensive in term of space disk required to encode the base in graph format. Our results confirm those reported by Diamantnini *et al.* Although, the model A requires the longest execution time (at least 7 times more than all other models), but not mentioned in Fig. 5. The qualitative performances of the A model depends on the dataset size; it can reach 0 % in terms of recall with the dataset size is important.

Regarding the C model, as expected, Fig. 4 shows that it require more than twice the number of edges and nodes required by the models that we propose, namely D and D1. In addition, the C model performs a recall rate that varies between 0 % and 61.54 % for all tested databases which confirms that it can, at best, discover only one alternative at a time (in our case there are 2 alternatives attached to the XOR node).

Qualitatively, the B model performs much better than the previous two models, A and C. On the other hand, models B and D led to very similar accuracy performances. Although, the B model B was able to discover more relevant

---

[1] http://www.myexperiment.org/home.

Input	Mod	V	E
	A	128	132
	B	79	80
9	C	123	102
	D	56	57
	D1	56	57
	A	610	604
	B	340	330
30	C	335	295
	D	268	250
	D1	268	250
	A	908	897
	B	511	496
42	C	473	421
	D	406	376
	D 1	406	376
	A	1560	1541
	B	886	863
71	C	777	706
	D	710	661
	D 1	710	661

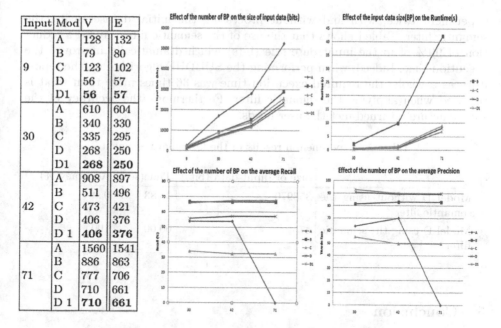

Fig. 4. Input Size   **Fig. 5.** Performances of the different Representation models

workflow elements than model D (about 10 % more), it returned more useless or irrelevant workflow elements (around 7 %). Regarding the disk space, the B model requires, between 25 % up to 40 % more than the model D and D1.

Based on results in Fig. 5, we can notice a common precision performance between models D and D1. This performance is due to the fact that these two models do not use control nodes, thereby avoiding a negative inference on the results (negative influence of the precision). Note also that labeling the edges lead to specializations of the same abstract workflow template and consequently affects the quality of results returned (negative impact on the recall).

As SUBDUE loads the input data and performs all calculations in main memory, reducing the search space and the input file size, would also reduce the amount of memory required and computation time. Moreover, the D1 model also requires the smallest space compared with the other models. We can therefore conclude from this first experiment that the D1 model was not only able to extract the most significant substructure but also in a relatively short execution time and required the least memory space. The performance achieved by our model D1 through this experiment has proven its effectiveness and efficiency. In the second experiment, we will be using model D1 for representing workflows.

4.2   Evaluation Results for the Second Experiment

Table 1 summarizes the results of the second experiment, which we ran to assess the impact of the semantic filter on the results. To this end, we repeated the experiment twice, with and without processing the initial dataset using the semantic filter. Table 1 shows that the use of the semantic filter caused a reduction of 99 % of in the input date size (bits) which dramatically improved the execution time. Indeed, when performing the SUBDUE algorithm on the repository as a whole, the required execution time was 36 times more than what is required when applying the semantic filter. Furthermore, the accuracy of the sub-structure returned met the user needs.

Table 1. Experimental results of the filtering experiment

	Size of Input data (bits)	Time(sec)	Accuracy(%)
Model D without using the semantic filter	353970	36.83	0
Model D using the semantic filter	47	00.00	100

5   Conclusion

We presented in this paper a methodology for improving the reusability of fragments within workflow repository, with the objective of allowing workflow designers to benefit from existing workflows (and the knowledge they encompass) when designing new workflows. Specifically, we examined the representation model that can be used for formatting workflows before they are mined. Moreover, we showed how semantic similarity can be used to improve the quality of the search conducted by the user. The experiment shows the effectiveness of the representation model and the semantic filtering in improving the performance of the mining task. The work presented in this paper is preliminary. Our ongoing work aims to examine how the user can formulate their search for fragments and how fragments from different workflow specification can be combined to meet user needs. We also intend to perform a larger scale evaluation to assess the performance of the solution proposed.

References

1. Roure, D.D., Goble, C.A., Stevens, R.: The design and realisation of the myExperiment virtual research environment for social sharing of workflows. Future Generation Comp. Syst. **25**(5), 561–567 (2009)
2. Mates, P., Santos, E., Freire, J., Silva, C.T.: CrowdLabs: social analysis and visualization for the sciences. In: Bayard Cushing, J., French, J., Bowers, S. (eds.) SSDBM 2011. LNCS, vol. 6809, pp. 555–564. Springer, Heidelberg (2011)
3. Giardine, B., Riemer, C., Hardison, R.C., Burhans, R., Shah, P., Zhang, Y., Blankenberg, D., Albert, I., Miller, W., Kent, W.J., Nekrutenko, A.: Galaxy: a platform for interactive large-scale genome analysis. Genome Res **15**, 1451–1455 (2005)

4. Bae, J., Caverlee, J., Liu, L., Yan, H.: Process mining by measuring process block similarity. In: Eder, J., Dustdar, S. (eds.) BPM Workshops 2006. LNCS, vol. 4103, pp. 141–152. Springer, Heidelberg (2006)
5. Goderis, A., Li, P., Goble, C.: Workflow discovery: the problem, a case study from e-science and a graph-based solution. In: International Conference on Web Services, ICWS 2006, pp. 313–19. IEEE, Chicago (2006)
6. Bergmann, R., Gil, Y.: Similarity assessment and efficient retrieval of semantic workflows. Inf. Syst. **40**, 115–127 (2014)
7. Burstein, M., Yaman, F., Oates, T.: A context driven approach for workflow mining. In: Proceedings of the 21st International Jont Conference on Artifical Intelligence, pp. 1798–1803. Morgan Kaufmann Publishers Inc., Pasadena (2009)
8. Leake, D.B., Kendall-Morwick, J.: Towards case-based support for e-science workflow generation by mining provenance. In: Althoff, K.-D., Bergmann, R., Minor, M., Hanft, A. (eds.) ECCBR 2008. LNCS (LNAI), vol. 5239, pp. 269–283. Springer, Heidelberg (2008)
9. Diamantini, C., Potena, D., Storti, E.: Mining usage patterns from a repository of scientific workflows. In: Fourth International Conference on Fuzzy Systems and Knowledge Discovery, FSKD 2007, vol. 4, pp. 629–635. IEEE, Haikou (2007)
10. Diamantini, C., Potena, D., Storti, E.: Mining usage patterns from a repository of scientific workflows. In: Proceedings of the 27th Annual ACM Symposium on Applied Computing, pp. 152–157. ACM, New York (2012)
11. Starlinger, J., Brancotte, B., Cohen-Boulakia, S., Leser, U.: Similarity search for scientific workflows. In: 40th International Conference on Very Large Data Bases, pp. 2150–8097. VLDB Endowment, Hangzhou (2014)
12. Cuzzocrea, A., Diamantini, C., Genga, L., Potena, D., Storti, E.: A composite methodology for supporting collaboration pattern discovery via semantic enrichment and multidimensional analysis. In: 2014 6th International Conference of Soft Computing and Pattern Recognition (SoCPaR), pp. 459–464. IEEE, Tunis (2014)
13. Garijo, D., Corcho, Ó., Gil, Y.: Detecting common scientific workflow fragments using templates and execution provenance. In: Proceedings of the Seventh International Conference on Knowledge Capture, pp. 33–40. ACM, New York (2013)
14. Diamantini, C., Genga, L., Potena, D., Storti, E.: Innovation pattern analysis. In: 2013 International Conference on Collaboration Technologies and Systems (CTS), pp. 628–629. IEEE, San Diego (2013)
15. Garijo, D., Corcho, Ó., Gil, Y., Gutman, B.A., Dinov, I.D., Thompson, P.M., Toga, A.W.: Fragflow automated fragment detection in scientific workflows. In: 10th IEEE International Conference on e-Science, pp. 281–289. IEEE, Sao Paulo (2014)
16. Diamantini, C., Gengaand, L., Potena, D., Storti, E.: Discovering behavioural patterns in knowledge-intensive collaborative processes. In: Proceedings of the ECML/PKDD 2014 Workshop on New Frontiers in Mining Complex Patterns (NFmcp 2014) (2014)
17. Jonyer, I., Cook, D.J., Holder, L.B.: Graph-based hierarchical conceptual clustering. J. Mach. Learn. Res. **2**, 19–43 (2001)
18. Spell, B.: Java api for wordnet searching (jaws). http://lyle.smu.edu/~tspell/jaws/index.html
19. P. University: Princeton university "about wordnet" (2010). http://wordnet.princeton.edu/wordnet/

AgileDBLP: A Search-Based Mobile Application for Structured Digital Libraries

Claudia Ifrim, Florin Pop$^{(\boxtimes)}$, Mariana Mocanu, and Valentin Cristea

Faculty of Automatic Control and Computers, Computer Science Department,
University Politehnica of Bucharest, Bucharest, Romania
claudia.ifrim@hpc.pub.ro,
{florin.pop,mariana.mocanu,valentin.cristea}@cs.pub.ro
https://cs.pub.ro

Abstract. Internet access on mobile devices used to be thought of as a service useful only for people on the move. Some mobile browser users are simply looking for quick access to specific information. They may be checking their online grocery list, looking up for an address, or trying to find the best Italian restaurant within a five minute walk. The abilities of applications on native platforms stayed rather consistent for over 10 years, but in the past several years we have seen the web platform increase its ability to handle web applications, with almost the same fidelity as native applications. Expose APIs and web services are available for a wide range of data sets or services like weather, maps and locations. In this paper, we propose an easy and fast alternative of mobile application development, using existing resources as web services or exposed APIs. We present the design of a search-based mobile application prototype (AGILEDBLP) using the exposed data set of DBLP Computer Science Bibliography. We consider that this application will be useful for scientists or common people.

Keywords: Keyword search · Digital libraries · Open data · Mobile application · Web APIs

1 Introduction

Digital Libraries that present scientific articles and publications like DBLP[1], ACM Portal[2] and Google Scholar[3] grow every year and are important for presenting overall scientific performance. Basic searches in these databases are providing results that match the keywords searched, but are affected by inconsistent information. The initiative of open data is also another good resource that could be considered when you want to create a new and innovative application or one that only promotes information [6].

---

[1] http://dblp.uni-trier.de.
[2] http://dl.acm.org/.
[3] https://scholar.google.com/.

© Springer International Publishing Switzerland 2015
J. Cardoso et al. (Eds.): KEYWORD 2015, LNCS 9398, pp. 88–93, 2015.
DOI: 10.1007/978-3-319-27932-9_8

The main objective of this paper is to show a method for an easy and fast development of a mobile application using existing services and exposed APIs. The main goal is to promote the development of mobile applications using existing resources. This application will be a prototype that will be extended in order to analyze the evolution of a scientific community.

We developed AGILEDBLP, a mobile application on Android (prototype) using the exposed API from DBLP database. The information is displayed in a simple and well-structured manner, in order to be easy for the user to access it. This application will be developed for the scientists that usually go to conferences and assist to presentations of new technologies, or new proof of concept designs. If the information presented is of interest for the attendee, then he will be able to search additional information about the presenter or about the author of that concept (he can verify what other papers the presenter published, who are the co-authors, what other conferences has he attended etc.), directly from his mobile phone or tablet. Another approach is based on semantic analysis for modeling profiles and interactions based on digital content [7].

AGILEDBLP prototype is proposed as a fast and intuitive way to access the DBLP web portal from mobile devices such as smart-phones and tablets. It will be a simple and efficient information tool customized by each user according to their preferences and interests.

The paper is structured as follows. Section 2 presents the background and related work in the field of digital libraries. Section 3 describes the AGILEDBLP prototype, while Sect. 4 highlights the user interface. The paper ends with Sect. 5 presenting conclusions and future work.

2 Related Work

There are two articles that describe the structure of the xml returned by DBLP exposed API and how to handle the requests: "DBLP - Some Lessons Learned" [4] and "DBLP-filter: effectively search on the DBLP bibliography" [1]. Those articles helped us understand the structure of the xml returned and passed by our custom parser. The DBLP service evolved from a small bibliography specialized in database systems and logic programming to a digital library covering most of the domains of computer science [5]. In June 2015, DBLP indexes 3 million publications from major information sources: VLDB, IEEE transactions, ACM transactions, etc.

Extended search capabilities are provided through Complete Search DBLP, which provides a fast search-as-you-type Interface to DBLP, as well as faceted search. Search features available: prefix search, exact word match, Boolean, phrase search, specify number of authors, only first- authored papers, etc.

Since we started our study it seems that the developer Ivano Malavolta has already published a mobile application named QuickDBLP on Google play App Store [2]. Because we want to extend our prototype in order to analyze scientific communities and DBLP is only our first data resource, we decide to develop our own application. Also, the entire idea of our application works around the concepts of open data and linked data, so we have conducted a research on these subjects in order to find out the rules that define open data, in which situations we can use the data we find on the web and if we can put it out openly, to be reused.

The publications of an author are typically identified by the author's name. The information that can be usually found in bibliographic digital libraries includes title, co-author(s), abstract, year of publication, number of citations, publication venues and links to the full-text document. Many scientists now organize their knowledge of the literature using some kind of computerized reference management system (BibTeX, EndNote, Reference Manager, RefWorks), and store their own digital libraries of full publications as PDF files [3].

In an era in which the development of technology allows collecting and storing information in electronic format, one would think that access to these databases is easier. Technically speaking, this might be true in most cases, but the main barriers today are security, economic and legal related.

With the amount of Internet search time spent on mobile devices continually increasing, its no surprise that various digital libraries and even applications for academic publications have extended their support on mobile platforms as well. On September 23, 2013, Mendeley announced iPhone and iPad apps that are free to install and recently announced (17 March 2015) the first version for Android 2. Also, ACM DL offers free apps for Android, iOS and Windows.

Although the research on mobile libraries is very recent, there have been some interesting findings regarding user perceptions on digital libraries in mobile context. X. Zha, J. Zhang and Y. Yan conducted a study in 2014, "Comparing digital libraries in the Web and mobile context from the perspective of the digital divide" [8], meant to explore and compare users perceptions of web digital libraries and mobile digital libraries in terms of ease of use and usefulness. The comparison of ease of use and usefulness employed by the authors showed that web digital libraries significantly exceed mobile digital libraries.

3   AgileDBLP Prototype

DBLP dataset is available from the location http://dblp.uni-trier.de/xml/dblp.xml and contains all the bibliographic records. The DBLP Computer Science Bibliography evolved from an early small experimental Web server to a popular service for the computer science community. Many design decisions and details of the public XML-records behind DBLP were never documented.

All the records from DBLP database are exposed in XML and JSON format, according with the schema presented in Fig. 1. When you search for a person in DBLP, the query is interpreted as a set of prefixes of a name. The result of the query could be a list of persons with names that include your searched words.

AGILEDBLP is an Android application that retrieves data from the DBLP database using the DBLP exposed API. At this stage, we intend to implement a prototype of this application and then, in the next stage, continue with an extension of this prototype. The first stage of our prototype will be an Android app with a graphical user interface that is simple to use and at the same time is able to provide all the important information to the users. Our application will be supported on Android version 4.0 and above, and the UI will stay consistent with Android design principles. The AGILEDBLP prototype specification contains primary and secondary characteristics.

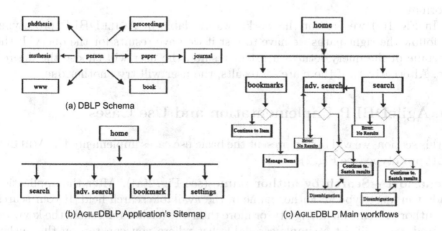

(a) DBLP Schema

(b) AGILEDBLP Application's Sitemap   (c) AGILEDBLP Main workflows

Fig. 1. AGILEDBLP prototype.

The *primary characteristics* are:

- Search for an item in the DBLP portal;
- Access the Articles bibliography;
- Access to the Article's electronic edition (if present);
- Save and organize a specific search (e.g. search by author John Nash) in order to repeat the search at any time without having to retype the name of the element to be searched.

The *secondary characteristics* are:

- Add to any item saved from its own resources, a small comment;
- Ability to identify every item that is saved (either a research or an article) with a label entered manually by the user;
- Ability to perform advanced searches, if the field author/title is not enough to identify the article, referring to other fields (Title, Author, Year, Venue, Type)
- Ability to customize the displays brightness without exiting the application.

The application is using the XML-based data set provided by DBLP. For each search operation, we will send a request to DBLP server with the parameters from the user's search. The server provides us with records that contain the bibliographic information needed to be saved locally if the user decides to store the element between its data. The heterogeneity of the sources for this type of data does not allow us to use an unique data structure, therefore the application will connect to the above link via a simple web browsing. Such content will not be saved locally, the only information that will be saved will be the link to the site. The application does not require a login to access the data so we do not need a server for the prototype. Referring to the AGILEDBLP sitemap scheme presented in Fig. 1(b) we consider the reading facilitation of the retrieved information.

In Fig. 1(c) we present the workflows available in AGILEDBLP prototype. To follow the right paths we have to test if we have results for the query. If the outcome of the query returns a list of results, the user will choose the desired one. Alternatively, if there are no results, the user will try another query.

4   AgileDBLP Implementation and Use Cases

In this section, we will briefly present the basic use cases implemented in AGILED-BLP prototype (see Fig. 2).

Scenario 1 - Search by author name (see Fig. 2(a)). After the application loads you must type an author name in the available search field. If your search by author presents an ambiguity, or more than one author references the keyword entered, you will get a simple scrollable list where you can tap on the author you searched for.

(a) Search Results   (b) Researcher Profile

Fig. 2. AGILEDBLP interface.

Scenario 2 - View author profile (see Fig. 2(b)). After the search by author name, you will see the list of returned results. To view the author profile, you must select one of the results included in the list. If you select an author from the co-authors list you will navigate to his profile.

Scenario 3 - Search an article by title. In order to search for an article you must enter the keywords in the available search textfield and check the title checkbox. We use that information to create a custom query for the DBLP API that will return an article object. The default search returns person objects.

5   Conclusions

In this paper, we have used an existing exposed API of the DBLP project to create a mobile application. We encourage the developers to use existing exposed APIs to create their mobile applications. AGILEDBLP is an useful application for people from the scientific community. More features for this application will be developed (e.g.: top co-authors of an author, aggregate other data sources like Google Scholar and ACM Portal, etc.) in the next iteration and we will publish an updated version on the Google play App Store, in order to be able to test the interest and the needs of our targeted users.

We plan to extend this application once we have a feedback from our users (using the reviews that we will receive on the Google Play application pagel).

Acknowledgments. The work has been funded by the Sectoral Operational Programme Human Resources Development 2007–2013 of the Ministry of European Funds through the Financial Agreement POSDRU/187/1.5/S/155536. The research was also supported by *"KEYSTONE - semantic KEYword-based Search on sTructured data sOurcEs* (Cost Action IC1302)"

We would like to thank the reviewers for their time and expertise, constructive comments and valuable insight.

References

1. Du, J., Jin, P., Zheng, L., Wan, S., Yue, L.: Dblp-filter: effectively search on the DBLP bibliography. In: Proceedings of the Companion Publication of the 23rd International Conference on World Wide Web Companion, WWW Companion 2014, pp. 255–256, Republic and Canton of Geneva, Switzerland (2014)
2. GooglePlay: QuickDBLP application
3. Hull, D., Pettifer, S.R., Kell, D.B., et al.: Defrosting the digital library: bibliographic tools for the next generation web. PLoS Comput. Biol. **4**(10), e1000204 (2008)
4. Ley, M.: DBLP: some lessons learned. Proc. VLDB Endow. **2**(2), 1493–1500 (2009)
5. Ley, M., Reuther, P.: Maintaining an online bibliographical database: the problem of data quality. In: Extraction et gestion des connaissances (EGC 2006), pp. 17–20, Lille, France (2006)
6. Pop, F., Negru, C., Cristea, V., Bessis, N.: Inspector: integrated service platform for management of academic and research communities over the internet. In: 2013 19th International Conference on Control Systems and Computer Science (CSCS), pp. 247–254, May 2013
7. Surdu, A.C., Pop, F.: Semantic approach for modeling profiles and interactions based on digital content. In: 2013 19th International Conference on Control Systems and Computer Science (CSCS), pp. 232–239, May 2013
8. Zha, X., Zhang, J., Yan, Y.: Comparing digital libraries in the web and mobile contexts from the perspective of the digital divide. J. Librarianship Inf. Sci. **47**(4), 330–340 (2014). doi:10.1177/0961000614532677

Support of Part-Whole Relations
in Query Answering

Piotr Kozikowski[1], Ekaterini Ioannou[2], Yannis Velegrakis[1(✉)],
and Francesco Guerra[3]

[1] University of Trento, Trento, Italy
piotr.kozikowski@gmail.com, velgias@disi.unitn.eu
[2] Technical University of Crete, Chania, Greece
ioannou@softnet.tuc.gr
[3] University of Modena and Reggio Emilia, Modena, Italy
francesco.guerra@unimore.it

Abstract. Part-whole relations are ubiquitous in our world, yet they do not get "first-class" treatment in the data managements systems most commonly used today. One aspect of part-whole relations that is particularly important is that of attribute transitivity. Some attributes of a whole are also attributes of its parts, and vice versa. We propose an extension to a generic entity-centric data model to support part-whole relations and attribute transitivity and provide more meaningful results to certain types of queries as a result. We describe how this model can be implemented using an RDF repository and three approaches to infer the implicit information necessary for query answering that adheres to the semantics of the model. The first approach is a naive implementation and the other two use indexing to improve performance. We evaluate several aspects of our implementations in a series of experimental results that show that the two approaches that use indexing are far superior to the naive approach and exhibit some advantages and disadvantages when compared to each other.

1 Introduction

Part-whole relations exist virtually everywhere and their modelling plays an important role in many application domains [6]. Despite this, they do not get "first-class" treatment in the data managements systems most commonly used today.

Part-whole relations have a number of properties and can be subdivided into different, more specific, kinds of relations. The conceptual modeling of part-whole relations and their different types and properties is a big challenge in itself and has been studied previously. The work in [1] provides a good summary of the difficulties and nuances involved. We believe that from all properties of part-whole relations the one that is most universal and deserves built-in support in a general-purpose data management system is that of attribute transitivity. It is very common to find that if some entity x is part of other entity y, some

© Springer International Publishing Switzerland 2015
J. Cardoso et al. (Eds.): KEYWORD 2015, LNCS 9398, pp. 94–107, 2015.
DOI: 10.1007/978-3-319-27932-9_9

attributes of x are also attributes of y and vice versa. For example, if Bob is an employee that works for the R&D department of company X, he also works for company X. Similarly, the person who owns a car usually also owns the car's engine. Query answering should take this transitivity into account: given that the contents of a database include "Bob works for R&D" and "R&D is part of company X", the answer to the question "who works for company X?" should include Bob, even though this fact is not explicitly stated in the data.

This transitivity does not always hold, though. The hand of a violinist is definitely a part of his or her, but it would make little sense to say that this hand plays for an orchestra given that the violinist does. Therefore, it is desired to have the ability to specify which attributes are transitive with respect to part-whole relations and which are not.

In schema-centric systems, such as relational databases, this kind of functionality can be achieved by using the schema to establish specific types of entities and attributes and define which types of entities are part of other types of entities and which type of attributes should be transitive. For example, a table *department* may be declared to be *part-of* the table *company* by having a column *part-of* containing a foreign key to *company*. If a third table *employee* is associated to *department* with the relationship *works-for*, the question "who works for company X?" can be answered with a predefined query that takes the semantics of the schema into account. The main limitation of this approach is that all the semantics have to be known a priori and defined in the schema, which imposes a rigid structure to which all data must conform. In many cases, the data is not structured enough for the design of such a schema to be practical, yet considering attribute transitivity when answering queries is still useful.

Entity-centric systems, which deal with unstructured or semi-structured data and do not rely on a schema, offer even less support for part-whole relations. Entities can have any number of arbitrary attributes, the values of which are other entities or atomic values such as strings and numbers. In such scenario the *part-of* relation is just like any other attribute.

In this paper we propose a new type of database that allows attributes to be transitive with respect to part-whole relations and takes this transitivity into account in query answering, all while preserving the flexibility and suitability for schema-less semi-structured data characteristic of entity-centric systems. We introduce a new data model to account for part-of relations and attribute transitivity, implement this model using existing database technology, suggest indexing techniques to speed-up query answering, and explore many aspects of the performance of our implementation in a series of experiments.

The paper is organized as follows. Section 2 provides a motivating example that illustrates why considering attribute transitivity with respect to part-whole relations is useful for answering queries. Section 3 describes the generic data model and our extension for supporting part-whole relations and attribute transitivity. We describe our implementation of this extended data model in Sect. 4, discussing three different approaches. We provide an experimental evaluation of our implementation in Sect. 5, concluding in Sect. 7.

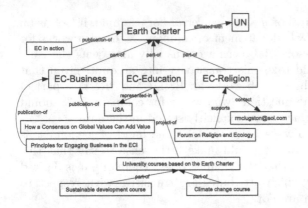
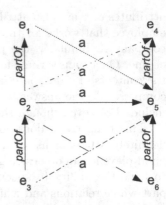

Fig. 1. A small fragment of the repository data.

Fig. 2. An example of attribute transitivity.

2   Motivating Example

Consider a system incorporating a repository that stores data related to non-governmental organizations (NGOs). NGOs typically represent and organize information in a very diverse way. This constitutes a challenge that the system needs to deal and especially when executing queries over the repository.

Figure 1 shows a small fragment of a repository that includes data related to the *Earth Charter*, one of the many NGOs affiliated with the United Nations. In the figure, each box represents an entity and each arrow represents an entity attribute. For example, the arrow labeled as *"affiliated-with"* denotes the *affiliation* of the entity *Earth Charter* with the *United Nations*. The arrows labeled as *"part-of"* denote that the *Earth Charter* is divided into the areas of *business*, *education*, and *religion*.

Consider now a user that wants to retrieve the *publications* of *Earth Charter*. Based on the information explicitly included in the repository, the answer to would only include *EC in action*. The publications *How a Consensus on Global Values Can Add Value* and *Principles for Engaging Business in the ECI* would not be included in the result set, since these are not directly associated with the entity *Earth Charter*. Of course, we could modify the model and associate the publications directly with the entity *Earth Charter* instead of *EC-Business*, but then a query asking for the publications of *EC-Business* would return no results. In addition, associating these publications with both entities would be cumbersome for the user of the repository, as she would have to figure out what is the hierarchy of areas and subareas of the Earth Charter before adding information about a publication.

Receiving inadequate query answers might frequently occur if we only use the information explicitly declared in the repository. Some additional examples with this issue appear when we try to retrieve the organizations that support the Earth Charter or the current projects of EC-Education.

To solve this problem, the repository should be able to reason about the implicit information implied by the *part-of* relations and be able to fully answer questions such as the ones discussed in the previous paragraphs. To do this in a sensible manner, we suggest incorporating additional knowledge for each attribute, and more specifically the transitivity of attributes with the *part-of* relations. We assume that the user of the repository does know this when inserting a new attribute. Note that this does not require the users to know what are the *part-of* relations themselves. For example, the user adding *Principles for Engaging Business in the ECI* as *publication-of* the entity *EC-Business* would know that this attribute has transitivity from part to whole. Thus, this publication should also be considered to be also a *publication-of* the entities that *EC-Business* is part of, i.e., the *Earth Charter* entity.

3   Data Model

3.1   Basic Database

We consider a generic data model that is centered around *entities* and *attributes*. An *entity* represents any object in the world, such as a person, a car or a school. No restrictions are imposed on the structure or characteristics of entities. An *attribute* describes some aspect of an entity and is composed of a name and a value. We assume the existence of an infinite set of entities $\mathcal{E}$, names $\mathcal{N}$, and atomic values $\mathcal{V}$. The latter contains values such as integers, strings, etc.

Definition 1. *Let pair $\langle n, v \rangle$ denote an attribute with $n \in \mathcal{N}$ being the attribute name and $v \in \mathcal{E} \cup \mathcal{V}$ the attribute value. A database is a tuple $\langle E, G \rangle$ where $E \subseteq \mathcal{E}$ is a finite set providing the entities (i.e., $\{e\}$). G is a finite set that provides the attributes of each entity as well as the relationships between entities, i.e., $G \subseteq \mathcal{N} \times \{E \cup V\}$.* ∎

Our definition can be used to represent structured data while also having the benefits of dataspaces [3] where data can be only partially structured.

It is easy to see that when all entities have at least one attribute, they will also be referred to in the G set. We can actually include a triple of the form $\langle e, -, - \rangle$ in G for each entity e that does not have an attribute, and then consider this G as the compact representation of the database. Given this compact representation, we can also retrieve the attributes of an entity e_α using the following function: $Attr(e_\alpha) = \{\langle n, v \rangle \mid \langle e_\alpha, n, v \rangle \in G\}$.

A query is described by a rule consisting of a head and a body. Both head and body are composed of a conjunction of atoms. The head can have only entity atoms of the form $e \, (n_1:v_1, \, n_2:v_2, \, \ldots, \, n_k:v_k)$, where e, n_i, and v_j are variables or constants. Variables appearing at the beginning of an atom (outside the parenthesis), i.e., e, correspond to entity variables and can only be bound to elements of $\mathcal{E}$. Variables on the left side of each colon, e.g., n_1 and n_2, stand for attribute names and can only be bound to elements of $\mathcal{N}$. Variables on the right side of each colon, e.g., v_1 and v_2, stand for attribute values and can be bound to either elements of $\mathcal{E}$ (entities) or elements of $\mathcal{V}$ (atomic values). In addition to entity atoms, the body of a query can also have atomic atoms, which are boolean conditions involving variables and constant values, e.g., $x{<}10$ or $x{=}y$.

Note that the variables appearing anywhere in the query are shared across all atoms from both the head and the body. Nesting is possible by using atoms as attribute values.

Given a binding of the variables e, n_i, and v_i to e^b, n_i^b, and v_i^b respectively, for every i from 1 to k, the entity atom e $(n_1{:}v_1, n_2{:}v_2, \ldots, n_k{:}v_k)$ is said to be *true* if there is an entity e^b in the database that has attributes $\langle n_i^b, v_i^b \rangle$, $\forall\, i \in [1,k]$. If all the atoms in the body of a query are true, the atoms in the head of the query are also considered to be true, in which case a set of entities and attributes as described in the head of the query is returned.

Example 1. Consider a user that want to detect an entity with the attribute `publication-of` having as value some entity, which in turn has the attribute `affiliated-with` with yet some other entity as value. She thus poses the following query:

Q 1 | $pub(related-to:$org) :- $pub(publication-of: $ngo),$ngo(affiliated-with: $org)

Executing **Q 1** over the data of Fig. 1 return the entity **EC in action** having the attribute `related-to` with the entity **UN** as value. ∎

3.2   Extension to Part-of Databases

We now extend the data model for the basic database (introduced in the previous paragraphs) to a model that accounts for the transitivity of attributes with respect to *part-of* relations.

The set $\mathcal{T} = \{\ up,\ down,\ both,\ none\ \}$ defines the four possible types of attribute transitivity. The elements *up* and *down* represent transitivity from part to whole, and whole to part, respectively. The element *both* denotes that both of the previous types of transitivity apply, and element *none* indicates that there is no transitivity. Additionally, the special name *partOf* is removed from the set of valid attribute names $\mathcal{N}$ and is reserved for part-of relations (Fig. 5).

Definition 2. *A part-of database is a tuple $\langle E,\ G,\ P \rangle$. E is the entity set, i.e., $E \subseteq \mathcal{E}$. P is a set of entity pairs, i.e., $P \subseteq E \times E$, with each pair $\langle e_i,\ e_j \rangle$ denoting e_i is partOf e_j. G provides relationships of an entity with its attributes or other entities, including also the transitivity type, i.e., $G \subseteq E \times \mathcal{N} \times \{E \cup \mathcal{V}\} \times \mathcal{T} \times \mathcal{T}$. Each element in G is $\langle e,\ n,\ v,\ et,\ vt,\ \rangle$ with $e \in \mathcal{E}$ being the entity, $n \in \mathcal{N}$ the attribute name, $v \in E \cup \mathcal{V}$ the attribute value, and $et, vt \in \mathcal{T}$ the transitivity for the entity that has the attribute and the attribute value v, respectively.* ∎

Each element of G states that an entity e has an attribute with name n and value v and that this attribute is transitive with respect to the part-of relations defined in P as specified by et and vt. Only one combination of n, v, et, and ev is allowed per attribute (i.e. the same attribute cannot be declared twice with conflicting types of transitivity). In addition, using the information of P,

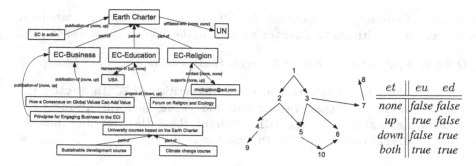

Fig. 3. Part-of database for Fig. 1 data.   **Fig. 4.** DAG example.   **Fig. 5.** Correspondence for transitivity.

et	eu	ed
none	false	false
up	true	false
down	false	true
both	true	true

i.e., *partOf* relationships between entities, we form a graph and we assume that there are no cycles in this graph.

As with the original model (Sect. 3.1), under the assumption that every entity in a part-of database has at least one attribute, the set E is no longer needed to represent the database and a more compact representation consisting of the quintuples in G and the pairs in P is possible. We denote this representation with tuple $\langle G, P \rangle$.

Figure 2 provides a graphical representation of the semantics of attribute transitivity. The entity e_3 is part of e_2, which in turn is part of e_1. Entities e_4, e_5, and e_6 have a similar configuration. The entity e_2 has an attribute a with e_5 as value. If $et=up$ or $et=both$ for attribute a, it is inferred that e_1 also has an attribute with name a and value e_5 by virtue of transitivity, even if such attribute is not explicitly declared in G. Similarly, if $et=down$ or $et=both$ for attribute a then e_3 has an attribute with name a and value e_5. The cases for the different values of vt are analogous.

Consider again our example with the NGOs repository. The data about Earth Charter can be represented using the part-of database shown in Fig. 3. All attributes have now values for et and vt. Part-of relations are no longer normal attributes but a special kind of relationship between entities. For instance, the attribute *publication-of* of the entity *Principles for Engaging Business in the ECI* has $et=none$ and $vt=up$. This means that this attribute has no transitivity on the entity's side, and transitivity of type *up* on the value's side. Since the value of this attribute is *EC-Business*, which is part of *Earth Charter*, an attribute *publication-of* is implicitly established for the entity *Principles for Engaging Business in the ECI* having *Earth Charter* as value.

The query language for part-of databases has the same elements and structure as the one defined in the previous section. The difference lies in the semantics of queries. Each atom in the body of a query can now be satisfied with the entities and attributes in the inferred closure of $\langle G, P \rangle$, defined as $\langle G \cup G', P \rangle$, where G' is the set of all triples $\langle e, n, v \rangle$ that can be inferred from the transitive attributes in G and the part-of relations in P by applying the inference rules described previously.

Example 2. Consider now searching for all entities that have an attribute publication-of with Earth Charter as value in the inferred closure of $\langle G, P \rangle$.

Q 2 | *$pub(publication-of: Earth Charter)* :- *$pub(publication-of: Earth Charter)*

If applied to the data of Fig. 3, this query returns entities: (i) EC in action, (ii) How a Consensus on Global Values Can Add Value, and (iii) Principles for Engaging Business in the ECI. Each of these three entities has an attribute publication-of with Earth Charter as value.   ∎

4 Our Solutions

We implemented the part-of database using Sesame[1], which is an open source framework for storing and querying RDF data. We chose RDF because it is a well established specification of a data model that is similar to the one we use. Sesame offers one of the most robust and mature implementations of an RDF repository available as open source.

4.1 Naive Approach

Our first implementation follows a lazy inference approach. All information is stored in a standard RDF repository and nothing is inferred at the time of insertion. When the database is queried, it analyzes the body of the query for patterns, inserts RDF statements corresponding to the inferred closure of those patterns, translates the query into SPARQL, executes it, and removes the inferred statements.

Update operations are uninteresting since they are direct mappings to the corresponding operations of the RDF repository. The only exception is that whenever a part-of relation is added, a check is made to ensure the addition does not introduce a cycle in the part-of graph G_p. Supposing that the function *addPartOfRelation*(e_1, e_2) is invoked, the part-of graph is traversed to ensure that there is no path from e_2 to e_1, in which case the operation fails.

Query answering involves several steps. The query is parsed and every entity atom is broken into one or more minimal atoms of the form *e(n:v)*. The atoms in the body of the query are classified according to which elements are constants and which are variables. If we denote variables with "?", the eight possible patterns are: *e(n:v)*, *e(n:?)*, *e(?:v)*, *e(?:?)*, *?(n:v)*, *?(n:?)*, *?(?:v)* and *?(?:?)*. If the pattern *?(?:?)* is found, the inferred closure of the entire database is computed, otherwise, only the implicit statements involving the constants in the query patterns are inferred.

The inferred closure of a pattern can be a subset of that of other pattern. In this case the former is considered redundant and only the latter is computed. For example, a query may contain the pattern e_1 *(?:v_1)*, which requires the inference of all the implicit statements that have e_1 as entity and v_1 as attribute value.

---

[1] http://www.openrdf.org/.

If the same query also contains the pattern $e_1(?:?)$, all the implicit statements that have e_1 as entity have to be inferred, which are a superset of those with e_1 as entity and v_1 as attribute value.

Figure 2 is helpful in visualizing how the inferred closure of a pattern can be obtained. To see the case for pattern $e(n:?)$, suppose a part-of database contains entities e_1, e_2, e_3, e_4, e_5 and e_6, with the part of relations shown in the figure, and that e_2's attribute with name a and value e_5 has full transitivity ($et=both$ and $vt=both$). The dashed lines represent the inferred closure of the database. First, every entity e' that is directly or indirectly a part of e (i.e. there is a path from e' to e in G_p) has to be checked for ownership of an attribute α with name n that has $et=up$ or $et=both$. If such attribute exists, the statement $\langle e, n, valueOf(\alpha) \rangle$ is added to the inferred closure. In the example, doing this for the pattern $e_1(a:?)$ would result in $\langle e_1, a, e_5 \rangle$ being added to the inferred closure. Next, every entity e'' that e is directly or indirectly part of (i.e. there is a path from e to e'' in G_p) has to be checked for ownership of an attribute β with name n that has $et=down$ or $et=both$. If such attribute exists, the statement $\langle e, n, valueOf(\beta) \rangle$ is added to the inferred closure. In the example, the statement $\langle e_3, a, e_5 \rangle$ would be added to the closure if this were done for pattern $e_3(a:?)$. Finally, every entity v that is the value of an attribute γ of e that has name n and $vt \neq none$ has to be checked for being directly or indirectly part of some entity v' (if $vt=up$ or $vt=both$), and/or an entity v'' being directly or indirectly part of v (if $vt=down$ or $vt=both$). If such entities exist, the statements $\langle e, n, v' \rangle$ and/or $\langle e, n, v'' \rangle$ are added to the closure. In the example, the statements $\langle e_2, a, e_4 \rangle$ and $\langle e_2, a, e_6 \rangle$ would be added to the closure after doing this for pattern $e_2(a:?)$.

The case for pattern $?(n:v)$ can be seen as a mirror of that for $e(n:?)$. The same steps are performed but the roles of e and v are interchanged. Other patterns require different steps but the underlying logic is the same and is not fully detailed for the sake of brevity.

Once the inferred closure of all the atoms in the body of a query is added to the repository, the equivalent SPARQL query is executed using Sesame's query engine. After the results of the query are available, all the inferred statements that were added are removed leaving the database in the same state as before executing the query.

4.2 Total Materialization

We now present another approach that follows an eager inference approach. Each time a statement or part-of relation is added, its inferred closure is computed. Similarly, when a statement or part-of relation is removed, the affected inferred statements are removed. The query execution is left entirely to Sesame's query engine, thus our main concern in this implementation is the speed of update operations.

Part-of Relations Index. Whenever a transitive attribute is inserted, the part-of graph has to be traversed to find all the relevant entities for the inferred closure. In the same way, deleting a transitive attribute requires a traversal of the part-of graph to find those inferred statements that should be removed. To speed-up this process, we propose an index dedicated to part-of relations.

The set of all part-of relations can be seen as a directed acyclic graph (DAG). We represent this graph with a double adjacency list that contains both the direct and indirect part-of relations. For example, the DAG in Fig. 4 is represented as follows:

```
 1 {2,3}   {4,5,6,7,8,9,10} {}      {}
 2 {4,5}   {6,9,10}         {1}     {}
 3 {5,6,7} {8,10}           {1}     {}
 4 {9}     {}               {2}     {1}
 5 {10}    {6}              {2,3}   {1}
 6 {}      {}               {3,10}  {1,2,5}
 7 {8}     {}               {3}     {1}
 8 {}      {}               {7}     {1,3}
 9 {}      {}               {4}     {1,2}
10 {6}     {}               {5}     {1,2,3}
```

There is an entry for every vertex in the DAG. The first column contains the list of vertices each vertex is connected to. The second column contains the list of vertices each vertex is indirectly connected to through other vertices. Columns three and four contain what the first and second columns would, if the direction of all edges were reversed. The idea is that a single look-up of this index is all that is needed for the insertion or deletion of any transitive statement. Depending on the type of transitivity, the lookup may include all columns or only some of them.

This index can be implemented with a key-value store. We used Ehcache[2], a system developed in Java meant primarily for caching the contents of some other larger and slower datastore, but it can also be used as a persistence solution to store very large datasets on disk without depending on any external database. The reason to prefer Ehcache over something such as Berkeley DB is that it performs object caching -Java objects are only serialized and deserialized when written to or read from disk-; Berkeley DB and other similar systems must serialize and deserialize Java objects every time they are inserted or retrieved, even if no access to disk is made. We found that object caching has a big influence on performance even if the amount of objects kept in memory is a relatively small part of all the stored data.

Transitive Attributes Index. The index for part-of relations is useful when inserting and deleting transitive statements, but the insertion and removal of part-of relations can benefit in turn from fast access to transitive attributes. This is because the inferred closure of transitive attributes already existing in the database can be affected by the addition or removal of a part-of relation. Given

---

[2] http://ehcache.org/.

e_1, n_1, v_1	$eu{=}true, ed{=}true, vu{=}false, vd{=}false$
e_1, n_2, v_2	$eu{=}true, ed{=}false, vu{=}false, vd{=}false$
e_1, n_3, v_3	$eu{=}false, ed{=}true, vu{=}false, vd{=}false$
e_2, n_4, v_4	$eu{=}false, ed{=}false, vu{=}true, vd{=}true$
e_2, n_5, v_5	$eu{=}false, ed{=}false, vu{=}true, vd{=}false$
e_2, n_6, v_6	$eu{=}false, ed{=}false, vu{=}false, vd{=}true$

Fig. 7. Index for eu. **Fig. 9.** Index for vu.

e_1	e_1, n_1, v_1		v_4	e_2, n_4, v_4
e_1	e_1, n_2, v_2		v_5	e_2, n_5, v_5

Fig. 6. Table with transitive attributes. **Fig. 8.** Index for ed. **Fig. 10.** Index for vd.

e_1	e_1, n_1, v_1		v_4	e_2, n_4, v_4
e_1	e_1, n_3, v_3		v_6	e_2, n_6, v_6

that transitive statements are stored as reified triples in RDF, their retrieval is not very efficient. Moreover, it is usually the case that only some of the transitive attributes are relevant for a given operation (e.g., only those with the transitivity type *up* and involving certain entity). It is therefore desired to have a fast way of retrieving transitive attributes with different characteristics.

To index transitive attributes, we propose to use an alternative representation of transitivity. Instead of having the two variables *et* and *vt* with four possible values each, we store four binary variables: *eu*, *ed*, *vu* and *vd*. Figure 5 shows the correspondence of the two representations for *et*, *eu* and *ed*. The correspondence between *vt*, *vu*, and *vd* is analogous.

Using this representation, the index consists of four tables, one for each of the binary variables *eu*, *ed*, *vu* and *vd*. To avoid having to modify the inner workings of the Sesame repository, we also added a fifth table containing all transitive attributes; this is the table that is indexed by the other four. Figures 7, 8, 9 and 10 show how the example contents of Fig. 6 are indexed. Naturally, in the real implementation the index tables contain pointers to entries in the main table rather than the entire triples as shown here.

Similarly to the part-of relations index, we implemented the transitive attributes index using a key-value store.

4.3 Smart Indexing

The previous approaches represent two extremes. The naive approach has fast update operations and the best possible space utilization given our choice of RDF repository, but much processing is required for answering queries, making them slow. The total materialization approach, on the other hand, achieves the fastest query answering possible given our choice of RDF repository and SPARQL query engine, but uses considerable extra space to have all the implicit information always readily available for queries, and needs to perform maintenance operations with every update.

We now present an approach that compromises the conflicting goals of fast query answering and fast update operations with low space requirements. Ideally, we should rewrite the query engine itself to compute the transitive closure of query patterns progressively and avoid the inference of statements that can be discovered to be unnecessary given the partial results already obtained from the query. This is, however, outside of the scope of our research. Instead, we still compute the inferred closure of all non-redundant patterns in the body of a query, as in the naive approach, but we try to do this as efficiently as possible with the help of an index.

In order to avoid traversing the part-of graph when computing the inferred closure of query patterns, we use the same part-of relations index used for the total materialization approach. We also need an index for transitive attributes, but the one from the total materialization approach is not very suitable for our current task. While inserting and deleting part-of relations is only concerned with transitive attributes involving either a specific entity or a specific attribute value, query answering often requires both entity and attribute value, and also the attribute name, depending on the query pattern. We could add a table for each of the query patterns, but this would result in at least six tables, requiring much extra space and defeating part of the purpose of not opting for the total materialization approach.

Instead, we propose to use B-trees -the basic data structure employed in Berkeley DB and many other databases- to simulate tries and allow prefix search. This way we can use a single index to search for relevant transitive attributes having one, two, or all three elements e, n, v of an attribute. This allows us to provide fast response time to all the access patterns required by query patterns using only three indexes: one sorted by env, other by vne, and the third by pev.

Using the entity, attribute name, and attribute value as key, and the attribute transitivity as value in a B-tree, just as Fig. 6 does, we achieve prefix search functionality by providing a custom comparator to be employed as the basis for sorting by the B-tree. A different comparator is used for each of the three sortings we need. For example, the index sorted by env employs a comparator that uses v as basis for comparison of two keys only if their respective values for e and n are equal; otherwise only e and n are considered. Likewise, the values of n are considered only if the keys have the same values of e. When searching the B-tree having only a prefix of the key, like en, we get the first key with the values of e and n that we specified, if such key exists, and can iterate through contiguous entries until we encounter a key that has a different value of some element of the prefix than what we specified. At this point we stop, having retrieved all attributes that share the prefix we searched for.

5   Experimental Results

We tested our implementations of the part-of database using synthetic datasets composed of entities connected to each other with part-of relations in a tree configuration. We used five parameters: n is the number of trees in a dataset, h the height of each tree, b the number of children per node, $attrs$ the number of non-transitive attributes per node, and t_attrs the number of transitive attributes. Transitive attributes are transitive either from part to whole ($et = up$ and $vt = up$), or from whole to part ($et = down$ and $vt = down$), with an equal number of each.

Each experiment consist in the creation of a synthetic dataset from scratch, a warm-up routine to ensure the database is fully initialized, and a set of measurements of different operations, each repeated several time selecting random nodes and the results averaged. In addition to measuring the time to complete

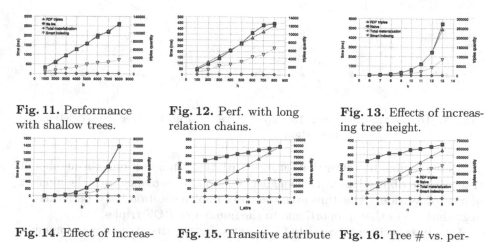

Fig. 11. Performance with shallow trees.

Fig. 12. Perf. with long relation chains.

Fig. 13. Effects of increasing tree height.

Fig. 14. Effect of increasing node children.

Fig. 15. Transitive attribute # vs. performance.

Fig. 16. Tree # vs. performance.

common operations, we also measured the size taken on disk by the database and its index, if any, after ensuring that all its contents were flushed to disk. In all graphs we provide the main variable being measured (i.e., time or space) on the vertical axis on the left, and the number of RDF triples used by the given configuration, not including any inferred triples, on the vertical axis on the right. This helps to observe the behavior relative to the size of the data.

Performance. Our main interest is the performance of queries. We evaluated all combinations of queries with the patterns $e(n:?)$, $e(?:v)$ and $?(n:v)$ using as e and n the root of the tree and a random node at the bottom of the tree, and transitive attributes as n.

Our first experiment focused on testing the behavior of trees with $n=1$, $h=1$, $attrs=0$ $t\_attrs=2$, and large numbers of children per node b. The results are shown in Fig. 11. In the following experiment we tested the opposite extreme: trees with $b=1$ (not really trees) and high values of h, the other parameters remaining unchanged. Figure 12 shows the results. As one may expect, the performance achieved with total materialization is much better than the other two approaches. The time taken for processing queries by the naive implementation seems to be directly proportional to the number of RDF statements. Smart indexing performs noticeable better and seems to be more resilient to wide and shallow trees than it is to long chains.

To try a more realistic scenario, we also tested trees that have more balanced ratios of h to b. Figure 13 shows the case where $b=2$ for various values of h. Figure 14 shows the inverse case with h fixed to 4 and various values of b. The results are very similar to the previous ones. Height has a slightly greater impact on performance than number of children, but performance is best correlated with the number of RDF triples, which in these experiments is directly proportional to the number of nodes in the tree.

Next, in experiment 5, we explored the effect of adding transitive attributes with other parameters fixed at $n = 1$, $h = 4$, $b = 5$ and $attrs = 0$. Figure 15

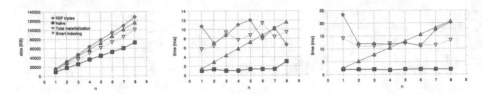

Fig. 17. Tree # vs. db size.

Fig. 18. Tree # vs. insertion.

Fig. 19. Tree # vs. deletion.

shows the results. It is clear that, at least with tree configurations, the number of transitive attributes has a much smaller effect on performance than the number of part-of relations. This time even the naive implementation has a performance degradation less than proportional to the number of RDF triples.

Finally, experiment 6 consisted in maintaining the tree structure and number of attributes fixed at $h = 4$, $b = 5$, $attrs = 50$ and $t\_attrs = 6$ and observing the effect of increasing the size of the database by adding trees. The results are shown in figure Fig. 16. In this experiment smart indexing had less of an advantage over the naive implementation. In both cases the time for answering queries grows less than proportionally to the number of RDF triples.

Overall, the result of all experiments are similar. Smart indexing has a big advantage over the naive implementation, but does not come anywhere even close to the levels of performance achieved by total materialization.

Database Size. Figure 17 shows the results of experiment 6 for database size. Evidently, the total materialization approach gets the worst results, but considering that it uses both an index and additional space in the RDF repository to store inferred statements, it is surprising that the amount of space it uses grows only slightly more than proportionally to the number of RDF triples. Obviously the naive approach is the best in terms of database size. Smart indexing is right in the middle.

In a typical RDF repository there are many more distinct object, predicates and objects than the URI prefixes they use. Therefore, storing the identifiers separately from URI prefixes can improve space utilization. This is most likely already done in Sesame's RDF repository and it is a simple way to improve the space efficiency of our indexing.

Update Operations. Update operations where tested by inserting a part-of relation between the root of a tree and a newly created entity and between a leaf node of a tree and other newly created entity. New transitive attributes were also inserted for the same nodes. The average time for those insertions was measured, after which the operations were undone with the corresponding deletions, the average time of which was also measured. Figures 18 and 19 show the results of doing this in experiment 6.

Maintaining the indexes imposes a noticeable overhead, but in a typical scenario in which queries are much more common than updates, it is well worth it.

6   Related Work

Part-whole relations have been studied from a conceptual modelling perspective [4,5,7]. The different cases that have been considered there are covered by our model. Modelling of part-whole relations has been studied in object oriented databases [1,2,6]. The main difference with our work is that they focus specifically on object oriented systems and their modelling of part-whole relations takes place at the schema level, as a mechanism to among other things improve the enforcement of the semantics defined in the schema. The model we consider does not require a schema and is more suited for semi-structured data. A similar line of work studied the information that can be inhereted across the different relations proposed for their epistemological layer of knowledge.

7   Conclusions

We proposed a new model to express part-of relations and the transitivity of attributes from whole to part and part to whole. Queries in this model take into account part-of relations and attribute transitivity to return more meaningful results, without any extra effort from the user. We implemented this model using an RDF repository and suggested two different approaches to index part-of relations and transitive attributes to improve query performance. Our experimental evaluation of these techniques indicates total materialization is unmatched in terms of query performance, but the performance of inferring implicit information in a lazy fashion can be improved significantly with an index with modest space requirements.

References

1. Artale, A., Franconi, E., Guarino, N., Pazzi, L.: Part-whole relations in object-centered systems: an overview. Data Knowl. Eng. **20**(3), 347–383 (1996)
2. Bertino, E., Guerrini, G.: Extending the ODMG object model with composite objects. SIGPLAN Not. **33**(10), 259–270 (1998)
3. Dong, X., Halevy, A.: Indexing dataspaces. In: Proceedings of the 2007 ACM SIGMOD International Conference on Management of Data, pp. 43–54. ACM, Beijing (2007)
4. Gerstl, P., Pribbenow, S.: Midwinters, end games, and body parts: a classification of part-whole relations. Int. J. Hum. Comput. Stud. **43**(5–6), 865–889 (1995)
5. Gerstl, P., Pribbenow, S.: A conceptual theory of part-whole relations and its applications. Data Knowl. Eng. **20**(3), 305–322 (1996)
6. Halper, M., Geller, J., Perl, Y.: An OODB part-whole model: semantics, notation and implementation. Data Knowl. Eng. **27**(1), 59–95 (1998)
7. Winston, M., Chaffin, R., Herrmann, D.: A taxonomy of Part-Whole relations. Cogn. Sci. **11**(4), 417–444 (1987)

Key-Phrases as Means to Estimate Birth and Death Years of Jewish Text Authors

Dror Mughaz[1,2(✉)], Yaakov HaCohen-Kerner[2], and Dov Gabbay[1,3]

[1] Department of Computer Science, Bar-Ilan University,
5290002 Ramat-Gan, Israel
myghaz@gmail.com, dov.gabbay@kcl.ac.uk
[2] Department of Computer Science, Lev Academic Center,
9116001 Jerusalem, Israel
kerner@jct.ac.il
[3] Department of Informatics, Kings College London,
Strand, London WC2R 2LS, UK

Abstract. In this study, we try to determine the time-frame in which the author of a given document lived. The discussed documents are rabbinic documents written in the Hebrew, Aramaic and Yiddish languages. The documents are usually undated and do not contain a bibliographic section, which leaves us with an interesting challenge to determine the desired time-frame. To do this, we define a set of key-phrases and formulate various types of rules: "Iron-clad", Heuristic and Greedy constraints, to define the time-frame. These rules are based on key-phrases and key-words in the documents of the authors. Identifying the time-frame of an author can help us determine the generation in which specific documents were written, can help in the examination of documents, i.e., to conclude if documents were edited, and can also help us identify an anonymous author. We tested these rules on two corpuses of documents, which were authored by 12 and 24 rabbinic authors, respectively, and the results are promising.

Keywords: Hebrew-Aramaic documents · Key-phrases · Key-words · Knowledge discovery · Time analysis · Undated documents · Undated references

1 Introduction

Determining the time frame of a book or a manuscript and identifying an author are important and challenging problems. Time-related key-words and key-phrases with references can be used to date and identify authors. Key-phrases and key-words have great potential to provide great information in many domains, such as academic, legal and commercial. Thus, the automatic extraction and analysis of key-phrases and key-words is growing rapidly and gaining momentum. Web search engines, machine learning, etc. are based on key-phrases and key-words. As a result, features are extracted and learned automatically; thus, the analysis of key-phrases and key-words has enormous importance. Key-phrases and key-words are essential features not only of the needs of scientific papers or for industry and commerce but also of rabbinic

© Springer International Publishing Switzerland 2015
J. Cardoso et al. (Eds.): KEYWORD 2015, LNCS 9398, pp. 108–126, 2015.
DOI: 10.1007/978-3-319-27932-9_10

responsa (answers written in response to Jewish legal questions authored by rabbinic scholars). Key-phrases and words included in rabbinic text are more complex to define and to extract than key-phrases and key-words in academic papers written in English because: (1) Natural Language Processing (NLP) in Hebrew, Aramaic and Yiddish has been studied relatively little; (2) there is a mixture of the complex morphology of Hebrew, Aramaic and Yiddish. For example, key-phrases and key-words can be presented with different types of prefixes (e.g., "and ...", "when ...", "and when ...", "in ...", "and when in ..."); (3) key-phrases and words in Hebrew, Aramaic and Yiddish texts may be ambiguous. Responsa texts present various interesting problems: (1) the morphology in Hebrew is richer than in English. Hebrew has 70,000,000 valid forms, while English has only 1,000,000 [1]. Declensions in Hebrew can be up to 7000 for one stem, while in English, there are only a few declensions; (2) responsa documents have a high rate of abbreviations (nearly 20 %) [2].

This research estimates the date of undated documents of authors using (1) the year (s) mentioned in the text, (2) "late" ("of blessed memory") key-phrases, (3) "rabbi" key-phrases, (4) "friend" key-phrases that are mentioned in the texts and (5) undated references of other dated authors that refer to the considered author or are mentioned by him. The assessments are with different degrees of certainty: "iron-clad", heuristic and greedy. The rules are based on key-phrases with and without references.

This paper is organized as follows: Sect. 2 gives background concerning the extraction and analysis of key-phrases and citation. Section 3 presents the boosting extraction key-phrases algorithm. Section 4 presents various rules of some degrees of certainty: "iron-clad", heuristic and greedy rules, which are used to assess writers' birth and death years. Section 5 presents the model description. Section 6 familiarizes the dataset, experiments, results and analysis. Section 7 includes the summary, conclusions and future works.

2 Related Research

Following the explosion of electronic information, there has been a growing need for extracting key-phrases and words automatically. Many studies have been made in this area for different purposes and from different perspectives. Key-words in documents allow for quick search on multiple large databases [3]. Key-words can also help to improve the NLP performance, as well as Information Retrieval performance in issues such as text summarization [4], text categorization [5], topic change during conversational text [6] and opinion mining [7].

Although key-words are important in many computer programs, there is still much to be done in this area, and the state-of-the-art methods underperform compared to other NLP core tasks [8].

There are several difficulties in extracting key-phrases and key-words. One is the length of the documents. In scientific articles, although there can only be approximately 10 key-words or key-phrases and approximately another 30 candidates in the abstract section, the rest of the article may contain hundreds of candidate key-phrases or key-words [9]. Moreover, key-words can also appear at the end of an article. If key-phrase or key-word appears at the beginning and at the end of an article, it indicates the importance of that key-phrase or key-word [10].

When documents are structured, key-words extraction is easier. For example, in scientific papers, most of the key-words appear in the abstract, in the introduction and in the title [11]. In other cases, key-phrases can be automatically extracted from web page text and from its metadata [12] for the purpose of advertisement.

Automatic extraction and analysis of references from academic papers was first proposed by Garfield [13]. Berkowitz and Elkhadiri [14] extracted writers' names and titles from articles. A knowledge-based system was used by Giuffrida et al. [15] to derive metadata, including writers' names, from computer science journal articles. Hidden Markov Models were used by Seymore et al. [16] to extract writer names from a limited collection of computer science articles. The use of terms leads to progress in the extraction of information. Selecting text before and after references to extract good index terms to improve retrieval effectiveness was done by Ritchie et al. [17]. Bradshaw [18] used terms from a fixed window around references.

In contrast with scientific articles, the documents we are working on are from the Responsa Project[1]; they are without any structural base, usually contain a mixture of at least two languages, and contain noise. Previous research on the Responsa Project dealt with text classification [19]. They checked whether classification could be done over the long axis of ethnic groups of authors with stylistic feature sets. HaCohen-Kerner and Mughaz [20] and Mughaz et al. [21] investigated in which era rabbis lived using undated Responsa, but they did not address the problem of how to extract time-related key-words or key-phrases. This article is a continuation research of this issue, i.e., determining when writers lived using key-phrases.

3   Semi-automatic Boosting Extraction of Key-Phrases

We want to automate the extraction of time-related key-phrases. We found that most of the sentences that contain time-related concepts (i.e., time-related words and phrases) to rabbinic literature (e.g., "late", "friend") are usually nearby rabbinic names/nicknames/acronyms/abbreviations/book-names. We developed a semi-automatic algorithm that boosts concepts extraction for extracting time-related concepts. The main idea is to extract sentences that contain names of rabbis so that the words and phrases that are nearby the rabbinic names are treated as the key-phrases (among others) that we look for. Now, we present a general description of our extraction algorithm.

3.1   The Algorithm

Notations:
    TW – vector of Time-related Words.
    RN – vector of Rabbinic Names.
    n – number of iterations of the algorithm.

---

[1] Contained in the Global Jewish Database (The Responsa Project at Bar-Ilan University). http://www.biu.ac.il/ICJI/Responsa.

TRC – set of Time-Related Concepts starting with, e.g., year, life, colleague, era.
TW ← TRC //initiate TW vector with TRC set
For i = 1 to n, do:

- Search for sentences that contain the last concepts added to TW.
- Extract new rabbinic names from those sentences.
- Add the new rabbinic names to RN.
- Search for sentences that contain the last rabbinic names added to RN.
- Extract time-related concepts from the new sentences:
  - Delete stop words.
  - Add the new time-related concepts to TW.
  - Add the new time-related words and phrases to TRC (with their frequency) and for the "old" time-related words and phrases only add their frequency. Sort TRC by the frequency of time-related words and phrases in decreasing order (normally, concepts have a large number of appearances).
- Select from the table the most frequent time-related concepts.

3.2   Algorithm Results

After using the algorithm, we extract time-related key-words, key-phrases and acronyms (a partial list is shown in Table 1). We divide them into three Hebrew and Aramaic key-words and key-phrases sets:

Rabbi – addressing another person as a rabbi/master, i.e., there is overlap between the lifetime of one author and the lifetime of another who is referred to by the first author as rabbi.

Friend – addressing another person as a friend, i.e., there is a large overlap between the lifetime of one author and the lifetime of another who is referred to by the first author as a friend.

Late – addressing a person who has already died.

Table 1 presents a partial list of Hebrew and Aramaic key-words and key-phrases and a few acronyms in Hebrew and their translation into English.

4   Rule-Based Constraints

This section presents the rules, based on key-phrases and references, formulated for the estimation of the birth and death years of an author X (the extracted results point to specific years) based on his texts and the texts of other writers (Yi) who mention X or one of his texts. We assume that the birth years and death years of all writers are known, excluding those that are under interrogation. Now, we will give some notions and constants that are used: X – The writer under consideration, Yi – Other writers, B – Birth year, D – Death year, MIN – Minimal age (at present, 30 years) of a rabbinic writer when he starts to write his response, MAX – Maximal age (at present, 100 years) of a rabbinic author, and RABBI_DIS – The gap age between rabbi and his student (at present, 20 years). The estimations of MIN, MAX, and RABBI_DIS constants are heuristic, although they are realistic on the basis of typical responsa authors' lifestyles.

Different types of references exist: general references with and without key-phrases, such as "rabbi", "friend" and "late". There are two types of references: those referring

Table 1. Hebrew and Aramaic cue words – a partial list

Set	Key-phrase in Hebrew	Translation of the key-phrase
Late	זכור לטוב	Remembered for good
	זכרו לברכה קדוש צדיק וטהור	of blessed memory; holy, righteous and pure
	זכרו לברכה	of blessed memory
	זכר קדוש וצדיק לברכה	may the holy and righteous be of blessed memory
	זצוק"ל	acronym: may the righteous and holy be of blessed memory
	זקוצ"ל	acronym: may the holy and righteous be of blessed memory
	יז"ל	acronym: May his memory be forever
	ז"ל	acronym: of blessed memory
Friend	ידידי הרב הגדול	My friend the Great Rabbi
	ידידי הרב הגאון	My friend the Gaon Rabbi
	ידידי הרב	My friend (the) Rabbi
	השם ישמרהו ויחיהו	may G-D preserve him and grant him life
	ידידו הקטן	his young friend
	ישמרהו השם ויחיהו	may G-D preserve him and grant him life
	ידידי הרה"ג	partially acronym: My friend the Gaon Rabbi
	יה"ו	acronym: may G-D preserve him and grant him life
Rabbi	יורנו רבנו	May the Rabbi guide us
	מרא דאתרא	the local rabbinic authority
	רבי ומורי	My Rabbi and teacher
	מרנא	Our teacher
	רבינו	Our Rabbi

to living authors and those referring to dead authors. In contrast to academic papers, responsa include many more references to dead authors than to living authors.

We will introduce rules based on key-phrases and references of different degrees of certainty: "iron-clad" (I), heuristic (H) and greedy (G). "Iron-clad" rules are always true, without any exception. Heuristic rules are almost always true. Exceptions can occur because the heuristic estimates for MIN, MAX and RABBI_DIS are incorrect. Greedy rules are rather reasonable rules for responsa authors. However, wrong estimates can sometimes be drawn while using these rules. Each rule will be numbered and its degree of certainty (i.e., I, H, G) will be presented in brackets.

4.1 "Iron-Clad" and Heuristic Rules with Key-Phrases

First, we present two general heuristic rules, which are based on regular references (i.e., without any key-phrase), based on authors that cite X.

General rule based on authors that were mentioned by X

$$D(X) > \; = \; MAX(B(Yi)) + MIN \; (1(H))$$

X must have been alive when he referred to Yi, so we can use the earliest possible age of publishing of the latest born author Yi as a lower estimate for X's death year.

General rule based on authors that referred to X

$$B(X) < \; = \; MIN(D(Yi)) - MIN \; (2(H))$$

All Yi must have been alive when they referred to X, and X must have been old enough to publish. Hence, we can use the earliest death year amongst such authors Yi as an upper estimate of X's earliest possible publication age (and thus his birth year).

General rules based on year mentioning Y that appeared in X's documents

$$D(X) > \; = \; MAX(Y) \, (3(I))$$

X must have been alive when he mentioned the year Y. We can use the most recent year mentioned by X to evaluate the death year of X as an estimation of X's death year.

Posthumous key-phrase rules. Posthumous rules estimate the birth and death years of an author X based on references of authors who refer to X with the key-phrase "late" ("of blessed memory") or on references of X that mention other authors with the key-phrase "late". Figure 1 describes possible situations where various types of authors Yi (i = 1, 2, 3) refer to X with the key-phrase "late". The lines depict writers' life spans; the left edges represent the birth years and the right edges represent death years. In this case (as all Yi refer to X with the key-phrase "late"), we know that all Yi passed away after X, but we do not know when they were born in relation to X's birth. Y1 was born before X's birth; Y2 was born after X's birth but before X's death; and Y3 was born after X's death.

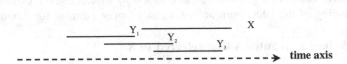

Fig. 1. References mentioning X with the key-phrase "late".

$$D(X) < = MIN(D(Yi))\ (4(I))$$

However, we know that X must have been dead when Yi referred to him with the key-phrase "late"; thus, we can use the earliest born Y's death year as an upper estimate for X's death year. Like all writers, dead writers of course have to comply with rule (2) as well.

Now, we look at the cases where the author X that we are studying refers to other authors Yi with the key-phrase "late". Figure 2 describes possible situations where X refers to various types of authors Yi (i = 1, 2, 3) with the key-phrase "late". All Yi passed away before X's death (or X may still be alive). Y1 died before X's birth; Y2 was born before X's birth and died when X was still alive; Y3 was born after X's birth and passed away when X was still alive.

Y₁ ——————— X
      Y₂
         Y₃
- → time axis

Fig. 2. References by X who mentions others with the key-phrase "late".

$$D(X) > = MAX(D(Yi))\ (5(I))$$

X must have been alive after the death of all Yi who were referred by him with the key-phrase "late". Therefore, we can use the death year of the latest-born Y as a lower estimate for X's death year.

$$B(X) > = MAX(D(Yi)) - MAX\ (6(H))$$

X was probably born after the death year of the latest-dying person that X wrote about. Thus, we use the death year of the latest-born Y minus his max life-period as a lower estimate for X's birth year.

Contemporary key-phrases rules. Contemporary key-phrases rules calculate the upper and lower bounds of the birth year of a writer X based only on the references of known writers who refer to X as their friend/rabbi. This means there must have been at least some period of time when both were alive together. Figure 3 shows possible situations where various types of writers Yi refer to X as their friend/rabbi. Y1 was born before X's birth and died before X's death; Y2 was born before X's birth and died after X's death; Y3 was born after X's birth and passed away before X's death; Y4 was

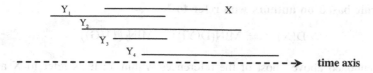

Fig. 3. References by authors who refer to X as their Friend/Rabbi.

born after X's birth and passed away after X's death. Like all writers, contemporary authors of course have to comply with rules 1 and 2 as well.

$$B(X) > = MIN(B(Yi)) - (MAX - MIN)(7(H))$$

All Yi must have been alive when X was alive, and all of them must have been old enough to publish. Thus, X could not have been born MAX-MIN years before the earliest birth year amongst all authors Yi.

$$D(X) < = MAX(D(Yi)) + (MAX - MIN)(8(H))$$

Again, all Yi must have been alive when X was alive, and all of them must have been old enough to publish. Hence, X could not have been alive MAX-MIN years after the latest death year amongst all writers Yi.

4.2 Greedy Rules

Greedy rules bounds are sensible but can sometimes lead to wrong estimates.

Greedy rule based on authors who are mentioned by X

$$B(X) > = MAX(B(Yi)) - MIN(9(G))$$

Many of the references in our research domain relate to dead authors. Thus, most of the references within X's texts relate to dead authors. Namely, many Yi were born before X's birth and died before X's death. Thus, a greedy assumption would be that X was born no earlier than the birth of the latest author mentioned by X; however, because there may be at least one case where Y was born after X was born, we subtract MIN.

Greedy rule based on references to year Y made by X

$$B(X) > = MAX(Y) - MIN(10(G))$$

When X mentions years, he usually writes the current year in which he wrote the document or a few years ahead. Most of the time, the maximum year, Y, minus MIN is larger than X's birth year.

Greedy rule based on authors who refer to X

$$D(X) < = MIN(D(Yi)) - MIN \quad (11(G))$$

As mentioned above, most of the references within Yi texts refer to X as being dead. Hence, most Yi died after X's death. Therefore, a greedy assumption would be that X died no later than the death of the earliest author who referred to X minus MIN.

Rules refinements 9–11 are presented by rules 12–17. Rules 12–14 are due to X referring to Yi and rules 15–17 are due to Yi referring to X.

Greedy rule for defining the birth year based only on authors who were referred to by X with the key-phrase "late"

$$B(X) > = MAX(D(Yi)) - MIN \quad (12(G))$$

When taking into account only references that were written in X's texts, most of the references are related to dead authors. That is, most Yi died before X's birth. Moreover, an author does not write from his birth; rather, he usually begins near his death. Thus, a greedy assumption would be that X was born no earlier than the death of the latest author mentioned by X minus MIN.

Greedy rule for defining the birth year based only on authors who are mentioned by X with the key-phrase "friend"

$$B(X) < = MIN(B(Yi)) + RABBI\_DIS \quad (13(G))$$

When taking into account only references that are mentioned by X, which are related to contemporary authors, a greedy rule could be that X was born no later than the birth of the earliest author mentioned by X with the key-phrase "friend". Because many times the older author refers to the younger author as "friend", we need to add RABBI_DIS.

Greedy rule for defining the birth year based only on authors who are mentioned by X with the key-phrase "rabbi"

$$B(X) < = MIN(B(Yi)) + RABBI\_DIS \quad (14(G))$$

When taking into account only references written in X's texts, which are related to contemporary authors, a greedy rule could be that X was born no later than the birth of the earliest author mentioned by X as a "rabbi". Due to the age difference between a student and his rabbi being approximately 20 years, we need to add RABBI_DIS.

Greedy rule for defining the death year of X based only on authors who referred to X with the key-phrase "late"

$$D(X) < = MIN(B(Yi)) + MIN \quad (15(G))$$

When taking into account only references written in Yi texts that refer to X with the key-phrase "late", a greedy assumption could be that X died no later than the birth of the earliest author who referred to X with the key-phrase "late"; because an author does not writes from birth, we need to add MIN.

Greedy rule for defining the death year of X based only on authors who referred to X with the key-phrase "friend"

$$D(X) > = MAX(D(Yi)) - RABBI\_DIS (16(G))$$

When taking into account only references written in Yi texts that refer to X with the key-phrase "friend", all Yi must have been alive when X was alive, and all of them must have been old enough to publish; also, many times, the older author refers to the younger author with the key-phrase "friend", and the opposite never occurs. Therefore, a greedy assumption would be that X died no earlier than the death of the latest author who referred to X with the key-phrase "friend" minus RABBI_DIS.

Greedy rule for defining the death year of X based only on authors who referred to X with the key-phrase "rabbi"

$$D(X) > = MAX(D(Yi)) - RABBI\_DIS (17(G))$$

This follows the same principle as the rule for defining the birth year, but because this time the student mentions the rabbi, we need to reduce RABBI_DIS.

4.3   Birth and Death Year Tuning

Application of the Heuristic and Greedy rules can lead to abnormalities, such as an author's death age being unreasonably old or young. Another possible anomaly is that the algorithm may result in a death year greater than the current year (i.e., 2015). Hence, we added some tuning rules: D – death year, B – birth year, age = D–B.

Current Year: if (D > 2015) {D = 2015}, i.e., if the current year is 2015, then the algorithm must not give a death year greater than 2015.

Age: if (age > 100), {z = age–100; D = D–z/2; B = B+z/2}, and if (age < 30), {z = 30 – age; D = D+z/2; B = B−z/2}. Our postulate is that a writer lived at least 30 years and no more than 100 years. Thus, if the age according to the algorithm is greater than 100, we take the difference between that age and 100, and then we divide that difference by 2 and normalize D and B to result in an age of 100.

5   The Model

The main steps of the model are presented below.

1. **Cleaning the texts.** Because the responsa may have undergone some editing, we
   must make sure to ignore the possible effects of differences in the texts resulting
   from variant editing practices. Therefore, we eliminate all orthographic variations.

2. **Boosting extracting key-phrases and key-words.**
3. **Normalizing the** references **in the texts.** For each author, we normalize all types of references that refer to him (e.g., various variants and spellings of his name, books, documents and their nicknames and abbreviations). For each author, we collect all references syntactic styles that refer to him and then replace them with a unique string.
4. **Building indexes,** e.g., authors, references to "late"/"friend"/"rabbi", and calculating the frequencies of each item.
5. **Performing various combinations of "iron-clad" and heuristic rules** on the one hand **and greedy rules** on the other hand **to estimate** the birth and death years of each tested author.
6. **Calculating averages** for the best "iron-clad", heuristic and greedy versions.

6 Examined Corpus, Experiments and Results

The documents of the examined corpus were downloaded from Bar-Ilan University's Responsa Project. The examined corpus contains 15,495 responsa written by 24 scholars, averaging 643 files for each scholar. The total number of characters in the whole corpus is 127,683,860 chars, and the average number of chars for each file is 8,240 chars. These authors lived over a period of 229 years (1786–2015). These files contain references; each reference pattern can be expanded into many other specific references [22].

Reference identification was performed by comparing each word to a list of 339 known authors and many of their books. This list of 25,801 specific references refers to the names, nicknames and abbreviations of these authors and their writings. Basic references were collected and all other references were produced from them.

We split the data into two corpora: (1) 10,512 responsa authored by 12 rabbis, with an average of 876 files for each scholar and each file containing an average of 1800 words spread over 135 years (1880–2015); (2) 15,495 responsa authored by 24 rabbis, with an average of 643 files for each rabbi and each file containing an average of 1609 words spread over 229 years (1786–2015) (the set of 24 rabbis contains the group of 12 rabbis). For more detailed information on the data set, refer to Table 2 in the appendix at the end of this article.

Because of the nature of the problem, it is difficult to appraise the results in the sense that although we can compare how close the system guess is to the actual birth or death years, we cannot assess how good the results are, i.e., there is no real notion of what a 'good' result is. For now, we use the notion Distance, which is defined as the estimated value minus the ground truth value.

The outcomes appear in the following histograms. Each histogram shows the results of one algorithm – Iron + Heuristic (I + H) or Greedy. Each algorithm was performed on two groups of authors: a group of 12 writers and a group of 24 writers. For both algorithm executions, there are outcomes containing estimated birth years and death years. The results shown in the histograms are the best birth/death date deviation results. In every histogram, there are eight columns; there are two quartets of columns in each histogram: the right quartet indicates the deviation from the death year, while the left quartet indicates deviations from the birth year. Each column represents a deviation without a key-phrase or with the year that was mentioned in the text, a deviation with the "late" key-phrase, with the "rabbi" key-phrase, and with the "friend" key-phrase. Moreover, we used two manipulations – Age and Current year. The column with a gray background contains the best results. Each histogram contains 8 columns (results); there are 16 histograms, so there are, in total, 128 results.

The Age manipulation is very helpful; we used it in 94.5 % of the experiments (i.e., 121/128 = 0.945) for all of the refinements, in both algorithms, with or without constants.

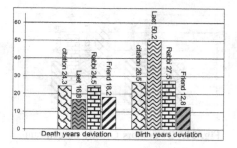

Fig. 4. 12 authors I + H no constant

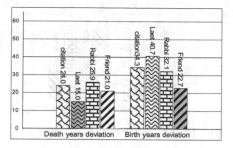

Fig. 5. 24 authors I + H no constant

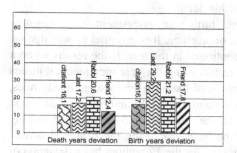

Fig. 6. 12 authors Greedy no constant

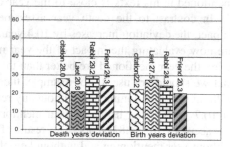

Fig. 7. 24 authors Greedy no constant

Examination of the effect of mentioning a year, listed in Figs. 4, 5, 6, and 7, compared with Figs. 8, 9, 10, and 11 regarding death year deviation, indicates that the contribution of referencing a year leads to an improvement of 2.8 years on average.

This phenomenon is more noticeable in Iron + Heuristic (average upswing of 4.2 years) than with Greedy (average deviation upswing of 1.4 years). The main reason for this is that a writer usually writes until close to his death. Additionally, when a year is mentioned in the text, it is often the year in which the writer wrote the document.

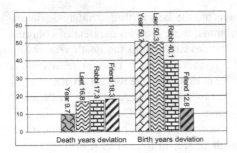

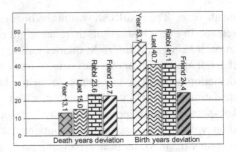

Fig. 8. 12 authors I + H no constant   **Fig. 9.** 24 authors I + H no constant

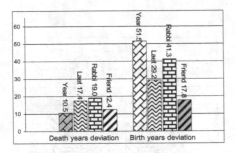

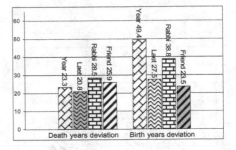

Fig. 10. 12 authors Greedy no constant   **Fig. 11.** 24 authors Greedy no constant

Because an author writes, in many cases, until near his death year, the maximum year mentioned in his texts is close to the year of his death.

In contrast to the death year assessment, birth year assessment has a negative impact; the deviation increases by 10.4 years, on average. It is essential to note that we are now evaluating the impact of the year mentioned in the text. If the results without using the year mentioned are better than the results using the year mentioned, it means that we should not use it. For example: the result of the birth year using Greedy rules, without year mentioning and without any refinement, for the 12 authors has a deviation of 16.7 years. After using the year mentioned, the deviation is 51.5 years, decreasing the accuracy by 34.83 years. The result of the birth year using the Iron + Heuristic, without year mentioning and without key-phrases, for the 12 authors has a deviation of 26.5 years. After using a reference to years, the deviation is 50.7 years, decreasing the accuracy by 24.2 years, i.e., the deviation with the use of year mentioning is greater. An analysis of the formulas shows that the formula that determines the birth year in the Greedy (10(G)) uses the most recent year the writer writes in his texts. The most recent year that the rabbi mentions is usually near his death, as explained above; therefore, very poor birth results are obtained, with a decline of 12.5 years. The results of the Greedy are better than Iron + Heuristic (decline of 8.4 years), but the effect of year mentioning on the results of Iron + Heuristic is less harmful. Thus, to estimate the death year, we will use the Iron + Heuristic algorithm with the use of year mentioning without any key-phrases.

The use of the key-phrase "friend" for birth year assessment gives the best results compared with the other key-phrases – "late", "rabbi" or none. This is because friends are of the same generation and more or less the same age; thus, they are born in roughly the same year. Thus, for a writer addressing another author as his friend, the assessment of his birth year will give good results. For the death year, however, this is not assured because there may be a much greater period between the deaths of friends (one may die at the age of 50, while his friend at the age 75). Hence, the "friend" key-phrase usually gives better birth year assessment than death year assessment (Figs. 12, 13, 14, and 15).

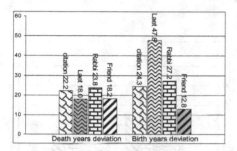

Fig. 12. 12 authors I + H with constant

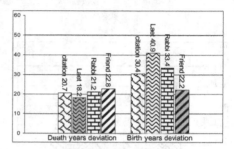

Fig. 13. 24 authors I + H with constant

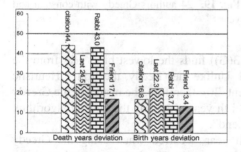

Fig. 14. 12 authors Greedy with constant

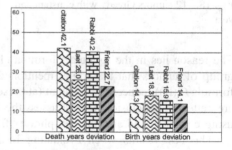

Fig. 15. 24 authors Greedy with constant

After we found that the best results for the birth year are always with the "friend" key-phrase (except for one case), we investigated at greater depth and found that this occurs specifically with the use of constants. Constants are important, resulting in an average improvement of 6.3 years in the case of Greedy (for the 12 and 24 authors). In general, a Posek is addressed in responsa after he has become important enough to be mentioned and regarded in the Halachic Responsa, which is usually at an advanced age.

We stated above that the use of Greedy rules with constants gives the greatest improvement. Even without the use of constants, Greedy produces the best results.

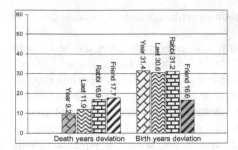

Fig. 16. 12 authors I + H with constant and year

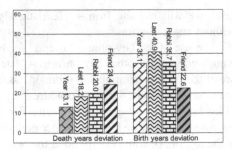

Fig. 17. 24 authors I + H with constant and year

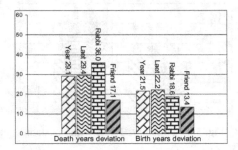

Fig. 18. 12 authors Greedy with constant and year

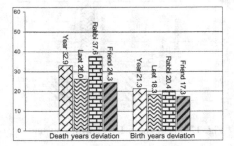

Fig. 19. 24 authors Greedy with constant and year

The reason lies in the formulae; formula (13(G)) finds the lowest birth year from the group of authors that the arbiter mentioned. Unlike the Greedy, the Iron + Heuristic formula (7(H)) reduces the constant (at present, 20); therefore, the results of the Greedy are better. In conclusion, to best assess the birth year, we apply the Greedy algorithm, using constants and also the key-phrase "friend".

The best results when evaluating birth year occurred when using the Greedy algorithm with constants and without mentioning years. The best results when evaluating death year occurred when using the Iron + Heuristic algorithm with constants and without mentioning years. When we compare these results with the results shown in Figs. 16, 17, 18, and 19 we find that in the case of Greedy, when we add more authors, there is an improvement only in one case, i.e., for the 12 authors using the "late" key-phrase; the remaining results show a decline in performance. The reason for this phenomenon may lie in the Greedy formula; when an author is more successful, in addition to being mentioned by others many times, he is mentioned at a younger age by authors that are older than him; therefore, the estimation is less accurate. For example: the estimation of the death year of the late Rabbi Ovadia Yosef has an error of 61 years (instead of 2014, the algorithm result is 1953), determining that he died at an age of 34;

using the Iron + Heuristic algorithm, there was a decrease in two results and an improvement in 5 results. For Iron + Heuristic, there is an average improvement of 0.64 years and, in fact, the best death year result estimation. The quality of the Greedy algorithm birth year results estimation using year mentioning pretty severely impairs the results (explained above). A possible explanation for this is that the improvement that comes from using constants cannot overcome the deterioration that comes from year mentioning. In contrast, when assessing the death year, using year mentioning with Iron + Heuristic significantly improves the results, and using constants improves them a little more; therefore, a combination of constants + year mentioning brings better assessment of the death year. Therefore, when assessing birth year and death year, it is not enough to use references; we have to use key-words and key-phrases. To estimate death year, we will use the year(s) mentioned in the text and constants with the Iron + Heuristic algorithm; to estimate birth year, we will run the Greedy algorithm using constants and the "friend" key-phrase without year mentioning.

7 Summary, Conclusions and Future Work

We investigated the estimation of the birth and death years of authors using year mentioning, the "late" ("of blessed memory") key-phrase, the "rabbi" key-phrase, the "friend" key-phrase and undated references that are mentioned in documents of other dated authors that refer to author being considered or those mentioned by him. This research was performed on responsa documents, where special writing rules are applied. The estimation was based on the author's texts and texts of other authors who refer to the discussed author or are mentioned by him. To do so, we formulated various types of iron-clad, heuristic and greedy rules. The best birth year assessment was achieved by using the Greedy algorithm with constants and the "friend" key-phrase. The best death year assessment was achieved by using the Iron + Heuristic algorithm with year mentioning.

We plan to improve this research by (1) testing new combinations of iron-clad, heuristic and greedy rules, as well as a combination of key-phrases (e.g., "late" and "friend"); (2) improving existing rules and/or formulating new rules; (3) defining and applying heuristic rules that take into account various details included in the responsa, e.g., events, names of people, new concepts and collocations that can be dated; (4) conducting additional experiments using many more responsa written by more authors to improve the estimates; (5) checking why the iron-clad, heuristic and greedy rules tend to produce more positive differences; and (6) testing how much of an improvement we can obtain from a correction of the upper bound of $D(x)$ and how much we will, at some point, use it for a corpus with long-dead authors.

Appendix

Data Set Information

Table 2. Full details about the data set

# of authors		Death year	Birth year	Author's name	# of files	# of words	# of characters
24	12	2015	1914	Vozner Shmuel	1807	1,490,463	7,768,059
		2014	1920	Yosef Ovadya	1283	4,578,049	22,933,473
		2006	1917	Waldenberg Eliezer	1639	3,197,662	16,589,888
		1995	1910	Auerbach Shlomo Zalman	229	793,706	4,087,592
		1989	1902	Weiss Yitzchak	1468	2,311,927	11,695,021
		1989	1911	Stern Bezalel	663	1,080,452	5,390,661
		1986	1895	Feinstein Moshe	1831	2,306,526	11,959,224
		1969	1890	Hadaya Ovadia	210	713,341	3,683,787
		1963	1898	Ades Yaakov	131	310,585	1,604,218
		1959	1901	Havita Rahamim	736	898,543	4,655,681
		1959	1889	Herzog Yitzchak	190	430,259	2,210,586
		1953	1880	Ben-Zion Meir Hai Uziel	374	899,617	4,621,414
		1948	1880	Boimel Yehoshua	129	237,093	1,227,007
		1942	1873	Baer Weiss Yitzchak	497	243,789	1,257,633
		1935	1865	Kook Abraham Yitzchak	681	750,145	3,892,610
		1921	1854	Allouch Faraji	112	205,258	1,069,460
		1911	1835	Schwadron Sholom Mordechai	1574	1,657,860	8,560,084
		1889	1813	Somekh Abdallah	86	80,508	412,486
		1896	1817	Spektor Yitzchak Elchanan	301	1,159,019	5,843,696
		1893	1820	Trunk Israel Yehoshua	281	132,257	689,598
		1880	1790	Abuhatzeira Yaakov	146	177,411	917,682
		1874	1801	Edery Abraham	119	176,849	918,564
		1866	1794	Assad Yehuda	882	880,361	4,565,230
		1843	1786	Birdugo Yaakov	126	218,402	1,130,206

References

1. Wintner, S.: Hebrew computational linguistics: past and future. Artif. Intell. Rev. **21**(2), 113–138 (2004)
2. HaCohen-Kerner, Y., Kass, A., Peretz, A.: HAADS: a Hebrew Aramaic abbreviation disambiguation system. J. Am. Soc. Inf. Sci. Technol. JASIST **61**(9), 1923–1932 (2010)
3. Gutwin, C., Paynter, G., Witten, I., Nevill-Manning, C., Frank, E.: Improving browsing in digital libraries with key-phrase indexes. Decis. Support Syst. **27**(1), 81–104 (1999)
4. Zhang, Y., Zincir-Heywood, N., Milios, E.: World wide web site summarization. Web Intell. Agent Syst. **2**(1), 39–53 (2004)
5. Hulth, A., Megyesi, B.B.: A study on automatically extracted key-words in text categorization. In: Proceedings of the 21st International Conference on Computational Linguistics and the 44th Annual Meeting of the ACL, pp. 537–544 (2006)
6. Kim, S.N., Baldwin, T.: Extracting key-words from multi-party live chats. In: Proceedings of the 26th Pacific Asia Conference on Language, Information, and Computation, pp. 199–208 (2012)
7. Berend, G.: Opinion expression mining by exploiting key-phrase extraction. In: IJCNLP, pp. 1162–1170 (2011)
8. Liu, Z., Huang, W., Zheng, Y., Sun, M.: Automatic key-phrase extraction via topic decomposition. In: Proceedings of the 2010 Conference on Empirical Methods in Natural Language Processing, ACL, pp. 366–376 (2010)
9. Hasan, K.S., Ng, V.: Conundrums in unsupervised key-phrase extraction: making sense of the state-of-the-art. In: Proceedings of the 23rd International Conference on Computational Linguistics: Posters, ACL, pp. 365–373 (2010)
10. Medelyan, O., Frank, E., Witten, I.H.: Human-competitive tagging using automatic key-phrase extraction. In: Proceedings of the 2009 Conference on Empirical Methods in Natural Language Processing: Volume 3, ACL, pp. 1318–1327 (2009)
11. Kim, S.N., Medelyan, O., Kan, M.Y., Baldwin, T.: Automatic key-phrase extraction from scientific articles. Lang. Resour. Eval. **47**(3), 723–742 (2013)
12. Yih, W.T., Goodman, J., Carvalho, V.R.: Finding advertising key-words on web pages. In: Proceedings of the 15th International Conference on World Wide Web, pp. 213–222. ACM (2006)
13. Garfield, E.: Can citation indexing be automated? In: Stevens, M. (ed.) Statistical Association Methods for Mechanical Documentation, Symposium Proceedings, National Bureau of Standards Miscellaneous Publication 269, pp. 189–142 (1965)
14. Berkowitz, E., Elkhadiri, M.R.: Creation of a style independent intelligent autonomous citation indexer to support academic research, pp. 68–73 (2004)
15. Giuffrida, G., Shek, E.C., Yang, J.: Knowledge-based metadata extraction from PostScript files. In: Proceedings of the 5th ACM Conference on Digital libraries, pp. 77–84. ACM (2000)
16. Seymore, K., McCallum, A., Rosenfeld, R.: Learning hidden markov model structure for information extraction. In: AAAI-99 Workshop on Machine Learning for Information Extraction, pp. 37–42 (1999)
17. Ritchie, A., Robertson, S., Teufel, S.: Comparing citation contexts for information retrieval. In the 17th ACM Conference on Information and Knowledge Management (CIKM), pp. 213–222 (2008)
18. Bradshaw, S.: Reference directed indexing: redeeming relevance for subject search in citation indexes. In: Koch, T., Sølvberg, I.T. (eds.) ECDL 2003. LNCS, vol. 2769, pp. 499–510. Springer, Heidelberg (2003)

19. HaCohen-Kerner, Y., Beck, H., Yehudai, E., Rosenstein, M., Mughaz, D.: Cuisine: classification using stylistic feature sets and/or name-based feature sets. J. Am. Soc. Inf. Sci. Technol. (JASIST) **61**(8), 1644–1657 (2010)
20. HaCohen-Kerner, Y., Mughaz, D.: Estimating the birth and death years of authors of undated documents using undated citations. In: Loftsson, H., Rögnvaldsson, E., Helgadóttir, S. (eds.) IceTAL 2010. LNCS, vol. 6233, pp. 138–149. Springer, Heidelberg (2010)
21. Mughaz, D., HaCohen-Kerner, Y., Gabbay, D.: When text authors lived using undated citations. In: Lamas, D., Buitelaar, P. (eds.) IRFC 2014. LNCS, vol. 8849, pp. 82–95. Springer, Heidelberg (2014)
22. HaCohen-Kerner, Y., Schweitzer, N., Mughaz, D.: Automatically identifying citations in Hebrew-Aramaic documents. Cybern. Syst. Int. J. **42**(3), 180–197 (2011)

Visualization of Uncertainty in Tag Clouds

Nikos Platis, Manolis Wallace$^{(\boxtimes)}$, and Thanos Triantos

Knowledge and Uncertainty Research Laboratory, Department of Informatics
and Telecommunications, University of the Peloponnese, 22 100 Tripolis, Greece
{nplatis,wallace}@uop.gr,thanos.tri@hotmail.com
http://gav.uop.gr

Abstract. Tag clouds provide an excellent means of visualization of
weighted semantic information. With their generation depending on given
or calculated weights, their use is not possible when these weights are not
known with certainty. In this paper we propose an extension of tag clouds
to support the notion of uncertainty and explore some properties of this
new representation. Furthermore, we present a tool implementing it.

Keywords: Tag cloud · Uncertainty · Visualization · Transparency

1 Introduction

Tag clouds are a very useful and intuitive way to present textual information.
They are consistently used as a way to visualize textual corpora, when frequency
of occurrence or some other measure of importance is of interest. More generally,
tag clouds can actually be (and often are) used in any context where weighted
textual information needs to be visualized. See for example Fig. 1 where free text
responses from 4000 individuals [3] are summarized in one brief picture.

In all existing applications of tag clouds, the information depicted is certain
and complete. However, real life semantic information rarely is, and various forms
of uncertainty are inherent in it. In this paper we propose the utilization of the
opaqueness of the tags to depict degrees of certainty on a tag cloud.

The rest of the paper is organized as follows: In Sect. 2 we outline related
background such as information visualization, uncertainty, and tag clouds. In
Sect. 3 we present our proposed approach using a simple example and discuss its
most important aspects. In Sect. 4 we focus on the software tool that implements
it. Finally, in Sect. 5 we list our concluding remarks.

2 Related Work

2.1 Information Visualization

Tag clouds are a characteristic tool of Information Visualization. Information
Visualization uses graphical representations of data in order to enhance human

© Springer International Publishing Switzerland 2015
J. Cardoso et al. (Eds.): KEYWORD 2015, LNCS 9398, pp. 127–132, 2015.
DOI: 10.1007/978-3-319-27932-9_11

Fig. 1. Word cloud of open ended responses from the Wikipedia Readers Survey [6].

cognition [7], to ease understanding of the data, to allow the viewer to form a mental model of it.

The graphical representations devised are most often able to convey, in an intuitive way, multiple properties (or dimensions) of the data at once, which would be impossible with a simple textual listing of the same data; for example, points on a x-y diagram could depict many more properties apart from those assigned to their x and y coordinates by varying their size, color, and shape.

2.2 Uncertainty

Uncertainty is an inherent feature of human life and we are accustomed to dealing with it in almost any information that we are faced with, often even subconsciously. In fact, the term "uncertainty" may refer to any situation in which something is not known certainly and/or accurately, which encompasses many heterogeneous types of information.

In this paper we deal only with uncertainty that refers to the very existence of the respective data. This includes, for instance, *probabilistic information* (events that may happen with known probability) and *possibilistic information* (events that may happen with unknown probability). Therefore, we deal with cases where uncertainty is orthogonal to the magnitude of the respective data and not correlated, i.e. it is an additional dimension of the data.

Other types of uncertainty, with which we do not deal here, refer to the magnitude of the data itself, for example *imprecision* stems from the finite precision of a measuring tool.

2.3 Tag Clouds

A tag cloud is a visualization of a set of tags, each of which is associated with a weight (frequency, importance, etc.) The tags are drawn using different *font sizes*, relative to their weight, and arranged so as not to overlap.

The other drawing parameters are chosen according to the application at hand. Tags may be arranged alphabetically (when discoverability is important), or such that the more important ones are placed near the center of the tag cloud (which emphasizes those with higher weights, cf. Fig. 1), or completely at random aiming at a more aesthetically pleasing result. They may be placed all horizontally or both horizontally and vertically (which leads to more interesting cloud shapes). Tags may be colored according to their weight (which, again, emphasizes those with higher weights, cf. Fig. 1), or with different colors according to some other characteristic (eg. category), or completely at random. Finally, the tag cloud may assume a specific shape or not.

3   Visualization of Uncertainty

As has been explained in the previous section, in the conventional tag cloud the weight of each tag is visualized by controlling the size of the font. In this work we aim to also visualize the uncertainty of each tag when it is not correlated to its weight; therefore we need to utilize a different graphical characteristic of the visualization.

Our proposal is to visualize the uncertainty of tags by controlling their *opaqueness*. Tags that are absolutely certain are printed "normally", absolutely improbable cases are not depicted at all, and intermediate cases are drawn with varying levels of transparency. Figure 2 demonstrates the concept.

Fig. 2. The uncertain tag cloud concept.

3.1   An Example

As an example, consider Table 1. In it we summarize the upcoming year's expected budget for a research group. There are three projects already running, for which next year's budget is secured, and an agreement with industry to implement a project next year with the contract still pending but almost certain. But there are also two proposals submitted to calls of different difficulties. And on top of that, there is the knowledge that some amount is typically allotted during the course of every year by the department.

Should we wish to depict this information in a tag cloud, we would be faced with the decision of how to visualize the different degrees of certainty related to each one of the table's entries. One way would be to only depict most probable options, as shown in Fig. 3(a); this clearly omits some information and we should certainly do better. Alternatively, in Fig. 3(b) we depict all entries in a simple tag cloud, choosing to hide the fact that we already know that some of these tags

Table 1. Expected budget of a research group for the next year.

Funding source	Amount (K euros)	P	Comments
Project A	50	1.0	Running project
Project B	100	1.0	Running project
Project C	150	1.0	Running project
Project D	30	0.9	Agreed project, to be contracted
Project E	100	0.5	Submitted proposal, easy call
Project F	200	0.1	Submitted proposal, very competitive call
Other	50	0.8	Additional funds typically attracted per year

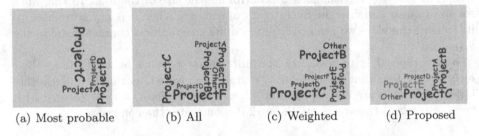

(a) Most probable   (b) All   (c) Weighted   (d) Proposed

Fig. 3. Different ways to visualize the data of Table 1.

correspond to improbable situations; again, not all the information available in the table is represented.

In Fig. 3(c) we incorporate uncertainty by weighing amounts proportionally to their probability. From an economic or risk analysis perspective this is the optimal approach, as what is depicted is the real economic value of each project at the present time. Still, from an information visualization point of view this is counterintuitive and misleading: for example, consider project F which is depicted as small in scale; this is inaccurate in all cases as project F will either bring in a large amount or none at all. The problem in this representation stems from joining volume and uncertainty, which in our case are unrelated, into one visualization parameter.

In order to overcome this, we apply our proposed solution of representing magnitude using font size, as usual, and degree of uncertainty using transparency; see Fig. 3(d). Compared to the previous approaches, we observe that this visualization contains all of the information in the table and communicates it accurately in a straightforward manner.

3.2   Discussion

Perhaps the greatest attractions of the conventional tag cloud are its simplicity and intuitiveness: larger tags stand out immediately as more important in the context of the image. Therefore, in extending the tool one has to be careful in order to retain these desirable properties.

We feel that our proposed extension of the tag cloud, which employs the opaqueness of the tags to convey their certainty, is very natural and intuitive as well: the less probable a tag, the more it faints into the background. The viewer can understand the relative certainty of the tags based on their opaqueness, while still being able to measure their relative importance based on their size.

The main parameter that influences the effectiveness of the uncertain tag cloud seems to be the choice of colors for the tags and for the background of the picture. In fact, our preliminary testing shows that if the tag color has enough contrast with the background color then the tag cloud delivers the information successfully. Figure 3(d) shows that even though the tag and the background color are both shades of green, the transparency effect is clear.

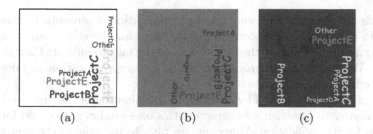

| (a) | (b) | (c) |

Fig. 4. Different color combinations.

Figure 4 demonstrates some other color combinations. Figure 4(a) uses a white background, which is possibly the safest one to use in conjuction with a strong tag color. Figure 4(b) utilizes two colors whose blending is rather well known, so the effect still gets through. Finally, Fig. 4(c) uses the colors of Fig. 3(d) inverted: a light green for the tags and a dark one for the background; we believe that the opacity effect is more intuitive with light backgrounds.

Another interesting aspect of the uncertain tag cloud would be to assess its effectiveness when many terms are depicted. Our simple test case uses few terms to convey the basic principle of this new representation; we believe that real-world uncertain tag clouds will be equally effective as conventional ones, since the effect of opacity is similar to the one of using different shades of color as in Fig. 1.

Of course, formal user evaluation of the proposed visualization would provide better insight into its properties, strengths and weeknesses.

4   Implementation

Several libraries are available for the creation of tag clouds [1,2,4,5], offering varied choices regarding the placement of words, text colors, overall size and shape, etc.

Our proposed approach to the representation of uncertainty is not related to these choices, and therefore it may be combined with any suitable software.

In order to experimentally demonstrate the effectiveness of the proposed approach we have chosen to extend the Kumo - Java Word Cloud library [5] to accept degrees of certainty as input and visualize it as degrees of opaqueness.

Kumo was chosen because it is open source software provided as a library, thus easily extensible. Furthermore, it provides enough flexibility for our purposes, allowing the user to customize all the graphical parameters of the tag cloud (dimensions, font size, colour palettes, tag direction, tag cloud shape).

Similarly to the Kumo library, our finalized tool and accompanying libraries will be made freely available under a GPLv3 licence.

5   Conclusions

Tag clouds are an established tool for the visualization of semantic textual information. In this work we proposed to extend them for the visualization of uncertain information by utilizing the opaqueness of the tags to indicate their degree of certainty. We discussed the properties of this new representation and developed a software library to showcase it.

This work will be followed by a formal user evaluation of the proposed visualization in order to establish its characteristics on sound evidence and formulate guidelines for its application. Moreover, we plan to investigate other metaphors for the transparency in tag clouds and investigate situations where it might be intuitive.

References

1. d3-cloud. http://github.com/jasondavies/d3-cloud/
2. OpenCloud. http://opencloud.mcavallo.org/
3. Research: Wikipedia Readership Survey 2011/Results (2011). https://meta.wikimedia.org/wiki/Research:Wikipedia_Readership_Survey_2011/Results
4. WordCram. http://github.com/danbernier/WordCram/
5. Cason, K.: Kumo - Java Word Cloud. http://kennycason.com/posts/2014-07-03-kumo-wordcloud.html
6. Pande, M.: Word Cloud of open ended responses from Wikipedia's readers survey. via Wikimedia Commons
7. Ware, C.: Information Visualization, Perception for Design, 3rd edn. Morgan Kaufmann, Amsterdam (2012)

Multimodal Image Retrieval Based on Keywords and Low-Level Image Features

Miran Pobar[✉] and Marina Ivašić-Kos

Department of Informatics, University of Rijeka, R. Matejčić 2, Rijeka, Croatia
{mpobar,marinai}@inf.uniri.hr

Abstract. Image retrieval approaches dealing with the complex problem of image search and retrieval in very large image datasets proposed so far can be roughly divided into those that use text descriptions of images (text-based image retrieval) and those that compare visual image content (content-based image retrieval). Both approaches have their strengths and drawbacks especially in the case of searching for images in general unconstrained domain. To take advantage of both approaches, we propose a multimodal framework that uses both keywords and visual properties of images. Keywords are used to determine the semantics of the query while the example image presents the visual impression (perceptual and structural information) that retrieved images should suit. In the paper, the overview of the proposed multimodal image retrieval framework is presented. For computing the content-based similarity between images different feature sets and metrics were tested. The procedure is described with Corel and Flickr images from the domain of outdoor scenes.

Keywords: Image retrieval · Multimodal query · Content-based similarity

1 Introduction

To help dealing with a huge number of images produced daily, different approaches for image search and retrieval have been proposed that can be roughly divided into those that use text descriptions of images (text-based image retrieval) [1, 2] and those that compare visual content (content-based image retrieval) [3, 4].

In content-based image retrieval approach images are retrieved and ranked based on visual similarity to a query image. The similarity between images is commonly computed based on low-level features so the consequence is that the similarity of semantics actually relies on the similarities of colors and other low-level features. On the specific domains such as criminalistics and medical diagnostics when search is performed among images that all have the same semantics, e.g. chest x-rays this approach gives excellent results because user is searching for exactly that query image or the most similar ones. When searching for images in general, it is more likely that the user is looking for images that are similar to the query image but differ in some aspect, i.e. the user is not actually looking for images that are as similar as possible to the query image but those images that semantically match the query image.

© Springer International Publishing Switzerland 2015
J. Cardoso et al. (Eds.): KEYWORD 2015, LNCS 9398, pp. 133–140, 2015.
DOI: 10.1007/978-3-319-27932-9_12

In most everyday cases where image semantics matter, image retrieval based on text has appeared to be easier and more suitable for image search and retrieval. This is because it is always possible to write a keyword-based query, and image examples are not always available. However, to be able to retrieve images using text, they must be labeled or described in the surrounding text, and most images are not.

Still, in some cases content-based image retrieval can be preferred to keyword-based search, especially when searching for images with very specific visual appearance that may be difficult to describe with a few keywords. Multimodal retrieval that uses both keywords and visual properties of images appears as a solution [4]. The approach in [5] uses either complex text queries describing relative configurations of objects in images, or use queries of different modalities (text, sketches and images) that are converted into a common semantic representation used for retrieval.

In this paper, we propose a multimodal image retrieval framework that integrates keyword-based image search with content-based ranking according to the visual simi-larity to a query image. In this way, users can provide both a reference example image to which the results should be similar, and keywords to specify the desired semantics of retrieved images, which can be different than in the example image. Visual similarity between candidate images and the example image is computed based on low-level visual features extracted from images. To present the perceptual information about the image, pixel-based and structure-based feature descriptors are used.

The overview of the proposed multimodal image retrieval framework is presented in Sect. 2. Section 3 presents the feature sets used for computing the content-based similarity between images and the content-based similarity measures are introduced in Sect. 4. The details about the experiment with examples from the outdoor image domain are given in Sect. 5 with the conclusion in Sect. 6.

2   Overview of Multimodal Image Retrieval Framework

The proposed pipeline for multimodal image retrieval is shown in Fig. 1. The user provides a query to the system consisting of a keyword and an example image. The expected results are images that match the given keyword because they contain a partic-ular word in the description or annotation and visually resemble the example image. The system first retrieves all the images from the image database that satisfy the query keyword. Then, low-level visual features are extracted from image regions of the example and retrieved images. Low-level visual features are then used to compare the example and all retrieved images by computing a similarity score. The retrieved images are then ranked by the similarity to the example image, yielding the final results that are presented to the user.

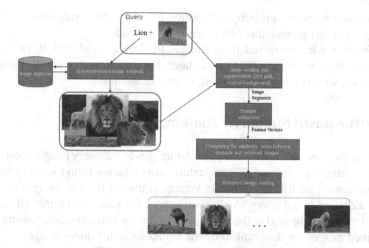

Fig. 1. Multimodal image retrieval pipeline.

3 Features

Most systems for content based image retrieval and image annotation perform feature extraction as a preprocessing step of presenting perceptual information about the image, obtaining global and local image features like dominant color or color histogram, structure, etc.

Here we have considered color histograms as pixel-based descriptors and GIST [6] as structure-based descriptors for computing the visual similarity of images during content-based image retrieval. Pixel-based descriptors are used because they are robust in position, translation and rotation changes and are useful for rapid detection of objects in image databases. Here, they are computed on the whole image, but also on two centrally symmetric regions to capture the information about the possible central image object and regions obtained by applying a 3 × 1 grid, to preserve the information about the color layout of an image.

To calculate the color histograms, the images were converted from RGB color space to indexed color, where the palette consists of 256 colors obtained by uniformly quantizing the RGB color space. The choice of number of colors in the palette depends on the number of desired bins in each histogram. Too few colors will lose accuracy by overestimating the overlap region, and too many colors will lose accuracy by creating individual bins with no values except in a densely populated sample space.

To represent coarse spatial information the GIST image descriptor was used. It is a structure-based image descriptor [7] that refers to the dominant spatial structure of the scene characterized by properties of its boundaries (e.g., the size, degree of openness, perspective) and its content (e.g., naturalness, roughness) [5]. The spatial properties are estimated using global features computed as a weighted combination of Gabor-like multi-scale oriented filters. In our case, we used 4 × 4 encoding samples in the GIST descriptor within 8 orientations per 4 scales of image components, so the GIST feature vector has 512 components.

For the content-based similarity calculation for image retrieval, subsets of features containing color histograms, and GIST descriptor is used.

The features were extracted from images that were sized 128 × 192 pixels or 192 × 128 pixels in the case of the Corel dataset. For the Flickr dataset, the images were rescaled to the width of 256 pixels before feature extraction.

4   Content-Based Similarity Ranking

To present to the user the most visually similar images to the query image, content-based similarity ranking is performed. Visual features are extracted from the query image and are compared with the low-level feature vectors extracted from all images obtained as results of keyword-based query. A similarity score between each retrieved image and the query image is computed as the distance between the corresponding feature vectors. The obtained images are then ranked by the similarity to the query image.

To compare the visual similarity of images, we used different features and suitable metrics. For histogram comparison we used the Bhattacharyya distance [8], histogram intersection [9], and the chi-squared histogram matching distance [8] and for distance between GIST features the Euclidean distance. Other metrics for comparing visual similarity can also be used, depending on the feature set, see [8] for a comprehensive review.

The Bhattacharyya distance is an appropriate distance measure for discrete probability distributions or normalized histograms p and q over the same histogram range, and it is defined as:

$$D_B(p, q) = -\ln(BC(p, q)),\tag{1}$$

where:

$$BC(p, q) = \sum_{i=1}^{n} \sqrt{p_i q_i},\tag{2}$$

is the Bhattacharyya coefficient, and for histograms p and q, n is the number of bins and p_i and q_i are the i-th bin values of histograms p and q.

The Bhattacharyya coefficient is a measurement of the amount of overlap between two histograms and can be used to determine the similarity of the two sample images being considered.

For Bhattacharyya distance, low scores indicate good matches, with perfect match being 0, and high scores indicate bad matches, with infinite value for total match.

The intersection of two histograms is the same as the minimum misclassification or error probability, which is computed as the overlap between two probability density functions [10]:

$$\text{histint}(p, q) = \sum_{i=1}^{n} \min(p_i, q_i),\tag{3}$$

where p and q are the compared normalized histograms, and n is the number of histogram bins.

To use histogram intersection as a distance measure, the inverse is computed:

$$D_I(p, q) = 1 - \text{histint}(p, q).$$ (4)

If both histograms are normalized to 1, then 0 indicates perfect match and 1 a total mismatch.

The chi-squared distance is defined as:

$$X^2(p, q) = \frac{1}{2} \sum_{i=1}^{n} \frac{[p_i - q_i]^2}{p_i + q_i},$$ (5)

where p, q, and n have the same meaning as in (3). For the chi-square distance, a perfect match is 0 and a total mismatch is unbounded and depends on the size of the histogram.

5 Experiments

The experiments of the keyword-based, content-based and multimodal image retrieval were performed on the Corel image dataset [11] and on a set of images from the Flickr website. We used images in the Corel dataset related to outdoor scenes, labeled with one or more keywords from a vocabulary of 27 keywords pertaining to natural and artificial objects, such as 'airplane', 'bird', 'lion', 'train' etc. The Flickr images were obtained by using the same set of 27 keywords as in the Corel dataset to query the Flickr website. For each of the chosen keywords, 100 most relevant image results were collected, resulting in a dataset of 2700 images belonging to 27 classes. Each of the Flickr images was annotated with the query keyword, but possibly also with other keywords or text descriptions. These labels are used for image retrieval when a user provides a keyword query.

An example of keyword based retrieval results from the Flickr image database is shown in Fig. 2. It shows the top nine images obtained for the keyword "tiger".

Fig. 2. Top nine results for keyword "tiger" obtained by text-based image retrieval.

To perform content-based similarity ranking and image retrieval, low-level visual features are extracted from Corel and Flickr images, as detailed in Sect. 3. The considered feature descriptors and combinations of appropriate distance measures were tested in isolation by querying the image databases using only the query images, and ignoring the text labels. As an example, Fig. 3 shows the results of visual similarity ranking of images when the color histogram is used as feature descriptor with histogram intersection distance measure and no keyword is specified. Similar results are obtained with other features and measures.

Fig. 3. Top five most similar images to the set target image (content-based retrieval).

Image retrieval is improved in comparison to text-based and content-based case by using multimodal query where both keywords and target image is used. Some examples of multimodal image retrieval are shown in Figs. 4 and 5 with different feature sets and distance measures. In Fig. 4, top three images are shown for the specified target image (wolf scene, same as in Fig. 3) and keyword "tiger" (as in Fig. 2), so the expected results should look like the target image, but a tiger should appear in the results. In this case, all obtained images correspond to the desired semantics (a tiger appears in the image), and the visual impression of the target image is preserved. This cannot be simply achieved with either text-based or content-based retrieval alone, although some of the images could appear among the results. In this example, color histograms were used as features with distance measures described in Sect. 4.

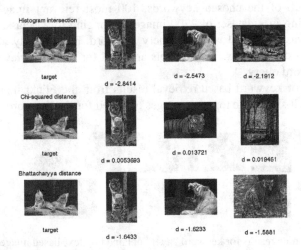

Fig. 4. Top three results for multimodal image retrieval using the target query image (left) and keyword "tiger", using color histograms for content-based ranking.

In Fig. 5, top three images are shown for the specified elephant scene as the target image and the keyword "lion". The obtained images have preserved the visual impression of the target image in both cases.

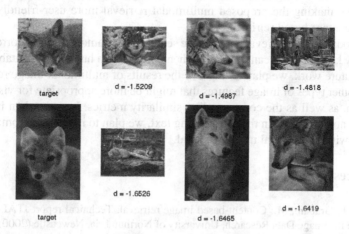

Fig. 5. Top three results for multimodal image retrieval using the target query image (left) and keyword "lion", using GIST descriptor with Euclidean distance measure for content-based ranking.

Fig. 6. Top three results for multimodal image retrieval using the target query image (left) and keyword "tiger", using color histograms for content-based ranking.

The influence of the target image in the multimodal image retrieval can be illustrated with an example shown in Fig. 6. The figure shows the results of two multimodal queries, both with the same keyword (wolf), but with different target images. Due to different feature values of the target images, the obtained results show different visual appearances of wolves. In both queries, the Bhattacharyya distance with color histograms was used.

6 Conclusion and Future Work

In this paper, a multimodal image retrieval framework was proposed, integrating keyword-based image search with content-based ranking according to the visual similarity to a query image. The semantics of the retrieved images are specified by keywords that are used to retrieve candidate images according to their textual annotations. The retrieved images are then ranked and sorted according to the visual similarity to the query image and presented to the user.

For content-based image ranking, different visual features extracted from images and distance measures were tested on image retrieval tasks on Corel and Flickr image databases of outdoor scenes. All tested measures and features have proven useful for improving the image retrieval. To choose the most suitable features and measure for the task of image retrieval in general domain, more formal evaluation will be performed since their performance in our experiment was similar to one another with many appearances of the same images in top 10 results.

The experiments have shown that multimodal image retrieval gives the user the opportunity to specify his query more easily and accurately, in terms of visual appearance and structure than with keywords alone. Simultaneously, the semantics are specified with keywords, so the query image does not have to be semantically related to the image the user is looking for. Thus, it is more likely that the user actually has a usable query image, making the proposed multimodal retrieval more user-friendly than the traditional content-based retrieval.

Multimodal image retrieval narrows the search results among images corresponding to the query keyword and can thus help when dealing with huge image databases.

In the future work, we plan to improve the results of multimodal image retrieval by exploring other types of image features that might be more appropriate for visual image comparison, as well as the corresponding similarity metrics. In case when images are not labeled nor described in the surrounding text, we plan to integrate automatic image annotation with multimodal image retrieval.

References

1. Eakins, J., Graham, M.: Content-based image retrieval. Technical report JTAP-039, JISC, Institute for Image Data Research, University of Northumbria, Newcastle (2000)
2. Hare, J.S., Lewis, P.H., Enser, P.G.B., Sandom, C.J.: Mind the gap: another look at the problem of the semantic gap in image retrieval. In: Multimedia Content Analysis, Management and Retrieval. IS&T/SPIE, Bellingham (2006)
3. Smeulders, A.W.M., Worring, M., Santini, S., Gupta, A., Jain, R.: Content-based image retrieval at the end of the early years. IEEE Trans. Pattern Anal. Mach. Intell. **22**(12), 1349–1380 (2000)
4. Datta, R., Joshi, D., Li, J.: Image retrieval: ideas, influences, and trends of the new age. ACM Trans. Comput. Surv. **20**, 1–60 (2008)
5. Siddiquie, B., White, B., Sharma, A., Davis, L.S.: Multi-modal image retrieval for complex queries using small codes. In: Proceedings of International Conference on Multimedia Retrieval, p. 321. ACM (2014)
6. Oliva, A., Torralba, A.: Modeling the shape of the scene: a holistic representation of the spatial envelope. Int. J. Comput. Vis. **42**(3), 145–175 (2001)
7. GIST. http://people.csail.mit.edu/torralba/code/spatialenvelope/
8. Cha, S.H., Srihari, S.N.: On measuring the distance between histograms. Pattern Recogn. **35**(6), 1355–1370 (2002)
9. Swain, M.J., Ballard, D.H.: Color indexing. Int. J. Comput. Vis. **7**(1), 11–32 (1991)
10. Pass, G., Zabih, R., Miller, J.: Comparing images using color coherence vectors. In: Proceedings of the 4th ACM International Conference on Multimedia, pp. 65–73. ACM (1997)
11. Duygulu, P., Barnard, K., de Freitas, J.F.G., Forsyth, D.: Object recognition as machine translation: learning a lexicon for a fixed image vocabulary. In: Heyden, A., Sparr, G., Nielsen, M., Johansen, P. (eds.) ECCV 2002, Part IV. LNCS, vol. 2353, pp. 97–112. Springer, Heidelberg (2002)

Toward Optimized Multimodal
Concept Indexing

Navid Rekabsaz[✉], Ralf Bierig, Mihai Lupu, and Allan Hanbury

Information and Software Engineering Group, Vienna University of Technology,
1040 Vienna, Austria
{navid.rekabsaz,ralf.bierig,mihai.lupu,allan.hanbury}@ifs.tuwien.ac.at

Abstract. Information retrieval on the (social) web moves from a pure
term-frequency-based approach to an enhanced method that includes
conceptual multimodal features on a semantic level. In this paper, we
present an approach for semantic-based keyword search and focus especially on its optimization to scale it to real-world sized collections in the
social media domain. Furthermore, we present a faceted indexing framework and architecture that relates content to semantic concepts to be
indexed and searched semantically. We study the use of textual concepts
in a social media domain and observe a significant improvement from
using a concept-based solution for keyword searching. We address the
problem of time-complexity that is critical issue for concept-based methods by focusing on optimization to enable larger and more real-world
style applications.

Keywords: Semantic indexing · Concept · Social web · Word2Vec

1 Introduction

The past decade has witnessed the massive growth of the social web, the contin-
ued impact and expansion of the world wide web and the increasing importance
and synergy of content modalities, such as text, images, videos, opinions, and
other data. There are currently about 200 active social networks[1] that attract
visitors in the range of the 100s of millions each month. Online visitors spend
considerable amounts of time on social network platforms where they constantly
contribute, consume, and implicitly evaluate content. The Facebook community alone, with over 1.2 billion members, shares the impressive amount of 30
billion pieces of content every month [15]. The knowledge contained in these
massive data networks is unprecedented and, when harvested, can be made useful for many applications. Although research has started to automatically mine
information from these rich sources, the problem of knowledge extraction from
multimedia content remains difficult. The main challenges are the heterogeneity
of the data, the scalability of the processing methods and the reliability of their
predictions.

---

[1] http://en.wikipedia.org/wiki/List_of_social_networking_websites.

© Springer International Publishing Switzerland 2015
J. Cardoso et al. (Eds.): KEYWORD 2015, LNCS 9398, pp. 141–152, 2015.
DOI: 10.1007/978-3-319-27932-9_13

In order to address these challenges in the social web domain, recent researches exploit the use of semantics in multimodal information retrieval and specially in image retrieval [11]. However, the focus resided on image processing and, so far, the methods used for text similarity for the purpose of multimodal retrieval are fairly mainstream [22]. In this work, we focus on semantic-based keyword search while specifically considering the optimization of the processing time, thus making our approach manageable in an information system.

This paper has two contributions. As the *first* contribution, we explored the effect of semantic similarity and optimization methods in text-based image retrieval in social media by applying Word2Vec [16] and Random Indexing (RI) [21]. This represents one possible form for a semantic concept index. We particularly focus on the optimization of these algorithms to allow them to scale to real-world collection sizes for more effective semantic-based keyword search on the (social) web. With an execution time that is about 40 times slower than standard TF-IDF in Solr, especially with longer documents, it is clear that optimization is paramount for allowing semantic search to become applicable and useful. We applied and evaluated two optimization techniques to contribute to this essential and important goal.

The *second* contribution is an architecture and test-bed for integrating and evaluating algorithms and methods for semantic indexing and keyword search. It is designed as a combined faceted index for multimodal content collections, such as MediaEval Diverse Images [9,10]. The framework is based on a flexible document model and incorporates concepts as an extension toward more generalized forms of information search that exceed the classic bag-of-words approach. The interlinked nature of these parts has the benefit of being flexible with respect to many kinds of multimodal and also multilingual documents. Each of these facets can be transformed into a semantic representation based on a dynamic set of algorithm. The index itself is implemented effectively by using flexible facet indices and a document index that can be combined and used based on the data at hand. The first contribution additionally serves as an application use-case for this architecture.

The following section describes the related work surrounding the domains of faceted, multi-modal and semantic indexing and search. In particular, we cover concept-based information retrieval. We describe our indexing architecture together with an application example of semantic index in Sect. 3. Focusing on questions of optimization, we explain two methods, followed by discussion and comparison in Sect. 4. We summarize our findings in Sect. 5, and subsequently elaborate on a range of future plans.

2   Related Work

While different modalities often occur together in the same document (scientific paper, website, blog, etc.), search through these modalities is usually done for each modality in isolation. It is well known that combining information from multiple modalities assists in retrieval tasks. For instance, the results of the

ImageCLEF campaign's photographic retrieval task have shown that combining image and text information results in better retrieval than text alone [17]. There are two fundamental approaches to fusing information from multiple modalities: early fusion and late fusion [7].

Late fusion is widely used, as it avoids working in a single fused feature space but, instead, fusing results by reordering them based on the scores from the individual systems. Clinchant et al. [3] propose and test a number of late fusion approaches involving the sum or product combination of weighted scores from text and image retrieval systems. Difficulties arise from

- weights that must be fixed in advance or that need to be learned from difficult to obtain training data
- modality weights that might be query dependent and
- weights that are sensitive to the IR system performance for the various modalities [7]

Separate queries are needed for each modality, so that for example to find a picture of a cat in a database of annotated images, one would need to provide a picture of a cat and text about the cat. There are ways of getting around this limitation, such as choosing the images for the top returned text documents as seeds in an image search [7], but these are generally ad-hoc.

With early fusion, a query would not have to contain elements from all modalities in the dataset. To continue the previous example, pictures of a cat could be found only with text input. Early fusion suffers from the problem that text tends to sparsely inhabit a large feature space, while non-text features have denser distributions in a small feature space. It is however possible to represent images sparsely in higher-dimensional feature spaces through the use of bags of 'visual words' [4] that are obtained by clustering local image features. The simplest approach to early fusion is to simply concatenate the feature vectors from different modalities. However, concatenated feature vectors become less distinctive, due to the curse of dimensionality [7], making this approach rather ineffective. A solution proposed by Magalhaes and Rüeger [14] is to transform the feature vectors to reduce the dimension of the text feature vectors and increase the dimension of the image feature vectors using the minimum description length (MDL) principle.

Textual features has been used in many multimodal retrieval systems. For instance, recently, Eskevich et al. [8] considered a wide range of text retrieval methods in the context of multimodal search for medical data, while Sabetghadam ct al. [20] used text features in a graph-based model to retrieve images from Wikipedia. However, these works do not particularly exploit text semantics.

In the text retrieval community, text semantics started with Latent Semantic Analysis/Indexing (LSA/LSI) [6], the pioneer approach that initiated a new trend in surface text analysis. LSA was also used for image retrieval [18], but the method's practicality is limited by efficiency and scalability issues caused by the high-dimensional matrices it operates on. Explicit Semantic Analysis (ESA) is one of the early alternatives, aimed at reducing the computational load [12].

However, unlike LSA, ESA relies on a pre-existing set of concepts, which may not always be available. Random Indexing (RI) [21] is another alternative to LSA/LSI that creates context vectors based on the occurrence of word contexts. It has the benefit of being incremental and operating with significantly less resources while producing similar inductive results as LSA/LSI and not relying on any pre-existing knowledge. Word2Vec [16] further expands this approach while being highly incremental and scalable. When trained on large datasets, it is also possible to capture many linguistic subtleties (e.g., similar relation between Italy and Rome in comparison to France and Paris) that allow basic arithmetic operations within the model. This, in principle, allows exploiting the implicit knowledge within corpora. All of these methods represent the words in vector spaces.

In order to compare the text semantic approaches, Baroni et al. [2] systematically evaluates a set of models with parameter settings across a wide range of lexical semantics tasks. They observe an overall better performance of state-of-the-art context-based models (e.g., Word2Vec) than the classic methods (e.g., LSA).

Approaching the text semantics, Liu et al. [13] introduced the Histogram for Textual Concepts (HTC) method to map tags to a concept dictionary. However, the method is reminiscent of ESA described above, and it was never evaluated for the purpose of text-based image retrieval.

3   Concept-Based Multimedia Retrieval

In this section, first we explain the architecture of our system for semantic indexing and keyword search. Thereafter based on the architecture, an application use-case is applied on the MediaEval Diverse Social Images task [9,10], using textual concepts. Our concept-based approach shows a significant improvement for keyword search on the test collection in the social media domain.

3.1   Framework for Extended Multimedia Retrieval

We introduce a framework for multimodal concept and facet-based information retrieval and, in the scope of this paper, focus on the indexing component, particularly the semantic indexing features. The interaction between the components of the indexing framework is depicted in Fig. 1. These components represent the conceptual building blocks of the indexing architecture as part of the general framework. The figure presents the document model, the concept model and the indexing model with its individual document facets, such as text-, tag-, and image-typed content. We additionally depicts the information flow between these parts in a simplified form.

The *document model* defines a document that functions as the basic unit for content that is composed of facets. A facet is either a text, a tag or an image. This allows many content structures to be created and organized, such as Wikipedia pages, scientific articles, websites, or blogs that often consist of such

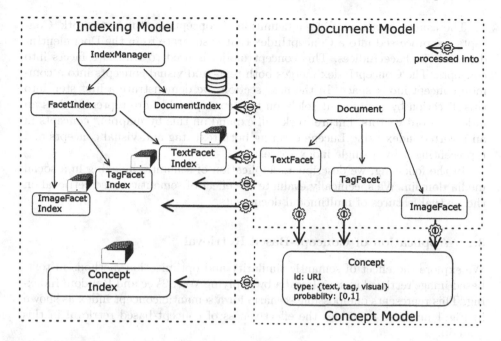

Fig. 1. Interaction between document model, concepts and (semantic) concept index

text, tag and image facets in various combinations. This structure also covers all unimodal variants, such as pure picture collections, since each document may contain any facet type in any order.

The *concept model* defines the structure of concepts. All concepts share a common identifier (usually a URI) that uniquely represents and differentiates them. A concept can describe either one of the three facet types, expressed as a type. That means, the concept can either be a text concept, a tag concept or a visual concept. Furthermore, a concept has a probability of being true, that allows a learning algorithm to store its confidence.

The *indexing model* is managed by the IndexManager, which controls the creation process of all indices, based on the configuration of the entire system. Facets are processed into respective indices that are all variations of a general FacetIndexer. TextFacets are indexed as a TextFacetIndex and TagFacets as a TagFacetIndex which are both based on Lucene[2] that stores it as separate, for their purpose optimized, inverted index file structures. ImageFacets are transformed into an ImageFacetIndex that is processed based on Lire, a Lucene derivative that is specialized on visual features. The indexing architecture therefore has three types of facet indexers, one per facet type, but maintains an arbitrary number of instances for each of them based on the structure of the content collection that is indexed. The DocumentIndex is a data structure that is implemented as a Database that connects all facets to make them accessible and usable for applications.

---

[2] http://lucene.apache.org/core.

The *concept model* provides a definition of concepts for the framework. Concepts are processed into a ConceptIndex that is separate from the DocumentIndex and the FacetIndices. This concept model is used to translate facets into concepts. The ConceptIndex merges both text- and visual concepts into a common concept index space. In the next section, we demonstrate a first step into this direction by applying it solely on text concepts that are represented as an index of word vectors. Future work will expand on this by mapping concepts in an inverted index using Lucene covering both text, tag and visual concepts and representing it by a single index space.

In the following, we describe an application of semantic indexing in a social media domain. We specifically evaluate the effect of semantic-based retrieval on the textual features of multimodal documents.

3.2 Application of Concept-Based Retrieval

We explore the effect of semantic similarity and optimization methods in text-based image retrieval in social media by applying Word2Vec and Random Indexing. This represents one possible scenario for a semantic concept index as shown in Fig. 1 and also examines the effectiveness of concept-based retrieval in this domain.

The evaluation was conducted using Flickr data, in particular in the framework of the MediaEval Retrieving Diverse Social Images Task 2013/2014 [9,10]. The task addresses result relevance and diversification in social image retrieval. We merged the datasets of 2013 (Div400) [10] and 2014 (Div150Cred) [9] and denoted it as MediaEval. It consists of about 110k photos of 600 world landmark locations (e.g., museums, monuments, churches, etc.). The provided data for each landmark location include a ranked list of photos together with their representative texts (title, description, and tags), Flickr's metadata, a Wikipedia article of the location and user tagging credibility estimation (only for 2014 edition). The name of each landmark location (e.g., Eiffel Tower) is used as the query for retrieving its related documents. For semantic text similarity, we focus on the relevance of the representative text of the photos containing title, description, and tags. We removed HTML tags and decompounded the terms using a dictionary obtained from the whole corpus.

We used the English Wikipedia text corpus to train our word representation vectors based on Word2Vec and Random Indexing, each with 200 and 600 dimensions. We trained our Word2Vec word representation using Word2Vec toolkit[3] by applying CBOW approach of Mikolov et al. [16] with context windows of 5 words and subsampling at $t = 1e^{-5}$. The Random Indexing word representations were trained using the Semantic Vectors package[4]. We used the default parameter settings of the package which considers the whole document as the context window. In both Word2Vec and Random Indexing we considered the words with frequency less than five as noise and filtered them out.

---

[3] https://code.google.com/p/word2vec/.
[4] https://code.google.com/p/semanticvectors/.

Table 1. MediaEval Retrieving Diverse Social Images Task 2013/2014 [9,10]. Models trained on Wikipedia using Random Indexing (RI) and Word2Vec (W2V). The sign †denotes statistical significant difference

Representation	Dimension	P@20
Random Indexing	200	†0.788
Random Indexing	600	†0.787
Word2Vec	200	†**0.795**
Word2Vec	600	†0.793
Solr (Baseline)		0.760

To measure the semantic-based text-to-text similarity, we applied an approach, denoted $SimGreedy$ [19]. The approach calculates the relatedness of document A to document B based on $SimGreedy(A, B)$ defined as follows:

$$SimGreedy(A, B) = \frac{\sum_{t \in A} idf(t) * maxSim(t, B)}{\sum_{t \in A} idf(t)} \tag{1}$$

where t represents a term of document A and $idf(t)$ is the Inverse Document Frequency of the term t. The function $maxSim$ calculates separately the cosine of the term t to each word in document B and returns the highest value. In this method, each word in the source document is aligned to the word in the target document to which it has the highest semantic similarity. Then, the results are aggregated based on the weight of each word to achieve the document-to-document similarity. $SimGreedy$ is defined as the average of $SimGreedy(A, B)$ and $SimGreedy(B, A)$. Considering n and m as the number of words in documents A and B respectively, the complexity of SimGreedy is of order $n * m$.

We used the evaluation metric as the precision at a cutoff of 20 documents (P@20) which was also used in the official runs. A standard Solr index was used as the baseline. Statistical significant difference at $p = 0.05$ or lower against the baseline (denoted by †) was calculated using Fisher's two-sided paired randomization test. The two-sided paired randomization test examines the significance of the difference between two sets of data by calculating the difference of each pair of the datasets and then passing them to a more common significance test such as 'one-sample t-test'.

The results of evaluating the SimGreedy algorithm with different word representations are shown in Table 1. We observed that using SimGreedy as a semantic-based similarity method outperforms the simple content-based approach. In addition, the word representation method or the number of dimensions does not have a significant effect on the result of the SimGreedy method.

In order to compare the results with the participating systems in the task, we repeated the experiment on test dataset 2014. As it is shown in Table 2 using SimGreedy and Word2Vec, we achieved the state-of-the-art result of 0.842 for P@20 between 41 runs including even the ones which used image features but not external resources.

Table 2. MediaEval Retrieving Diverse Social Images Task 2014 Results using query expansion. Models are trained on Wikipedia corpus with 200 and 600 dimensions. Our semantic-based approach only uses the textual features. *Best* indicates the state-of-the-art performing system in the 2014 task for different runs

Representation	Dimension	P@20
Random Indexing	200	0.813
Random Indexing	600	0.817
Word2Vec	200	0.833
Word2Vec	600	**0.842**
Best text (Run1)		0.832
Best text-visual (Run3)		0.817
Best all resources (Run5)		0.876

Considering the achieved results, in the next section we focused on optimizing the performance of the algorithms provided to match with the practical requirements of real-world application problems.

4   Optimizing Semantic Text Similarity

Although SimGreedy shows better performance in comparison to the content-based approach, based on the time complexity discussed before, it has a much longer execution time. We observed that SimGreedy is approximately 40 times slower than Solr so that SimGreedy generally has the query processing time of about 110 to 130 min while it takes about 3 min for Solr. The method can be especially inefficient when the documents become longer. Therefore in the following, we apply two optimization techniques for SimGreedy in order to achieve better execution time without degrading its effectiveness.

4.1   Two-Phase Process

In the first approach, we turn the procedure into a two-phase process [5]. In order to do this, we choose an alternative method with considerably less execution time in comparison to SimGreedy such as using Solr. Then, we apply the faster algorithm to obtain a first ranking of the results and afterwards, the top n percent of the results is re-ranked by applying SimGreedy. Therefore, the SimGreedy algorithm computes only on a portion of the data which is already filtered by the first (faster) one.

Considering that the alternative algorithm has the execution time of t and is k time faster than SimGreedy, applying this approach takes $t + t \cdot k \cdot n/100$ where n is the percentage of the selected data. In fact, this approach is $k/(1 + k \cdot n/100)$ times faster than running the SimGreedy algorithm standalone. While achieving better execution time, the choice of the parameter n can reduce the effectiveness of the SimGreedy method. Finding the optimal n such that performance remains in the range of significantly indifferent to the non-optimized SimGreedy is a special problem of this method.

Table 3. Execution time in minutes of the standard, Two-Phase, and Approximate Nearest Neighbor (ANN) approaches of SimGreedy. Models are trained on the Wikipedia corpus with 200 dimensions. There is no statistically significant difference between the achieved results of the evaluation metric (P@20).

Repres.	Algorithm	Indexing Time	I/O	Query Time	Overall	P@20
W2V	SimGreedy	-	0:16	1:50	2:06	0.795
	SimGreedy + Two-Phase	-		0:50	1:06	0.772
	SimGreedy + ANN	0:28		0:17	1:01	0.782
RI	SimGreedy	-	0:14	2:07	2:24	0.788
	SimGreedy + Two-Phase	-		1:00	1:14	0.770
	SimGreedy + ANN	0:21		0:19	0:54	0.782

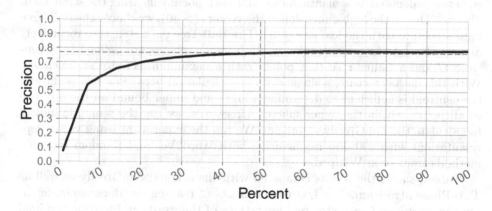

Fig. 2. Average performance of the Two-Phase approach with best value at around 49 %

In order to apply this technique on the MediaEval collection, we selected Solr as the first phase. SimGreedy as the second phase uses vector representations trained on Wikipedia by Word2Vec and Random Indexing methods, both with 200 dimensions. For all the integer values of n from 1 to 100, we found an extremely similar behaviour between the two methods summarized in Fig. 2. In order to find the best value for n as the cutting point, we identified the highest precision value that is not significantly different (using Fisher's two-sided paired randomization test with $p = 0.05$) from the best one (i.e. when n is 100 percent). This corresponds to $n = 49$. Giving the second phase (SimGreedy) is about 40 times slower than the first (Solr), using this approach improves the execution time to almost two times (48 percent) while the performance remains the same.

4.2 Approximate Nearest Neighborhood

In this technique, we exploit the advantages of Approximate Nearest Neighbor (ANN) methods [1]. Similar to Nearest Neighbor search, ANN methods attempt to find the closest neighbors in a vector space. In contrast to the Nearest Neighbor method, ANN approaches approximate the closest neighbors using pre-trained data structures, while in a significantly better searching time. Considering these methods, we can adapt the *maxSim* function of *SimGreedy* to an approximate nearest neighbor search where it attempts to return the closest node to a term. Therefore in this approach, first we create an optimized nearest neighbor data structure (indexing process) for each document and then use it to find the most similar terms.

The overhead time of creating the semantic indices depends on different factors such as the vector dimension, the number of terms in a document, and the selected data structure. While this excessive time can influence the overall execution time, it can be especially effective when the indices are used frequently by many queries.

We apply this technique on MediaEval by first creating an ANN data structure—denoted as semantic index—for each document using the scikit-learn library[5]. Due to the high dimension of the vectors (> 30), we choose the Ball-Tree data structure with the leaf size of 30. The Ball-Tree data structure recursively divides the data into hyper-spheres. Such hyper-spheres are defined by a centroid C and a radius r so that points with a maximum leaf size are enclosed. With this data structure, a single distance calculation between a test point and the centroid is sufficient to determine a lower and upper bound on the distance to all points within the hyper-sphere. Afterwards, we use the semantic indices to calculate the SimGreedy algorithm. We run the experiment using vector representations with 200 dimensions using both Word2Vec and Random Indexing methods trained on Wikipedia.

Table 3 shows the results compared with the original SimGreedy as well as Two-Phase algorithm. The I/O time consists of reading the documents, fetching the corresponding vector representations of the words and writing the final results which is common between all the approaches. Although the ANN approach has the overhead of indexing time, its query time is significantly less than the original SimGreedy and also Two-Phase approach. We therefore see an improvement of approximately two times in the overall execution time in comparison to the original SimGreedy method. In spite of the time optimization, there is no significant difference between the evaluation results of the methods.

It should also be noted that since in MediaEval task, each topic has its own set of documents, the semantic index of each document is used only one time by its topic. Considering this fact, we expect a larger difference between the overall execution times when the indexed documents are used by all the topics as is the normal case in many information retrieval tasks.

---

[5] http://scikit-learn.org/stable/.

5 Conclusions and Future Work

We explored the effect of textual semantic and optimization methods in the social media domain as an example of a semantic index. We ran experiments on the MediaEval Retrieving Diverse Social Images Task 2013/2014 using Word2Vec and Random Indexing vector representations. Beside achieving state-of-the-art results, we show that SimGreedy—a semantic-based similarity method—outperforms a term-frequency-based baseline using Solr. We then focused on two optimization techniques: Two-Phase and Approximate Nearest Neighbor (ANN) approaches. Both the methods reduced by half the processing time of the SimGreedy method while keeping precision within the boundary of statistically insignificant difference.

Although these techniques similarly optimize the processing time, they show different characteristics in practice. While the Two-Phase approach needs pre-knowledge on the performance of the other search methods for setting the parameters, the ANN method can easily be applied on new domains with no need for parameter tuning. In addition, in the ANN approach, despite the overhead time of creating semantic-based data structures, the query time is significantly faster which is a great benefit in real-time use-cases.

In future work, we exploit the semantics of different facets (e.g. text, image, etc.) by first indexing and then combining them in the scoring process of our multimodal information retrieval platform. The concept index is achieved differently for text and image: For image facets, it represents the probability of a visual concept that has been learned from an image (e.g. from a visual classifier). For text facets, it represents the probability of a term being conceptually similar to its context (e.g., document, window of the terms, and etc.). Despite the effectiveness of SimGreedy (as an approach for semantic similarity), for each term in the source document, it only finds the highest similar term in the destination and ignores the others with less similarity value. We therefore want to study new, alternative similarity measures that match terms with groups of related terms.

References

1. Arya, S., Mount, D.M., Netanyahu, N.S., Silverman, R., Wu, A.Y.: An optimal algorithm for approximate nearest neighbor searching fixed dimensions. J. ACM (JACM) **45**(6), 891–923 (1998)
2. Baroni, M., Dinu, G., Kruszewski, G.: Dont count, predict! a systematic comparison of context-counting vs. context-predicting semantic vectors. In: Proc. of the 52nd Annual Meeting of the Association for. Comput. Linguist. **1**, 238–247 (2014)
3. Clinchant, S., Ah-Pine, J., Csurka, G.: Semantic combination of textual and visual information in multimedia retrieval. In: Proceedings of the 1st ACM International Conference on Multimedia Retrieval (2011)
4. Csurka, G., Dance, C.R., Fan, L., Willamowski, J., Bray, C.: Visual categorization with bags of keypoints. In: Workshop on Statistical Learning in Computer Vision (at ECCV) (2004)
5. Dang, V., Bendersky, M., Croft, W.: Two-stage learning to rank for information retrieval. In: Proceedings of European Conference on Information Retrieval (2013)

6. Deerwester, S.C., Dumais, S.T., Landauer, T.K., Furnas, G.W., Harshman, R.A.: Indexing by latent semantic analysis. J. Am. Soc. Inf. Sci. (JASIS) **41**, 391–407 (1990)
7. Depeursinge, A., Müller, H.: Fusion techniques for combining textual and visual information retrieval. In: Müller, H., Clough, P., Deselaers, T., Caputo, B. (eds.) ImageCLEF. The Information Retrieval Series, pp. 95–114. Springer, Berlin (2010)
8. Eskevich, M., Jones, G.J., Aly, R., et al.: Multimedia information seeking through search and hyperlinking. In: Proceedings of the Annual ACM International Conference on Multimedia Retrieval (2013)
9. Ionescu, B., Popescu, A., Lupu, M., Gînsca, A.L., Boteanu, B., Müller, H.: Div150cred: a social image retrieval result diversification with user tagging credibility dataset. In: ACM Multimedia Systems Conference Series (2015)
10. Ionescu, B., Radu, A.-L., Menéndez, M., Müller, H., Popescu, A., Loni, B.: Div400: a social image retrieval result diversification dataset. In: Proceedings of ACM Multimedia Systems Conference Series (2014)
11. Jia, Y., Shelhamer, E., Donahue, J., Karayev, S., Long, J., Girshick, R., Guadarrama, S., Darrell, T.: Caffe: convolutional architecture for fast feature embedding. In: Proceedings of the ACM International Conference on Multimedia, pp. 675–678. ACM (2014)
12. Liu, C., Wang, Y.-M.: On the connections between explicit semantic analysis and latent semantic analysis. In: Proceedings of Conference on Information and Knowledge Management, New York, NY, USA (2012)
13. Liu, N., Dellandréa, E., Chen, L., Zhu, C., Zhang, Y., Bichot, C.-E., Bres, S., Tellez, B.: Multimodal recognition of visual concepts using histograms of textual concepts and selective weighted late fusion scheme. Comput. Vis. Image Underst. **117**, 493–512 (2013)
14. Magalhaes, J., Rüger, S.: Information-theoretic semantic multimedia indexing. In: Proceedings of the 6th ACM International Conference on Image and Video Retrieval, pp. 619–626. ACM (2007)
15. Manyika, J., Chui, M., Brown, B., Bughin, J., Dobbs, R., Roxburgh, C., Byers, A.H.: Big data: the next frontier for innovation, competition, and productivity. McKinsey Global Institute (2011)
16. Mikolov, T., Chen, K., Corrado, G., Dean, J.: Efficient estimation of word representations in vector space (2013). arXiv preprint arXiv:1301.3781
17. Paramita, M.L., Grubinger, M.: Photographic image retrieval. In: Müller, H., Clough, P., Deselaers, T., Caputo, B. (eds.) ImageCLEF: Experimental Evaluation in Visual Information Retrieval, pp. 141–162. Springer, Berlin (2010)
18. Pham, T.-T., Maillot, N., Lim, J.-H., Chevallet, J.-P.: Latent semantic fusion model for image retrieval and annotation. In: Proceedings of Conference on Information and Knowledge Management (2007)
19. Rekabsaz, N., Bierig, R., Ionescu, B., Hanbury, A., Lupu, M.: On the use of statistical semantics for metadata-based social image retrieval. In: Proceedings of the 13th International Workshop on Content-Based Multimedia Indexing (CBMI) (2015)
20. Sabetghadam, S., Lupu, S., Bierig, R., Rauber, A.: A combined approach of structured and non-structured IR in multimodal domain. In: Proceedings of ACM International Conference on Multimedia Retrieval (2014)
21. Sahlgren, M.: An introduction to random indexing. In: Methods and Applications of Semantic Indexing Workshop in the Proceedings of Terminology and Knowledge Engineering (2005)
22. Thomee, B., Popescu, A.: Overview of the ImageCLEF 2012 flickr photo annotation and retrieval task. In: Proceedings of Cross-Language Evaluation Forum (CLEF) (2012)

Semantic URL Analytics to Support Efficient Annotation of Large Scale Web Archives

Tarcisio Souza[1](✉), Elena Demidova[1], Thomas Risse[1], Helge Holzmann[1], Gerhard Gossen[1], and Julian Szymanski[2]

[1] L3S Research Center and Leibniz Universität Hannover, Hannover, Germany
{Souza,Demidova,Risse,Holzmann,Gossen}@L3S.de
[2] Gdansk University of Technology, Gdańsk, Poland
julian.szymanski@eti.pg.gda.pl

Abstract. Long-term Web archives comprise Web documents gathered over longer time periods and can easily reach hundreds of terabytes in size. Semantic annotations such as named entities can facilitate intelligent access to the Web archive data. However, the annotation of the entire archive content on this scale is often infeasible. The most efficient way to access the documents within Web archives is provided through their URLs, which are typically stored in dedicated index files. The URLs of the archived Web documents can contain semantic information and can offer an efficient way to obtain initial semantic annotations for the archived documents. In this paper, we analyse the applicability of semantic analysis techniques such as named entity extraction to the URLs in a Web archive. We evaluate the precision of the named entity extraction from the URLs in the Popular German Web dataset and analyse the proportion of the archived URLs from 1,444 popular domains in the time interval from 2000 to 2012 to which these techniques are applicable. Our results demonstrate that named entity recognition can be successfully applied to a large number of URLs in our Web archive and provide a good starting point to efficiently annotate large scale collections of Web documents.

1 Introduction and Motivation

Web archives are a unique source of data reflecting rapid evolution of the digital world. Recently, an increasing interest in using the data stored within the Web archives for research purposes has been observed in several disciplines such as history or digital sociology [14]. For example, as discussed in [6], Web archives can be an important source for communication and media history and within historiography in general.

Unfortunately, existing Web archives are very difficult to use since most often only a URL based access is provided. Researchers are typically interested in a few relevant Web sites regarding a given topic, domain or time frame to be selected for manual analysis. Finding such relevant data for a specific purpose within the Web archive is still very challenging. This is mainly attributed to the very large

© Springer International Publishing Switzerland 2015
J. Cardoso et al. (Eds.): KEYWORD 2015, LNCS 9398, pp. 153–166, 2015.
DOI: 10.1007/978-3-319-27932-9_14

size of the data coupled with the lack of efficient tools for annotation, search and exploration. Indexing existing Web archives, which often contain hundreds of terabytes of data, is difficult and hence, full-text search capabilities are rarely available, not to mention more sophisticated semantic content analytics.

In this context, we look at different ways to obtain relevant documents from a Web archive efficiently and analyse the role of URLs of the archived documents towards this goal. The advantage of using URLs is twofold: First, the URLs of the archived documents can be retrieved from the archive efficiently, using CDX files (i.e. standard index files that contain URLs and additional metadata, such as mime type and capture dates). Second, URLs can contain important hints about the document content. In this context, related work on URL analytics on the Web shows that URLs can provide accurate estimates of the document language [3], location relevance [2] and topic classification [9].

In this paper we analyse the applicability and precision of Named Entity Extraction (NER) in the context of URLs. Furthermore, we analyse the distribution of the extracted named entities within the URLs in the Popular German Web dataset - a subset of the Internet Archive data covering popular domains in the ".de" top level domain over a period of 12 years. This analysis confirms the precision of NER in the context of URL analytics and helps to better understand which domains can be efficiently accessed using such light-weight annotation methods for a Web archive. Our results demonstrate that state-of-the-art NER tools, such as Stanford NER[1], can achieve high precision (up to 85 % in our dataset) if applied to the URLs after performing sufficient pre-processing and post-filtering described in this paper. We also observed that the number of extracted entities differs significantly across the domain categories and along the temporal dimension. In some years, the dataset contains dominant domains - i.e. the domains within a domain category that contribute the majority of captures in the specific year. In most cases, the variations in the extraction results can be explained by the varying number of captures from such dominant domains as well as by the entity-rich URLs in such domains (i.e. the domains like *dblp.uni-trier.de* - an open computer science bibliography, where the URLs typically contain named entities of the type person, *dict.tu-chemnitz.de* - a dictionary domain, that frequently presents entities of miscellaneous type).

Overall, our results confirm that NER is a useful method of semantic URL analytics and can provide precise results and high coverage in several domain categories.

2   The Popular German Web: A Dataset Description

The dataset used in this study is referred to as "Popular German Web". This dataset is a subset of the '.de' top-level domain (tld), as it has been archived by the Internet Archive[2] and provided to us in the context of the ALEXANDRIA[3]

---

[1] http://nlp.stanford.edu/software/CRF-NER.shtml.
[2] http://archive.org.
[3] http://alexandria-project.eu/.

project. This dataset comprises the most prominent domains in 17 categories from 2000 to 2012 selected according to the Alexa ranking[4].

Terminology: A *URL (uniform resource locator)* identifies a Web resource (for example a Web page) and specifies its location on the Web. Over time, the content of the Web page under any given URL may change. Therefore, Web archives often re-assessed the URLs after a period of time to collect new content. In the following we refer to a particular copy of the URL assessed at a certain time and stored in the archive as a *capture*. This way, a Web archive can possess several captures of the URL, whereas each capture can be uniquely identified through the URL and the date.

These captures are stored as CDX files that contain meta information about the crawls in a space-separated format with one line per capture, i.e. one snapshot of one URL at a given time. The corresponding line in the CDX file presents the structure illustrated by Fig. 1. We consider "original url" as the input for NER, "timestamp" provides the exact time when the URL was crawled and "status code" tells us whether or not a successful response was returned. The other fields are ignored since they do not represent useful information for our analysis.

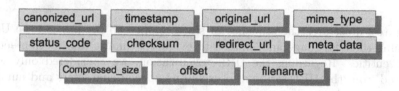

Fig. 1. CDX structure

2.1 Domain Extraction

There is an interest in these domains as they are impacting most users of the Web today and at the same time they have the biggest impact on upcoming research. The selection of domains was taken from different categories on Amazon's Alexa. In order to match our dataset we fetched only websites from those categories on that comprise German websites[5]. In addition to the 15 top categories, we picked *news* and *universities* as two sub-categories that seemed particularly relevant to analyze separately in our study.

As the available dataset only included domains under the German tld '.de', we filtered out all websites on Alexa's list that are German but use a different tld. Out of the remaining, we extracted up to 100 from the top of every category. The final state of this ranking, which is analyzed here, was retrieved on July 10th, 2014 at 09:26 CET.

---

[4] http://www.alexa.com.
[5] http://www.alexa.com/topsites/category/Top/World/Deutsch.

2.2   Dataset Cleaning and Pre-Processing

Following the domain extraction we performed a few cleaning steps at the URL level to filter out malformed URLs as well as those that are inappropriate for our analysis:

- In this analysis we focus on the html content of the Web archive. Therefore, we discarded all captures that do not represent the html content (identified by .html or .htm extensions in the URLs).
- We discarded all captures of the URLs that never returned a successful status code (i.e. a status code starting with "2", according to the official HTTP status codes).

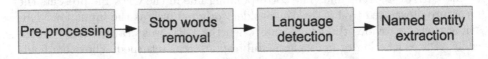

Fig. 2. URL processing pipeline

Figure 2 illustrates the sequence of steps applied to pre-process the URLs, determine their language and, finally, to extract semantic information such as named entities. Regarding the URL tokenization, we considered only words extracted from the URL string also excluding special characters and numbers, based on a simple regular expression.

- **Pre-processing:** From the pre-processing perspective, we consider only the URL path, discarding the extension. We exclude other parts such as domain name, parameters and numbers (e.g. port number, session id, etc.) from further consideration. These fields are not expected to contain semantic information specific to the particular Web document.
- **Stop Words Removal:** In next step we detect stop words within the parsed URLs and eliminate them. In order to determine stop words, we randomly sample URLs and manually select the most frequent terms extracted from that sample. This is required, as no pre-defined stop word lists for URLs exists. Short terms (i.e. the terms with the length less than three characters) are also discarded in this step. Stop words filtering is particularly important to increase precision of the language detection performed in the next step.
- **Language Detection:** We apply an n-gram language detection model to the remaining tokens in the URLs to detect the language of the URL and to select the correct language configuration for the extractors applied in the next step.
- **Named Entity Extraction:** We apply Stanford NER to extract named entities mentioned in the preprocessed URLs. The language-specific named entity extractor (German or English) is selected based on the determined URL language.

2.3   Dataset Statistics

Ultimately, we obtained a dataset consisting of 17 categories with today's popular domains from the '.de' top level domain, as presented in Table 1. The resulting Popular German Web dataset covers 1,444 domains with more than 320 million captures in total. Table 1 presents the number of domains and captures in each domain category as well as the percentage of captures from which we could extract named entities using our method. As we can observe, the highest coverage of captures containing entities is attributed to the *education* category with 73%, followed by the *regional* and *sports* categories with around 40%. The dominating domains for the *education* category were *stayfriends.de* and *werweiss-was.de*, with 20–50% of captures dependent on the year. These domains typically contain entity-rich URLs that explains the high percentage of entities extracted from this category. For many other domain categories the coverage of captures containing named entities exceeds 20%. Overall, we can say that our method can efficiently produce annotations for a significant number of captures in many domain categories.

Table 1. The Popular German Web dataset details: the number of domains and captures per category.

Category	# Domains	# Captures	Entities(%)
Education	100	12,406,130	73.36
Regional	100	34,204,862	44.79
Sports	100	17,358,130	39.33
Business	100	25,457,639	36.39
Recreation	100	8,260,029	30.95
Media	100	11,277,003	28.20
Universities	100	14,299,856	25.09
News	40	41,710,500	23.13
Shopping	100	33,045,310	20.14
Culture	100	6,822,986	19.69
Society	100	9,968,534	18.37
Games	99	13,518,500	16.40
Computer	100	26,298,534	15.90
Home	100	45,488,255	14.07
Kids & Teens	10	1,682,848	10.45
Health	100	6,260,340	9.31
Science	100	13,651,913	7.86
TOTAL	*1444*	*321,711,369*	

In order to obtain a better understanding of the temporal dimension of the dataset, we analyse the distribution of captures over time. Figure 3 illustrates

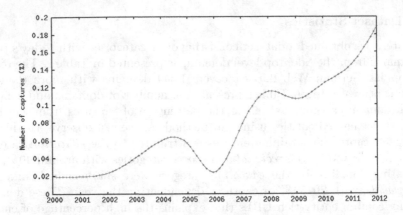

Fig. 3. Overall distribution of the number of captures per year.

the overall distribution of the number of captures per year in the time period from 2000 to 2012 normalized by the total number of captures in the Popular German Web dataset, where X axis represent the years and Y axis the percentage of captures.

This graph illustrates that the number of captures in the dataset is rapidly increasing over time, in particular starting from 2007, although at some points (2005–2006 and 2009) temporary decreases in the data collection rate can be observed. The total number of captures are more equally distributed for the majority of years per domains, where *spiegel.de* appears at the first position from 2001 to 2012, representing 7.72 % of all captures per year, on average. The university domain *tu-berlin.de* dominates the crawl by representing 47.30 % of all captures in 2000.

Figure 4 shows the distribution of all captures through five selected domain categories including *shopping, sports, business, news* and *universities* normalized by the total number of captures. As we can observe, various domain categories have different dynamics within the archive: Whereas the proportion of the *news* cites is relatively high and is only slowly increasing over time, the proportion of *shopping* cites increased rapidly in recent years. In contrast, the proportion of the *universities* cites is slowly decreasing, in particular starting from 2007.

Even the total number of captures of *spiegel.de* (a german *news* domain) exceeds total captures from top *universities* domains (e.g. *uni-leipzig.de* and *cert.uni-stuttgart.de*) from 2002 to 2003, the overall number of captures from *universities* is greater than *news* for those years. In this period the majority of domains belongs to *universities* (140) and only 40 belongs to *news*. From 2008 to 2011, captures from *shopping* (532 domains) are more frequent followed by *news* (136 domains) and *business* (588 domains).

Overall Fig. 4 shows the behavior of captures within five selected categories, where the quantity of captures in general is growing, except for *universities* starting in 2007. We also observed several *business* domains from 2008 to 2011, but the majority of captures belongs to *shopping* in this period.

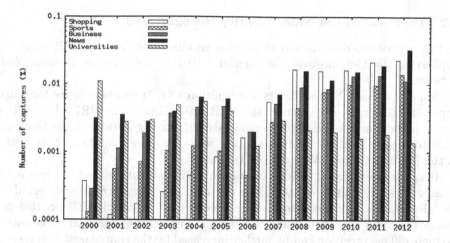

Fig. 4. Number of captures within selected domain categories.

3 URL Analytics

In this section we describe the results of the URL analysis we obtained by applying the pipeline described in Sect. 2.2 to the Popular German Web dataset described in Sect. 2.3. The goal of the analysis is two-fold: First, we evaluate the precision of the named entity extraction method for URLs proposed in this paper to confirm its effectiveness; Second, we would like to better understand the domain coverage and the temporal coverage of the proposed method while applied to our dataset. In this section we present the evaluation results of the method and statistics we collected while applying the method to the Popular German Web dataset.

3.1 Language Detection Statistics

In order to detect the language of a URL, we applied state-of-the-art techniques to language detection using n-grams [3]. The URL pre-processing described in Sect. 2.2, such as URL splitting and removal of URL-specific stop words makes it possible to apply the n-gram analysis on the relevant part of the URL only and to increase precision of the language detection. The stop words typical for the URLs are identified using a random sample from the whole URL collection and a manually identified frequency threshold.

According to the results of the language detection analysis, 52.89 % of the URLs in our Popular German Web dataset are in German, 27.96 % in English and 19.14 % in other languages. After applying the URL pre-processing, we obtained 89 % of precision for language detection. We measure this precision choosing a random sample of 100 URLs and manually checking the returning language.

3.2 Precision of the Named Entity Recognition for URLs

In this section we describe our evaluation results regarding the NER precision applied to the German and the English URLs in the Popular German Web dataset.

State-of-the-art Named Entity Recognition (NER) techniques are language dependent. Therefore, we restrict the NER processing to the URLs detected as German and English and apply language-specific configurations of the Stanford NER to these URLs. With this restriction, we cover more than 80 % of the URLs in the Popular German Web dataset (s. above).

In order to evaluate precision of Stanford NER on this dataset, we manually chose a random sample of 100 URLs out of those that have been detected to contain entities. Initially, the average precision of Stanford NER on this set reached 60 % for the German and 56 % for the English configuration of the entity extractor. This precision can be further increased by the simple post-processing, including two steps:

1. Removal of the entities with long labels (i.e. the labels containing more than 2 terms). Our manual examination has shown that in many cases such long labels result from the extraction errors.
2. Removal of the entities that rarely occur in the URLs (the number of the URLs detected to contain the entity is less than 3 in the entire dataset). According to our observations, entities extracted from very few URLs are often incorrect as opposed to the entities that are repeatedly observed in URLs.

After applying these corrections and re-evaluating the results, we observed the precision increase to 85 % for the German and to 82 % for the English extractor on this dataset.

Table 2. The most frequent named entities of type "location" and "person" in the urls of the Popular German Web dataset.

Label	Type	Frequency
deutschland	location	2,301,917
berlin	location	628,300
hamburg	location	557,000
nordrhein	location	430,939
muenchen	location	405,845

Label	Type	Frequency
michael jackson	person	30,210
tommy hilfiger	person	25,943
harald schmidt	person	25,176
heidi klum	person	21,291
merkel	person	17,835

3.3 Domain and Temporal Coverage of NER

In this section we summarize the extraction results to better understand the domain coverage and the temporal coverage of the proposed method for this dataset.

Whereas some domains and domain categories possess entity-rich URLs, others do not. In addition, the number of URLs that contain entities in the Web archive can vary along the temporal dimension. Therefore, in addition to the evaluation of the precision of the extraction method, it is important to better understand the domain coverage of NER applied to the URLs in the Web archive. This analysis can help to better understand which parts of the Web archive can be made accessible using the proposed light-weight named entity annotation.

Overall 42,547,734 captures containing named entities have been identified by the extractor. The frequencies of the named entities extracted from the URLs of these captures range from 2,301,917 to 3. We decided a limit of 3 as a way to maximize the NER precision, which is one of the post-processing steps described above.

The majority of the extracted entities are of type "location", followed by the type "person". The most frequent locations are local to Germany, whereas the person names are in many cases internationally known celebrities. Table 2 presents the most frequent entities of types "location" and "person" extracted from the Popular German Web dataset and their frequencies (i.e. the number of captures).

As an example of entities extracted from URLs, the Table 3 illustrates some URLs containing entities. Up to two different entities could be extracted from those URLs. Entities of type location as *Berlin* and *Prenzlauer-Berg* were found in the same URL and persons as *Franz Maget* (german politician) and *Katja Kessler* (german journalist).

Table 3. URLs containing entities

URL	Entities
http://www.hna.de/nachrichten/welt/costa-concordia-zahl-vermissten-gestiegen-1565391.html	Costa Concordia
http://www.wg-gesucht.de:80/wohnungen-in-Berlin-Prenzlauer-Berg.1529789.html	Berlin Prenzlauer-Berg
http://www.stern.de:80/video/:Video-Franz-Maget3A-Der-AuDFenseiter/638474.html?	Franz Maget
http://forum.gofeminin.de:80/forum/matern1VERKAUFE-mein-DAS-MAMI-BUCH-katja-kessler.html	Katja Kessler

Distribution of Entities by Domain Category. Figure 5 illustrates the distribution of captures containing entities in several selected domain categories.

In this figure we normalized the total number of entities by the total number of captures per year for each specific category where X axis represent the years and Y axis the percentage of captures with entities. We focus on those categories as they indicate interesting patterns with respect to the temporal dimension. We can observe that between 2001 and 2006 the distribution remains overall stable while after 2006 several peaks can be observed.

In the *universities* category a first significant increase can be observed between 2004 and 2005. By looking into the data it turns out that the domain *uni-leipzig.de*

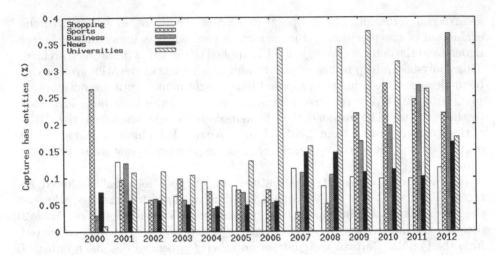

Fig. 5. Captures having entities within categories

dominates the crawl representing 19.81 % of the captures in 2005. In 2006 the *dblp.uni-trier.de*, a popular computer science bibliography, dominates the captures regarding *universities* representing 42.73 %.

Continuing the analysis for *universities*, in 2007 the same domain (*dblp.uni-trier.de*) represents only 6.48 % of the total number of captures, and in that year all domains are more equally distributed. From 2008 to 2011 the *dict.tu-chemnitz.de* - a dictionary domain - dominates the collection and then gradually decreases from 33.26 % to 26.46 % of the total number of captures, respectively. In 2012 *dblp.uni-trier.de* dominates again, but only represents 12.47 % of the captures.

A first significant increase of entities in news can be observed in 2007. The detailed analysis shows that in 2006 and 2007 the *news* category was dominated by *spiegel.de* followed by *openpr.de*, a press release portal. The portal uses the titles of the news articles as names for their html pages. Since the number of crawled pages from this domain significantly increases from 200k pages in 2006 to 700k pages in 2007 we assume that the number of title-based URLs in the archive also increased in this period.

The *sports* category shows a significant increase from 2007 to 2010 due to a particular domain about transfer market of soccer players - *transfermarkt.de*.

Crawled pages from this domain increased from 500 k in 2007 to 1.5 million in 2010, thus we expect that more players' names were mentioned and more entities of type person and location were found. The quantity of captures from such domain decreased in following years, therefore we expect that less entities were extracted, as shown by the graph.

Regarding *business*, the majority of captures belong to *postbank.de* - a postal bank domain in Germany, which increased from 680 k in 2008 to 1.1 million in 2011 and it constitutes an entity-rich domain for type location.

Overall Fig. 5 reveals a number of peaks from 2006 onwards. In the above example the reason was always the domination of a certain site. We assume that this is also the case for most of the other peaks that we observed in previous analyses.

Distribution of Entities by Type. Figure 6 illustrates the distribution of entity types through the years where the X axis represent the years and the Y axis the portion for each entity type we extracted, normalized by the total number of entities.

As mentioned above, the most common entities are of type location followed by the types person, and organization. In previous sections, we showed that while the amount of captures significantly increased starting in 2006, many entity-rich sites increased as well (e.g. *postbank.de*, *openpr.de*, *transfermarkt.de*). Thus the number of entity types also increases, as illustrated by Fig. 6, starting in 2006. Since the majority of domains contains entity-rich URLs of type location, such type represent the most frequent one from all entities.

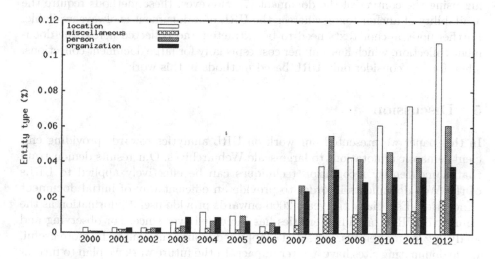

Fig. 6. Entities types retrieved through years

4   Related Work

The information contained in URLs has been analysed already in previous work, however it is the first time that entities have been extracted using only the information within URLs, the majority of current work rely on classification tasks and do not consider entity extraction in URLs. There are several works that classify the content of a document only based on its URL. Baykan et al. conducted an extensive set of URL features and classification methods to detect the topic of a Web document [4]. They report a precision of around 0.86 and a recall between 0.36 and 0.4 on a multi-class topic classification using a combination of character n-grams of length 4-8. In their datasets they have about 32 % "empty URLs", i.e. URLs whose tokens or n-grams did not occur in the training set, which bounds the recall achievable using this data. Similarly, Kan and Thi discuss the applicability of URLs for general classification tasks [11]. They also consider sequential features that take the typically hierarchical nature of URLs into account.

Special applications of URL classification are the detection of the document language [5], genre [1] or locational relevance [2]. In web crawling systems the information in URLs is used to detect duplicates [12] or documents containing relevant types of information [8,10]. Furthermore, URLs have been used to detect malicious content [15] as well as online advertising [13].

A related field considers the anchor texts of links to a document. Similarly to URL classification, this approach allows a performance comparable to content-based methods on many task at a lower processing cost. For example, anchor-text based document ranking is significantly better for site finding tasks than a ranking using the content of the document [7]. However, these methods require the availability of anchor texts, whereas the URL of a document is always available. Furthermore, anchor texts need to be extracted and collected across the document collection, which has a higher cost especially for large document collections. Therefore we consider only URL based methods in this work.

5   Discussion

In this paper we presented our work on URL analytics towards providing efficient semantic annotations to large-scale Web archives. Our results demonstrate that named entity recognition techniques can be effectively applied to URLs of the Web documents in order to provide an efficient way of initial document annotation. Especially the years 2006 onwards provide useful information as the number of URLs providing entities has increased ever since. For observing and analyzing longer periods, news and shopping domains turn out to be more useful, while dominating sites have a lower impact. In the future work we plan to further analyse term extraction techniques for the URLs and to combine these techniques with light-weight content annotations to incrementally increase annotation coverage while maintaining scalability and efficiency of the annotation process as well as detecting temporal expressions still using the URL.

Understanding the dinamic of entities over time is important since we need to know which part of our dataset has most promising entities. Therefore, when a more specific search is needed, we should previously check which domains or domains categories had the most entities and generate a subset on this specific domains, instead of considering the entire archive, which sometimes is computationally unfeasible. The information we extracted from URLs can be further analysed in the document content, as where in the HTML page (title, paragraphs, etc.) the same entities or temporal expressions can be detected.

This URL level analysis can support further keyword-based search algorithms in our web archive, also providing an overview of potential entity-rich domains (as those showed in last sections).

Acknowledgments. This work was partially funded by the European Research Council under ALEXANDRIA (ERC 339233) and the COST Action IC1302 (KEYSTONE). Tarcisio Souza is sponsored by a scholarship from CNPq, a Brazilian government institution for scientific development.

References

1. Abramson, M., Aha, D.: What's in a URL? genre classification from URLs. In: Proceedings of AAAI workshop on Intelligent Techniques for Web Personalization and Recommender Systems (2012)
2. Anastácio, I., Martins, B., Calado, P.: Classifying documents according to locational relevance. In: Lopes, L.S., Lau, N., Mariano, P., Rocha, L.M. (eds.) EPIA 2009. LNCS, vol. 5816, pp. 598–609. Springer, Heidelberg (2009)
3. Baykan, E., Henzinger, M., Weber, I.: Web page language identification based on URLs. PVLDB Endow. **1**(1), 176–187 (2008)
4. Baykan, E., Henzinger, M., Marian, L., Weber, I.: A comprehensive study of features and algorithms for URL-based topic classification. ACM Transactions Web (2011)
5. Baykan, E., Henzinger, M., Weber, I.: A comprehensive study of techniques for URL-based web page language classification. ACM Transactions Web (2013)
6. Brügger, N.: Probing a nation's web sphere: a new approach to web history and a new kind of historical source. In Proceedings of the 2014 ACM conference on Web science (2014)
7. Craswell, N., Hawking, D., Robertson, S.: Effective site finding using link anchor information. In: Proceedings of the 24th Annual International ACM SIGIR, SIGIR 2001, ACM, New York (2001)
8. Hernández, I., Rivero, C.R., Ruiz, D., Corchuelo, R.: A statistical approach to URL-based web page clustering. In: Proceedings of the 21st International Conference Companion on World Wide Web, WWW 2012, ACM, New York (2012)
9. Hernández, I., Rivero, C.R., Ruiz, D., Arjona, J.L.: An experiment to test URL features for web page classification. In: Rodríguez, J.M.C., Pérez, J.B., Golinska, P., Giroux, S., Corchuelo, R. (eds.) Trends in PAAMS. AISC, vol. 157, pp. 109–116. Springer, Heidelberg (2012)
10. Hernndez, I., Rivero, C.R., Ruiz, D., Corchuelo, R.: CALA: an unsupervised URL-based web page classification system. Knowl. Based Syst. **57**, 168–180 (2014)
11. Kan, M.-Y., Thi, H.O.N.: Fast webpage classification using URL features. In: Proceedings of the 14th ACM International Conference on Information and Knowledge Management, CIKM 2005, ACM, New York (2005)
12. Koppula, H.S., Leela, K.P., Agarwal, A., Chitrapura, K.P., Garg, S., Sasturkar, A.: Learning URL patterns for webpage de-duplication. In: Proceedings of the Third ACM International Conference on Web Search and Data Mining, WSDM 2010, New York (2010)
13. Raju, S., Udupa, R.: Extracting advertising keywords from URL strings. In: Proceedings of the 21st International Conference Companion on World Wide Web, WWW 2012, ACM, New York (2012)

14. Risse, T., Demidova, E., Gossen, G.: What do you want to collect from the web? In: Proceedings of the Building Web Observatories Workshop, BWOW 2014 (2014)
15. Zhao, P., Hoi, S.C.H.: Cost-sensitive online active learning with application to malicious URL detection. In: Proceedings of the 19th ACM SIGKDD International Conference on Knowledge Discovery and Data Mining, KDD 2013, ACM, New York (2013)

Indexing of Textual Databases Based on Lexical Resources: A Case Study for Serbian

Ranka Stanković[1]([✉]), Cvetana Krstev[2], Ivan Obradović[1],
and Olivera Kitanović[1]

[1] Faculty of Mining and Geology, University of Belgrade, Belgrade, Serbia
{ranka,ivan.obradovic,olivera.kitanovic}@rgf.bg.ac.rs
[2] Faculty of Philology, University of Belgrade, Belgrade, Serbia
cvetana@matf.bg.ac.rs

Abstract. In this paper we describe an approach to improvement of information retrieval results for large textual databases by pre-indexing documents using bag-of-words and named entity recognition. The approach was applied on a database of geological projects financed by the Republic of Serbia for several decades now. Each document within this database is described by a summary report, consisting of metadata on the geological project, such as title, domain, keywords, abstract, and geographical location. A bag of words was produced from these metadata with the help of morphological dictionaries and transducers, while named entities were recognized using a rule-based system. Both were then used for pre-indexing documents for information retrieval purposes where ranking of retrieved documents was based on several tf_idf based measures. Evaluation of ranked retrieval results based on data obtained by pre-indexing were compared to results obtained by informational retrieval without pre-indexing with precision-recall curve, showing a significant improvement in terms of the mean average precision measure.

1 Introduction

Three basic problems related to Information Retrieval (IR) are the presentation of document content, the presentation of information needs and the comparison of these two representations. If the search is performed by scanning textual documents, then their additional representation is not required. However, in order to increase efficiency, especially in the case of large collections, a formal representation surrogate of each document is usually formed. Representation of a document as a rule contains metadata about the document, such as title, abstract, author and assigned index terms referring to document content. Automatic assigning of a surrogate can also be performed by extracting and selecting specific terms (words) that appear in the document text. To that end, many natural language processing (NLP) methods and techniques are used: determining the boundaries of sentences, tokenization, stemming, tagging, recognition of nominal phrases and named entities and, finally, parsing [7].

Based on these representations, during the preparatory phase an index of the collection of documents is formed, which is then used in the search phase.

© Springer International Publishing Switzerland 2015
J. Cardoso et al. (Eds.): KEYWORD 2015, LNCS 9398, pp. 167–181, 2015.
DOI: 10.1007/978-3-319-27932-9_15

Finding and ranking of relevant documents on basis of the index is realized using the model of approximate matching, based on the frequency distribution of terms and documents. Two basic approaches are the vector space model, based on weight coefficients of terms, and the probabilistic model, based on relevance feedback [18].

Serbian belongs to a group of Less-Resourced Languages for which many lexical resources and language technology tools are still lacking or have not reached the mature state. The META-NET extensive survey performed in 2012 [17] showed that nevertheless for Serbian some important lexical resources were developed (corpora and e-dictionaries), as well as applications for basic NLP operations (tokenization, Part-Of-Speech (POS) tagging, morphological analysis), information retrieval and extraction [21]. Resources and tools used in our research will be presented in more details in Subsect. 3.1, here we will mention some other successful applications.

At the University of Novi Sad a system for PhD dissertation meta-data and full-text search was developed. It uses an index based on Lucene that integrates a Porters stemmer for Serbian [6]. Furlan and associates [2] also use Porter's stemmer and min-max normalization for logarithm of tf_{log} (the log-number of times the given word appears in a document) for calculating semantic similarity of short texts. Graovac [3] uses lexical resources for Serbian — morphological dictionaries and the WordNet — for text categorization. Mladenović and associates [15] use the same resources for document-level sentiment polarity classification using maximum entropy modeling. Zečević and Vujičić-Stanković [22] use various language-identification tools to distinguish Serbian among other closely related languages.

In the next section we describe the motivation for creating a textual database on geological projects and the initial IR system in this domain based on text scanning, along with its shortcomings. An improved system developed using NLP methods is outlined in Sect. 3, while the evaluation of this improvement is given in Sect. 4, followed by some concluding remarks.

2   The Geological Information System of Serbia

2.1   Motivation

Constant increase of geological data and information in Serbia was not accompanied by adequate development and introduction of modern information technologies until recently. Thus the management of various geological documentation relied on traditional libraries and archives, where obtaining specific information was difficult or time consuming. An analysis of the way geological research results, stored in numerous archives and document libraries, were used, showed that their usage was inefficient, due to inadequate organization, limited access and general lack of readiness for introducing modern information technology.

As a result of this analysis, the Ministry of Natural Resources and Environment Protection, now the Ministry of Mining and Energy of the Republic of

Serbia, launched in 2004 the project of the Geological Information System of Serbia (*GeolISS*), which has been developed in several phases over the past decade. The aim of such an information system was to establish an object-oriented database for digital archiving of geologic data, as a modern and efficient information basis for planning, design and decision-making in the geological domain.

Within the *GeolISS* project a web portal[1] was developed that allows quick and easy access to geological data and information in the field of general geology, exploration of mineral deposits, hydrogeology and engineering geology. Users, whether professionals or ordinary citizens, can use this geo-portal for search and access to available information according to their needs.

The content on the portal can be grouped into several categories: cartographic content, multimedia, dictionaries and textual databases. The "core" of *GeolISS* is the Geological Dictionary (Thesaurus) containing about 4,000 geological terms described by definitions, of which about 3,000 have a translation into English. The most important cartographic content is: the basic geological map, maps of national parks, map of endangered groundwater bodies, geomorphological map, map of exploration-mining fields, while within multimedia content the most prominent are the gallery of photos and movies, geoheritage, and jeweler mineral resources. The web portal supports access to applications for search of textual databases (catalogs): projects, archival documents and bibliographies, library of geological projects documentation and exploration-exploitation approvals for water and solid mineral resources.

One of the textual databases is the database of geological projects documentation that contains metadata in the form of a project summary, namely structured descriptions of over 4,900 geological projects financed by the Republic of Serbia from 1956 to the present day, with: title, year, location, name of the company that developed the project, the authors, abstract, keywords, geological field, prospects, application of mineral resource and possibilities for its use, field works, geomechanics, mining works, geodesic works, and prospective exploration. Each project summary contains on the average about 30 % of text from projects themselves, obtained basically by removing pictures, maps, tables, and the like, and is thus a reasonably accurate representation of the textual content of the geological project. Digitalization and full text archiving of the project content is planned, and the approach described in this paper will be expanded and implemented on future full text database.

2.2 The Initial Solution

The initial solution for searching the textual databases in *GeoliSS* (which is in use for several years) is based on input of keywords, single or multi-word units (MWU), which can be combined into Boolean expressions. In addition to general search, which goes through all metadata fields in the summary report, the search can also be performed using specific criteria. For example, if the user

---

[1] http://geoliss.mre.gov.rs; search of fund documentation http://geoliss.mre.gov.rs/index.php?page=fodib.

chooses the criterion *mineral raw material* then only the following fields in the database are taken into consideration: title, field, keywords, and abstract, while for *location* criterion other fields are searched: municipality, county, name of the cartographic sheet, location and chronological number of the document, and the sheet signature. The search system takes into account the field where the keyword was found as this information is used for document ranking.

The users express their information need by selecting the criteria and entering keywords, where they can add any number of criteria, of the same or different type. The criteria are linked by conjunction and when there are more keywords within one criterion a disjunction is generated. For example, if the user is interested in projects that deal with the research of "gold in the Bor region", then *mineral resource* is selected as one criterion and the words *zlato* 'gold' and *Au* are defined for search, and the system will search for any of these two words. If another criterion is added, for example *location*, then keywords which define the desired location are entered, e.g. *Bor* (the name of a city) or *Borski okrug* 'Bor county'. If we want a MWU to treated as a whole, then it is entered under quotation marks.

The search is performed by scanning the text of appropriate fields with given keywords, while word boundaries are not taken into consideration. This partially solves the problem of rich morphology that is characteristic for Serbian, as a language belonging to the South-Slavic Language family. For instance, scanning with *lignit* 'lignite' will also retrieve inflected forms *lignita, lignitu, lignitom*, etc.

Search results are ranked on the basis of weight factors assigned to individual fields in the function of search criteria. Given the information available in the database, it is possible to add criteria and fine-tune the ranking output based on the number of occurrences of a keyword or phrase and the sum of the weight factors of the search fields. Namely, each search criterion fits several different entities and their attributes within the database, and each entity/attribute includes weight factors that determine the relevance of the appearance of the resource within the result set. One example can illustrate this: *location* is one search criterion. When searching with this criterion the weights of corresponding fields are: Municipality 8, County 7, Title 4, Keywords 3, Abstract 2, Appendices 1. Thus, if search is performed with the location criterion *Bor*, documents in which *Bor* occurs in Municipality field will be better ranked than those in which it occurs in the Abstract field. The ranking of results is performed in descending order according to the total sum of the product of weight factors and the number of occurrences of the corresponding keywords.

A specific feature of Serbian is the common use of two alphabets: Cyrillic and Latin, so a user can initiate her/his search using any of the two, and the method on the server automatically expands the search query with the other, while the results are shown in the original alphabet used in the documents, and that is Cyrillic.

Query processing on the server side expands the query by creating a matrix of key words, fields that are searched, and weight factors, and then translates this query into SQL (Structured Query Language) form. The query generated in such a way searches the text of the subset of attributes in the database that correspond to the selected criteria of search.

The initial solution has been used from 2008, while the development of the improved solution started at beginning of 2015 and is available for use since June 2015, with new features for evaluation and relevance feedback in the development phase.

3   The Improved Solution

One of the problems of full text search in Serbian is its rich morphology, as the keyword for search is always entered in the nominative singular, while in the texts that are searched it can occur in different inflectional forms.

For languages such as Serbian, some kind of normalization of morphological forms has to be performed both for document indexing and query processing. One soultion is to use stemmers. For Serbian, work on several stemmers was reported: a stemmer as a part of a larger system for information retrieval, PoS tagging, shallow parsing and topic tracking [12], a stemmer and lemmatizer based on suffix stripping [8], the same basic idea being used in the stemmer presented in a later paper [14]. The only stemmer available for use is the last one since its code is available from the paper itself. However, although the author claims accuracy of 92 % it was evaluated on a very small text (522 words) so its reliability is not confirmed. Also, as Hiemstra states [5] "Stemming tends to help as many queries as it hurts." The other possibility is statistical lemmatization for which TreeTagger trained for Serbian is available, already used for lemmatization of the Corpus of Contemporary Serbian [20]. However, this lemmatizer was trained on a corpus that differs significantly from our collection, and additionally it does not take into account MWUs.

The approach described in this paper bases lemmatization on morphological electronic dictionaries and finite-state transducers for Serbian [9].

3.1   Used Resources

Lexical Resources. The resources for natural language processing of Serbian consisting of lexical resources and local grammars are being developed using the finite-state methodology as described in [1,4]. The role of electronic dictionaries, covering both simple words and multi-word units, and dictionary finite-state transducers (FSTs) is text tagging. Each e-dictionary of forms consists of a list of entries supplied with their lemmas, morphosyntactic, semantic and other information. The forms are, as a rule, automatically generated from the dictionaries of lemmas containing the information that enable production of forms. For this purpose almost 1,000 inflectional transducers were developed. The system of Serbian e-dictionaries covers both general lexica and proper names and all inflected forms are generated from 135,000 simple forms and 13,000 MWU lemmas. Approximately 28.5 % of these lemmas represent proper names: personal, geopolitical, organizational, etc.

Named Entity Recognition. According to [16] the term "Named Entity" (NE) usually refers to names of persons, locations and organizations, and numeric expressions including, time, date, money and percentage. Recently other major types are being included, like "products" and "events", but also marginal ones, like "e-mail addresses" and "book titles".

The NE hierarchy in our Named Entity Recognition (NER) system consists of five top-level types: persons, organizations, locations, amounts, and temporal expressions, each of them having one or more levels of sub-types. Our tagging strategy allows nesting, which means that a named entity can be nested within another named entity, e.g. a persons name within an organization name, like in *<org> Institut za vodoprivredu "<persName> Jaroslav Èerni </persName>" </org>* 'Institute for waterpower engineering Jaroslav Èerni'.

The Serbian NER system is a handcrafted rule-based system that relies on comprehensive lexical resources for Serbian described in the previous subsection. For recognition of some types of named entities, e.g. personal names and locations, e-dictionaries and information within them is crucial; for others, like temporal expressions, local grammars in the form of FSTs that try to capture a variety of syntactic forms in which a NE can occur had to be developed. However, for all of them local grammars were developed that use wider context to disambiguate ambiguous occurrences as much as possible [10]. These local grammars were organized in cascades that further resolve ambiguities [13]. NER system was evaluated on a newspaper corpus and results reported in [10] showed that F-measure of recognition was 0.96 for types and 0.92 for tokens.[2]

For the purpose of indexing, we applied our NER system to title and abstract fields of our geological structured data. The whole collection consisted of 4,902 documents (900,403 simple word forms). Almost all documents contained at least one NE — in only 61 (1.24%) not a single NE was recognized. On the average, 4 NEs of all types were recognized per document, with as many as 47 NEs for one of them. For indexing we used only three top level types: personal names, locations and organizations and their distribution is presented in Table 1.

Table 1. Distribution of three top-level NEs: persons, locations and organizations

NE type	Frequency	Average per doc	% of the text
Person	11,991	2.45	1.33
Location	49,414	10.08	5.49
Organization	2,882	0.59	0.32
Total	64,287	13.11	7.14

---

[2] Tokens are all occurrences (in this case, NEs) in a given texts, types are different occurrences.

3.2   The Architecture of the New System

Indexing of documents on geological projects is done so that for each document a text is generated of all the fields and records in the project summary database, where the title and geological field are given extra weight. Two types of "representative items" or indexes that are used for search are generated: a bag of words and named entities. They are equally treated for indexing. Figure 1 presents the architecture of the new system, where the left side depicts the preprocessing phase for document indexing, based on lexical resources and NLP tools, and the right side the query processing including calculation of similarity between information need (query) and document representations.

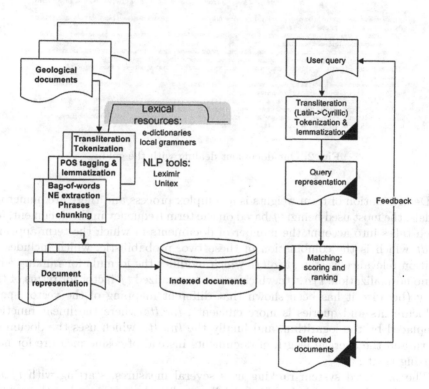

Fig. 1. The Architecture of the improved system.

The bag of words implies the representation of the document by a set of ungrammatical words — in our case nouns, adjectives, adverbs and acronyms — followed by their frequencies. Thus, the text is lemmatized and lemmas (simple and multi-word) are extracted and their frequency is calculated. In that way 12,204 simple lemmas (with 450,418 occurrences) and 271 MWUs (with 6,525 occurrences) were extracted.

Recognized NEs that belong to 3 selected types — location, organization, persons — are entered in the index. Figure 2 represents one document from our collection in which recognized NEs are highlighted in different shades of gray.

DokumentID: 6314
Извештај Студија истраживања злата са оценом минералне потенцијалности за 2002. годину..
БЕОГРАД БЕОГРАД Србија - 1/1 "Геозавод" Институт за истраживање минералних сировина Београд Проф.др. Раде Јеленковић, руд.геол.фак., Предраг Мијатовић, дипл.инж.геол., Горан Златановић, дипл.инж.геол. Кучево
Злато (Au), рудоносни рејон Благојев Камен.
I Књига - Студија истраживања злата Србује са оценом минералне потенцијалности аутора др Радета Јеленковића, редовног професора. Пројектним задатком је планирана реализација следећег обима активности које, истовремено представљају и и циљ израде Студије|
- Прикупљање геолошких података о лежиштима злата и значајнијим појавама злата у Србији односно лежиштима других минералних сировина у којим злато представља једну од водећих компоненти или компиенту чија је валоризација успутна уз основне рудне компоненте.
- Синтезу анализу прикупљених података.
- Класификовање лежишта и појава злата Србује са аспекта а) географског положаја, б) металогенетске припадности и ц) мерфогенетских типова орудњења,
- Прикупљање података о резервама злата у појединачним објектима, односно њихову синтезу, класификација и категоризација у виду табеларног приказа.
- Дефинисање типова руда у лежиштима злата Србије са аспекта парагенетских карактеристика рудне минерализације - анализу минералних фаза носилаца злата
- Дефинисање основних генетских карактеристика издвојене рудне минерализације, односно услова њиховог стварања и контролни фактора просторног положаја орудњења као основе за оцену потенцијалности
- Приказ резерви злата у претходно издвојеним рудним пољима са прогнозним оценом њихове потенцијалности и перспективности.
- Истражни простор који је обухваћен истражним геолошким радовима у оквиру овог пројекта захвата следећа подручја: Бор-Доње Њевље у оквиру Борске металогенетске зоне.
II Књига - Студија истраживања злата са оценом минералне потенцијалности у 2002. години аутора Предрага Мијатовића и Горана Златановића, дипл.инж.геологије, петставља синтезу досадашњих примењених методологија на лежиштима Шута - Расовача, Језерина, као и прорачун рудних резерви у лежишту Леце, оцена потенцијалности лежишта Леце, оцена потенцијалности рудних поља Туларе, Ђавоља Варош и Краварска Планина.

Fig. 2. One document dealing with the gold.

Determination of term weights is a complex process and there are numerous models, the most used being: tf based on the term frequency in the document, idf which takes into account the number of documents in which the term appears, tf_idf which is the combination of these two, probabilistic, which includes in addition relevance weights, tfc_tfc which modifies the formula for ranking with cosine normalization, tfc_nfc which uses a normalized tf factor for terms of the query (because it has been shown that different mapping of the vector space of documents and queries is more efficient), lnc_ltc where the linear function is replaced by the logarithm, and finally the lnu_ltu which uses the document length and the average length of documents instead of cosine measure for normalizing length [5].

The improved system ranking uses several measures, starting with tf_idf measure based on frequencies of words allocated to the text, text length, and the document frequency [11]. Further development included modification of tf_idf with cosine normalisation (tfc_tfc), tfc_nfc term weighting algorithm with normalized tf factor for the query term weights, lnc_ltc measure where l stands for weights with a logarithmic tf component, lnu_ltu where normalization is based on the number of unique words in text, as well as several measures used in Inquery system. Indexing is performed in the following steps:

1. Generating a text (D_i) from records and fields of the project summary related to a particular project document, where $i = 1, \ldots N$ and N is the size of the document collection;

2. Lemmatizing and POS tagging of all D_i texts;
3. Recognizing NEs and assigning the chosen types to documents;
4. Selecting ungrammatical words t_{ij} for each D_i and calculating:
   (a) n_{ij} as frequencies of t_{ij},
   (b) average and maximal term frequency (avg_tf_i, max_tf_i),
   (c) number of unique words in document (no_uw_i) and document length (l_i),
   (d) relative frequency tf_{ij} for each term t_{ij} in a text D_i as n_{ij}/l_i where l_i is the length of the text in the number of simple words;
5. Creating a dictionary of the whole document collection from all words selected in Step 4. For each term T_k in the document collection, $k = 1, \ldots M$, where M is the size of the dictionary of document collection:
   (a) calculating document frequency df_k as the number of documents in the collection in which the term T_k appears,
   (b) calculating the acceptable indicator idf_k of term value as a document discriminator as $log(N/df_k)$ (lnc_ltc algorithm uses for ltc expression $idf1_k = log((N + 1)/df_k)$),
   (c) $nidf_k = idf_k/log(N)$;
6. Calculating the document vector combined measure:
   (a) $tf\_idf = tf \cdot idf$, and vector intensity int_tf_idf,
   (b) $ltf = 1 + log(tf)$ and vector intensity int_ltf,
   (c) $tfc = tf\_idf/int\_tf\_idf$,
   (d) $lnc = ltf/int\_ltf$,
   (e) $lnu = (ltf/(1 + log(avg\_tf)))/((1 - s) + s \cdot (no\_uw))$, with the constant value $s = 0.25$.

   In the search stage the similarity of the search query vector and the document are determined as follows:

1. the query is analyzed, tokenization is performed (separating into words, where a MWU within quotation marks is treated as one word) followed by calculating:
   (a) maximal term frequency max_tf and number of unique words no_uw from query,
   (b) $nfc = (0.5 + 0.5 \cdot tf/max\_tf) \cdot lema\_idf$,
   (c) $ltc = (1 + log(tf)) \cdot lema\_idf1$,
   (d) $ltu = ltc/((1 - s) + s \cdot no\_uw)$;
2. for each document and for each word in the query depending of the selected method the weight is calculated, where d stands for document and q for query:
   (a) 'tfc_nfc': $d\_tfc \cdot q\_nfc$,
   (b) 'lnc_ltc': $d\_lnc \cdot q\_ltc$,
   (c) 'lnu_ltu': $d\_lnu \cdot q\_ltu$;
3. the similarity between the query and the document is ranked based on the sum of weights for all words in the query.

   Document in Fig. 2 is about a project that deals with gold. When searching with the keyword *zlato* 'gold' the old system ranks the document as 125th within general search and as 84th when searching in the category *mineral deposits* because the keyword matches only that particular form of the word (two matches highlighted in gray in Fig. 2). The new system ranks it as the first because the *tf_idf* of this term for this document is calculated on the basis of its frequency $n_j = 12$ (ten additional matches are in Fig. 2 highlighted in light gray). Due to its simple pattern matching the old system finds the positive match *zlatonosna žica* 'gold vein' when searching with *zlato*, which the new system misses (*zlato* and *zlatonosan* are two different lemmas); however, for the same reasons, the old system has the negative match *Zlatokop* (the name of one settlement), which the new system again misses.

4 Evaluation

The goal of evaluation was to assess the efficiency of the old and new search method. The evaluation was performed over the entire collection of documents and a set of 15 information needs, represented by respective queries. For query selection the log of the existing system was used, while also consulting geologist about their most common information needs. It turned out that most frequent requests are for a mineral resource type like coper, gold, coal, optionally at some location, or a geological event like landslide or earthquake. For example, the first informational need "gold in Bor and the surrounding area" is converted into formal Boolean query *(zlato OR Au) AND (Bor OR Borski okrug)* '(gold OR Au) AND (Bor OR Bor district)'. For evaluation standard measures were used, namely precision $P = tp/(tp + fp)$, recall $R = tp/(tp + fn)$, and F1-measure $F = 2 \cdot P \cdot R/(P + R)$, where tp – *true positive* is the number of relevant documents retrieved, fp – *false positive* is the number of non-relevant documents retrieved, and fn – *false negative* is the number of relevant documents that were not retrieved. During the evaluation ranked responses were offered to users, and the measures P and R were calculated for sets containing the first i choices offered, where $i \in [1, 100]$ [11]. In this way, curves showing the dependency between precision and recall for all 15 queries were obtained, as illustrated in Fig. 3 for the abovementioned query. The charts show that the search precision of the old system is significantly better among first-ranked documents, while the recall is better with the new system: among the first 100 documents the old system had 22 relevant responses, and the new had 25.

If the Interpolated Average Precision for 11 levels of recall $0.0, 0.1, 0.2, ..., 0.9,$ 1.0 is calculated, a comparative graph is obtained of the relationship between precision and recall presented (a graph in Fig. 4(a) represent this relationship for the first query). The same procedure was applied for all 15 information needs (queries) and the results are presented in Table 2. In the columns the Average Precision $AP = \sum_{k=1}^{n} P(k)\Delta(k)$ is given for a particular query using the current system and several indexing methods, where $n = 100$ is the number of retrieved documents, $P(k)$ is the precision in the intersection point k, and $\Delta(k)$ is the change in the recall from items $k - 1$ to k. The results show that for 3 queries AP was higher in the current system, while for 12 queries AP was higher when indexing was used. Mean Average Precision (MAP) for the current

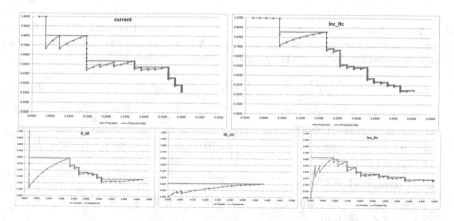

Fig. 3. Precision-recall curve for the first query *(zlato OR Au) AND (Bor OR Borski okrug)*: top left, retrieval without index; top right, retrieval with the best index *lnc_ltc*, bottom from left to right: index with *tf_idf*, *tfc_nfc* and *lnu_ltu*.

system is lower than MAP when indexing methods are used, being more than 38.7 % higher for the best performing method *lnc_ltc*.

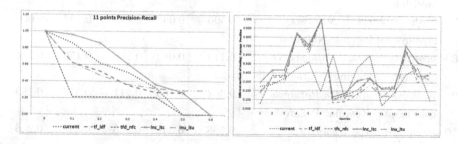

Fig. 4. Comparison of the current system and new methods based on indexing: (a) 11-point Interpolated Average Precision for the first query; (b) Average Precision for 15 queries.

The evaluation, as well as the analysis of the results showed that the current system achieves good results when searching with terms that occur as discipline and mineral resources classifiers, which are thus listed in the appropriate fields in the same form in which the users formulate their query (e.g. the nominative singular). However, a large number of other forms cannot be found by scanning the text, for example, the form *zlata* (genitive singular) cannot match the query keyword *zlato* (nominative singular). The disadvantage of the system based on text scanning which affects the precision is especially visible when short words that could be parts of other words are used in a search. As explained before, the current system does not require match with whole words precisely in order to recognize at least some inflectional forms. This problem is generated by query

Table 2. Average Precision per query and Mean Average Precision (MAP) for the current system and various indexing methods. A space in a query stands for an OR operator, a semicolon for an AND operator (relevant for the old system).

	Query	Current	tf_idf	tfc_nfc	lnc_ltc	lnu_ltu
1	*zlato*; *Au*; *Bor*; *Borski okrug*	0.247	0.178	0.056	0.294	0.199
	gold; Au; Bor; Bor county					
2	*opekarska keramička glina*;	0.270	0.352	0.369	0.432	0.29
	Geozavod Geoinstitut					
	brick ceramic clay; Geozavod					
3	*opekarska keramička*; *glina*;	0.339	0.352	0.369	0.432	0.29
	Geozavod Geoinstitut					
	brick ceramic; clay; Geozavod					
4	*poplava plavljenje izlivanje*	0.446	0.848	0.834	0.849	0.843
	flood flooding spills					
5	*nestabilna padina*	0.521	0.658	0.680	0.711	0.619
	unstable slopes					
6	*klizište*	0.193	1.000	1.000	1.000	1.000
	landslide					
7	*geofizički karotaž*; *Naftagas*	0.596	0.068	0.109	0.134	0.096
	geophysical logging; Naftagas					
8	*geofizički karotaž*; *Naftagas NIS*	0.113	0.083	0.155	0.176	0.144
	geophysical logging; Naftagas NIS					
9	*ugalj lignit*; *Kostolac Požarevac*	0.461	0.165	0.211	0.317	0.158
	coal lignite; Kostolac Požarevac					
10	*glina*; *Geozavod Geoinstitut*	0.598	0.349	0.335	0.348	0.266
	clay; Geozavod Geoinstitut					
11	*hidrogeologija*; *istraživanja*; *Beograd*	0.043	0.135	0.238	0.228	0.152
	hydrogeology; research; Belgrade					
12	*"rezerve uglja"*; *"Sjenički basen"*	0.183	0.255	0.253	0.234	0.141
	"coal reserves"; "Sjenica basin"					
13	*kvarcni*; *pesak*; *bušotina*	0.385	0.673	0.646	0.709	0.640
	quartz; sand; well					
14	*jezgro*; *bušenje*; *Arandjelovac*	0.460	0.300	0.369	0.519	0.406
	core; drilling; Arandjelovac					
15	*Dunav*; *Sava*; *podzemni*	0.093	0.413	0.378	0.478	0.322
	Danube; Sava; underground					
	MAP	0.330	0.389	0.400	**0.457**	0.371
	Improvement		17.8 %	21.3 %	**38.7 %**	12.5 %

keywords such as the chemical symbol for gold "Au" or the acronym of company "NIS". The average precision for query 8 (obtained by adding "NIS" to query 7), drops from 0.596 (for query 7) to 0.113 for the current solution, while results for methods based on indexing are improved (see Table 2). The opposite happens for queries that contain terms that are missing from e-dictionaries, e.g. *karotaž* 'logging' or terms for which inflected forms are missing, e.g. the plural form *ugljevi* of *ugalj* 'coal' that is specific to the mining terminology. Graph presented in Fig. 4(b) gives average precisions for all 15 queries used for evaluation. The comparison of current system and new indexing methods shows that *lnc_ltc* method is superior for majority of queries over current system and other indexing methods.

The evaluation revealed that some NEs referring to the same entity occur in various forms which can deteriorate search results. For instance, the name of one particular person that documents refer to frequently occurs in 12 different forms:[3] *Dr Petar Petrović, Mr Petar Petrović, Prof. dr Petar Petrović, Prof. Dr Petar Petrović, dr Petar Petrović, Mr. Petar Petrović, PETROVIĆ PETAR, Dr Petar Petrović, docent, Mr Petar Petrović, asistent, docent Dr Petar Petrović, Mr. Petar Petrović, asistent, Petrović.* The biggest problem of the new system are specific technical terms that are not found in electronic dictionaries as well as quite a number of typographical errors in the document collection. However, this shortcoming can be rectified by correcting errors (based on the list of words unrecognized by the vocabulary), and by continuous enhancement of the vocabulary by adding new words.

5   Conclusion and Future Work

The evaluation showed that the initial solution has its advantages: besides being simple to apply, it performs well for certain types of queries. However, although the new solution based on pre-indexing already outperforms it, its main advantage is that it can be improved and there are various means to do that:

- Enriching morphological e-dictionaries of simple words and MWUs with terms from geological domain;
- Using named entities for faceted search;
- Addapting NERs to the new domain and text type (projects rather than newspapers) and adding named entity normalization;
- Experimenting with different term weight measures;
- Experimenting with different comparison of document and information need representations.

Further research will be done by applying the new solution to other textual and spatial databases and data collections, as well as by enabling map visualization of location of recognized named entities using geodatabases. An analysis of queries in the full sentence form is planned, which would eliminate stop words —

---

[3] The name of the person was de-identified for privacy reasons.

prepositions, followed by lemmatization to produce a bag of words for the query. Finally, query expansion is planned, by adding synonyms and other related terms from available resources, such as the geologic dictionary [19] for terminological query terms and WordNet for more general terms.

Acknowledgements. This research was supported by the Serbian Ministry of Education and Science under the grant #47003 and KEYSTONE COST Action IC1302. The authors would also like to thank the anonymous reviewers for their helpful and constructive comments.

References

1. Courtois, B., Silberztein, M.: Dictionnaires électroniques du français. Larousse, Paris (1990)
2. Furlan, B., Batanović, V., Nikolić, B.: Semantic similarity of short texts in languages with a deficient natural language processing support. Decis. Support Syst. **55**(3), 710–719 (2013)
3. Graovac, J.: Wordnet-based Serbian text categorization. INFOtheca **14**(2), 2a–17a (2013)
4. Gross, M.: The use of finite automata in the lexical representation of natural language. In: Gross, M., Perrin, D. (eds.) Electronic Dictionaries and Automata in Computational Linguistics. LNCS, vol. 377, pp. 34–50. Springer, Berlin/Heidelberg (1989). http://dx.doi.org/10.1007/3-540-51465-1_3
5. Hiemstra, D.: Using language models for information retrieval. Taaluitgeverij Neslia Paniculata (2001)
6. Ivanović, D., Milosavljević, G., Milosavljević, B., Surla, D.: A CERIF-compatible research management system based on the MARC 21 format. Inf. Knowl. Manage. **44**(3), 229–251 (2010)
7. Jackson, P., Moulinier, I.: Natural Language Processing for Online Applications: Text Retrieval, Extraction and Categorization, vol. 5. John Benjamins Publishing, Amsterdam (2007)
8. Kešelj, V., Šipka, D.: A suffix subsumption-based approach to building stemmers and lemmatizers for highly inflectional languages with sparse resources. INFOtheca **9**(1–2), 23a–33a (2008)
9. Krstev, C.: Processing of Serbian - Automata, Texts and Electronic Dictionaries. Faculty of Philology. University of Belgrade, Belgrade (2008)
10. Krstev, C., Obradović, I., Utvić, M., Vitas, D.: A system for named entity recognition based on local grammars. J. Logic Comput. **24**(2), 473–489 (2014)
11. Shrimpton, J.: Introduction. In: Shrimpton, J. (ed.) Charge Injection Systems. Heat, Mass Transfer, vol. 1, pp. 1–4. Springer, Heidelberg (2009)
12. Martinović, M.: Transfer of natural language processing technology: experiments, possibilities and limitations case study: english to Serbian. INFOtheca **9**(1–2), 11a–21a (2008)
13. Maurel, D., Friburger, N., Antoine, J.Y., Eshkol, I., Nouvel, D., et al.: Cascades de transducteurs autour de la reconnaissance des entités nommées. Traitement Automatique des Langues **52**(1), 69–96 (2011)
14. Milosevic, N.: Stemmer for Serbian language. CoRR abs/1209.4471 (2012)

15. Mladenović, M., Mitrović, J., Krstev, C., Vitas, D.: Hybrid sentiment analysis framework for a morphologically rich language. J. Intell. Inf. Syst. **45**(129), 1573–7675 (2015). doi:10.1007/s10844-015-0372-5. Springer, ISSN 0925-9902
16. Nadeau, D., Sekine, S.: A survey of named entity recognition and classification. In: Sekine, S., Ranchhod, E. (eds.) Named Entities: Recognition, Classification and Use, pp. 3–28. John Benjamins Pub. Co., Amsterdam/Philadelphia (2009)
17. Rehm, G., Uszkoreit, H. (eds.): META-NET. White Paper Series. Springer, Heidelberg (2012). http://www.meta-net.eu/whitepapers
18. Salton, G., McGill, M.J.: Introduction to modern information retrieval. McGraw-Hill Inc, New York (1983)
19. Stanković, R., Trivić, B., Kitanović, O., Blagojević, B., Nikolić, V.: The development of the geolissterm terminological dictionary. INFOtheca **12**(1), 49a–63a (2011)
20. Utvić, M.: Annotating the corpus of contemporary Serbian. INFOtheca - J. Inf. Librariansh. **12**(2), 36a–47a (2011)
21. Vitas, D., Popović, L., Krstev, C., Obradović, I., Pavlović-Lažetić, G., Stanojević, M.: Srpski jezik u digitalnom dobu - the Serbian language in the digital age. In: Rehm, G., Uszkoreit, H. (eds.) META-NET. White Paper Series. Springer, Heidelberg (2012). http://www.meta-net.eu/whitepapers
22. Zečević, A., Stanković-Vujičić, S.: Language identification-the case of Serbian. In: Pavlović-Lažetić, G., Krstev, C., Vitas, D., Obradović, I. (eds.) Natural Language Processing for Serbian - Resources and Applications, pp. 101–112. Faculty of Mathematics. University of Belgrade, Belgrade (2014). http://jerteh.rs/wp-content/uploads/2015/05/Zecevic.pdf

Domain-Specific Modeling: Towards a Food and Drink Gazetteer

Andrey Tagarev[✉], Laura Toloşi, and Vladimir Alexiev

Ontotext AD, 47A Tsarigradsko Shosse, 1124 Sofia, Bulgaria
andrey.tagarev@ontotext.com

Abstract. Our goal is to build a Food and Drink (FD) gazetteer
that can serve for classification of general, FD-related concepts, efficient faceted search or automated semantic enrichment. Fully supervised
design of a domain-specific models *ex novo* is not scalable. Integration of
several ready knowledge bases is tedious and does not ensure coverage.
Completely data-driven approaches require a large amount of training
data, which is not always available. For general domains (such as the FD
domain), re-using encyclopedic knowledge bases like Wikipedia may be
a good idea. We propose here a semi-supervised approach that uses a
restricted Wikipedia as a base for the modeling, achieved by selecting a
domain-relevant Wikipedia category as root for the model and all its subcategories, combined with expert and data-driven pruning of irrelevant
categories.

Keywords: Categorization · Wikipedia · Wikipedia categories ·
Gazetteer · Europeana · Cultural heritage · Concept extraction

1 Introduction

Our work is motivated by the Europeana Food and Drink (EFD) project[1], which
aims at categorizing food and drink-related concepts (FD), in order to digitalize,
facilitate search and semantically enrich Cultural Heritage (CH) items pertaining to the 'food and drink' theme. Even though driven by the application to
FD, our approach is easily generalizable to any domain that is encyclopedic in
nature. For example, we can apply the approach for categorizing 'Arts', 'Sports',
'History' etc.

Modeling a domain from scratch requires interdisciplinary expertise, both in
the particular domain and in knowledge-base modeling. Also, it is a tedious,
time-consuming process. When the domain is very specialized, for example 'Art
Nouveau', 'Performance Arts' or 'Human Genes', probably the process is
unavoidable. However, for broader domains like FD we believe that using encyclopedic, LOD data is a better, more scalable approach. To model FD concepts
we used Wikipedia.

---

[1] http://foodanddrinkeurope.eu/.

© Springer International Publishing Switzerland 2015
J. Cardoso et al. (Eds.): KEYWORD 2015, LNCS 9398, pp. 182–196, 2015.
DOI: 10.1007/978-3-319-27932-9_16

Wikipedia is a great collection of general knowledge concepts. It is freely available and easily editable by anyone. The volume of information is enormous. E.g. the English wiki has a total of 35 M pages, of which 30 M are auxiliary (discussions, sub-projects, categories, etc.). Overall, Wikipedia has some 35 M articles in over 240 languages. Multilingualism is a very important aspect that recommends the usage of Wikipedia, as CH objects in EFD come in eleven languages.

In this paper we describe the method, we show preliminary results and we present a critical discussion on the suitability of Wikipedia for the purpose of FD categorization. In Sect. 2, we describe the EFD application. In Sect. 3, we present the steps of the method. Section 4 presents some insightful (from both technical and application perspective) properties of the sub-hierarchy generated from the *Food_and_drink* root. We continue by describing the supervised curation of the domain in Sect. 5 and by showing the results of the data-driven enrichment analysis in Sect. 6. We will conclude the paper with comments and outlook in Sect. 7.

Next, we mention previous work that has addressed domain-specific modeling in the past.

1.1 Related Work

Much work has been dedicated to building domain specific knowledge bases. Earliest approaches were fully supervised, domain experts defining *ex-novo* the classification model. With the development of modern NLP techniques such as concept disambiguation, concept tagging or relation extraction, semi-supervised and even unsupervised methods are emerging. For example, there are many methods for automated merging and integration of already existing ontologies ([3,4,11]). In [10], a semi-supervised method for enriching existing ontologies with concepts from text is presented. More ambitious approaches propose unsupervised generation of ontologies ([8,9]), using deep NLP methods. In [5], a method is described, for generating lightweight ontologies by mapping concepts from documents to LOD data like Freebase and DBpedia and then generating a meaningful taxonomy that covers the concepts.

Classification of FD has been approached before. Depending on the purpose of the classification, there exist models for cooking and recipes, models for ingredients and nutrients, food composition databases (EuroFIR classification[2]), models that classify additives (Codex Alimentarius GSFA[3]), pesticides (Codex Classification of Foods and Feeds[4]), traded food and beverages nomenclature (GS1 standard for Food and Beverages[5]), national-specific classification systems, etc. [12] have proposed a cooking ontology, focused on: food (ingredients), kitchen utensils, recipes, cooking actions. BBC also proposed a lightweight

---

[2] http://www.eurofir.org/.

[3] http://www.codexalimentarius.org/standards/gsfa/.

[4] ftp://ftp.fao.org/codex/meetings/ccpr/ccpr38/pr38CxCl.pdf.

[5] http://www.gs1.org/gdsn/gdsn-trade-item-extension-food-and-beverage/2-8.

food ontology[6], that classifies mainly recipes, including aspects like ingredients, diets, courses, occasions.

The purpose of the EFD project is to classify food and drink objects from a cultural perspective, which is not addressed by existing models.

2   Europeana Food and Drink

The EFD Classification scheme [2] is a multi-dimensional scheme for discovering and classifying Cultural Heritage Objects (CHO) related to Food and Drink (FD). The project makes use of innovative semantic technologies to automate the extraction of terms and co-references. The result is a body of semantically-enriched metadata that can support a wider range of multilingual applications such as search, discovery and browse.

The FD domain is generously broad and familiar, in the sense that any human can name hundreds of concepts that should be covered by the model: 'bread', 'wine', 'fork', 'restaurant', 'table', 'chicken, 'bar', 'Thanksgiving dinner', etc. In our particular application however, the model is required to cover a large variety of cultural objects related to FD, some of which exist nowadays only in etnographic museums. These are described in content coming from a variety of CH organizations, ranging from Ministries to academic libraries and specialist museums to picture libraries. The content represents a significant number of European nations and cultures, it comprises objects illustrating FD heritage, recipes, artworks, photographs, some audio and video content and advertising relating to FD. It is heterogeneous in types and significance, but with the common thread of FD heritage and its cultural and social meaning. Metadata are available partly in English and native languages, with more than half of the metadata only available in native languages.

Content is heterogeneous and varied. Examples include [2]: books on Bovine care and feeding (TEL[7]), book on tubers/roots used by New Zealand aboriginals (RLUK[8]), self-portraits involving some food (Slovak National Gallery[9]), traditional recipes for Christmas-related foods (Ontotext), colorful pasta arrangements (Horniman[10]), mortar used to mix lime with tobacco to enhance its psychogenic compounds (Horniman), food pounder cut from coral and noted for its ergonomic design (Horniman), toy horse made from cheese (Horniman), a composition of man with roosters/geese made from bread (Horniman), poems about food and love, photos of old people having dinner, photos of packers on a wharf, photos of Parisian cafes, photos of a shepherd tending goats, photos of a vintner in his winery, medieval cook book (manuscript), commercial label/ad for consommé, etc.

---

[6] http://www.bbc.co.uk/ontologies/fo.
[7] http://www.theeuropeanlibrary.org/tel4/.
[8] http://www.rluk.ac.uk/.
[9] http://www.sng.sk/en/uvod.
[10] http://www.horniman.ac.uk/.

2.1 Wikipedia Categories Related to FD

Wikipedia categories live in the namespace 'https://en.wikipedia.org/wiki/ Category:' (note the colon at the end). We discovered a number of FD categories, amongst them: *Food and drink, Beverages, Ceremonial food and drink, Christmas food, Christmas meals and feasts, Cooking utensils, Drinking culture, Eating parties, Eating utensils, Food and drink preparation, Food culture, Food festivals, Food services occupations, Foods, History of food and drink, Holiday foods, Meals, Works about food and drink, World cuisine.* Other interesting categories: *Religious food and drink, Food law*: topics like halal, kashrut, designation of origin, religion-based ideas, fisheries laws, agricultural laws, food and drug administration, labeling regulations, etc., *Food politics, Drink and drive songs, Food museums.* We selected https://en.wikipedia.org/wiki/Category:Food_and_ drink as the root of our FD restricted model, considering that all the above-mentioned categories are its direct or indirect subcategories.

3 A Method for Domain-Specific Modeling

Wikipedia is loosely structured information. It has very elaborate editorial policies and practices, but their major goal is to create modular text that is consistent, attested (referenced to primary sources), relatively easy to manage. A huge number of templates and other MediaWiki mechanisms are used for this purpose. The structured parts of Wikipedia that can be reused by machines are: (*i*) Links (wiki links, inter-language links providing language correspondence, inter-wiki links, referring to another Wikipedia or another Wikimedia project e.g. Wiktionary, Wikibooks, external links), (*ii*) Informative templates, in particular Infoboxes; (*iii*) Tables; (*iv*) Categories; (*v*) Lists, Portals, Projects.

There are several efforts to extract structured data from Wikipedia. E.g. the Wikipedia Mining software[11] [6] allows extraction of focused or limited information. For our purpose, we prefer to use data sets that are already structured, like DBpedia. The data in RDF format is easily loaded in Ontotext GraphDB[12], which allows semantic integration of both Europeana and classification data, and easier querying using SPARQL.

3.1 Wikipedia Categories

Category statistics for Wikipedia are presented in Table 1. The counts are obtained from DBpedia (see [2] Sect. 3.11.2). The columns have the following meaning:

- 'Wikipedia' specifies for which language the statistics are computed;
- 'art' is the number of content pages (articles);
- 'cat' is the number of category pages;

---

[11] http://sourceforge.net/projects/wikipedia-miner.
[12] http://ontotext.com/products/ontotext-graphdb/.

Table 1. Wikipedia: statistics concerning categories.

Wikipedia	art	cat	art→cat	cat per art	art per cat	cat→cat	cat per cat
English	4,774,396	1,122,598	18,731,750	3.92	16.69	2,268,299	2.02
Dutch	1,804,691	89,906	2,629,632	1.46	29.25	186,400	2.07
French	1,579,555	278,713	4,625,524	2.93	16.60	465,931	1.67
Italian	1,164,000	258,210	1,597,716	1.37	6.19	486,786	1.89
Spanish	1,148,856	396,214	4,145,977	3.61	10.46	675,380	1.7
Polish	1,082,000	2,217,382	20,149,374	18.62	9.09	4,361,474	1.97
Bulgarian	170,174	37,139	387,023	2.27	10.42	73,228	1.97
Greek	102,077	17,616	182,023	1.78	10.33	35,761	2.03

- 'art→cat' is the number of assignments of a category as parent of an article;
- 'cat per art' is the average number of category assignments per article, computed as art→cat/art;
- 'art per cat' is the average number of articles assigned per category, computed as art→cat/cat;
- 'cat→cat' is the number of assignments of a category as parent of another category;
- 'cat per cat' is the average number of parent categories per category, computed as cat→cat/cat.

As you can see, there is a great variety of categorization practices across languages. Polish uses a huge number of categories (relative to articles) and assignments. Dutch has a very small number of categories, and their application is not very discriminative ('art per cat' is very high).

Despite these differences, the categorization presents a wealth of information that our method uses for classification.

3.2 Method Overview

Our approach to domain-specific modeling is aimed at selecting a sub-hierarchy of Wikipedia, rooted at a relevant category, that covers well the domain concepts. Following Wikipedia, our model is hierarchical and parent-child relations follow SKOS principles [7]. The procedure follows the steps below:

1. Start by selecting the maximally general Wikipedia category that best describes the domain to ensure coverage. We will refer to this category as *root*.
2. Traverse Wikipedia by starting from the *root* and following `skos:broader` relations between categories to collect all *children* (i.e. sub-categories of the *root*). We also remove cycles to create a directed acyclic graph and calculate useful node metadata such as *level* (i.e. shortest path from root), number of unique subcategories, etc.
3. Top-down curation: perform manual curation by experts of the top (few hundred) categories to remove the ones irrelevant to the domain.

4. Bottom-up enrichment: map domain-related concepts to Wikipedia articles and evaluate enrichment in concepts mapped to each category. Thus, we automatically evaluate the relevance of categories, by direct evidence.

Technical details:

Step 1. Breadth-first (BF) traversal selects all categories reachable from the root. In order to obtain the domain categorization, we keep all possible edges defined by the `skos:broader` relation, but remove edges that create cycles. Cycles are logically incompatible with the SKOS system, but are not forbidden and exist in Wikipedia (sometimes due to bad practices or lack of control). In order to remove cycles, we check that a potential child of the current node of the BF procedure is not also its ancestor before adding the connection. The average number of children of a category is 2.02, therefore we expect the number of categories to grow exponentially with each level until the majority of connections start being discarded for being cyclical.

Step 2. We generate a list of the few hundred most important categories (based on being close to the *root* and having many descendants) that are judged for relevance by an expert. Ones judged irrelevant are marked for removal. Removal of a category consists of a standard node-removal procedure in a directed graph, meaning that all node metadata including all incoming and outgoing edges are deleted and the node is marked as irrelevant in the repository (to be omitted in future builds). As a consequence, the sub-hierarchy may split into two or more connected components, one of which contains the root, the others being rooted at the children of the removed category. In such a case, we discard all connected components, except for the one starting at the initial *root*. The expert curation drastically reduces the size of the sub-hierarchy with minimal work, thus being an efficient early method for pruning.

Step 3. Moving away from the *root*, the number of categories of the domain hierarchy grows exponentially. Manually checking the validity of the categories w.r.t. the domain becomes infeasible. We propose a data-driven approach here: given a collection of documents, thesauri, databases, etc. relevant to the domain, we use a general tagging algorithm to map concepts from the collection to the hierarchy. Categories to which concepts are mapped are likely to belong to the domain, supported by evidence. For the categories to which no concepts have been mapped, we can infer their validity by using evidence mapped to children or even more distant descendants. For a leaf category (with no children) X with t concepts directly mapped to it, the score is computed as:

$$score(X) = 1 - e^{-t} \tag{1}$$

For a category Y with children $Y_1, ..., Y_n$ and t directly mapped concepts, the score is computed as:

$$score(Y) = \max\{1 - e^{-t}, \max_{i=1}^{n}\{\gamma score(Y_i)\}\}, \tag{2}$$

where $\gamma \in (0,1)$ is a decay factor, that decreases the score of categories as they get further away from descendants with evidence (i.e. mapped concepts). Figure 1 illustrates an example, where the scores of leaf categories D, E, F are computed based on Eq. 1 and the scores of categories E and B are computed using Eq. 2. The scores can be used for automatically pruning categories that have a score under a certain threshold, where the threshold is level-specific.

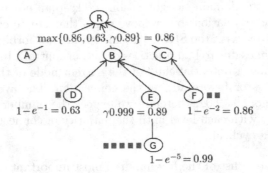

Fig. 1. Scoring categories bottom-up. Concepts mapped to categories are marked with red squares. Categories are marked with circles and named with capital letters (Color figure online).

4 Properties of the FD Classification Hierarchy

Following the method described in Sect. 3.2 we generated the *FD hierarchy*. We retrieved $887,523$ categories or about 80% of all categories in the English Wikipedia (see Table 1). The categories span 26 levels below the FD root. The distribution of the number of categories by level is unimodal, peaking at the 16th level, where we retrieve about $200,000$ categories (see Fig. 2). The average number of subcategories of a category is 2.36.

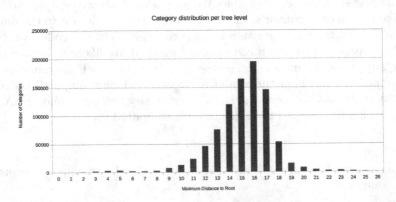

Fig. 2. Distribution of the shortest-path length from categories to the FD root category.

Most subcategories reachable from the selected root are *not relevant* to the domain. E.g. all the top 10 most populous categories at level 5 are irrelevant: Oceanography, Water pollution, Physical exercise, Bodies of water, Natural materials, Country planning in the UK, etc. We discuss below reasons and examples for such a disappointing initial hierarchy.

4.1 Reasons for Irrelevant Inclusions

Semantic Drift. The main reason for irrelevance is "semantic drift": since the meaning of the Wikipedia "parent category" relation is not well-defined, the longer path one follows, the harder it becomes to see any logical connection between the two categories (ancestor and descendant). E.g. following the chain

Food_and_drink → *Food_politics* → *Water_and_politics* →
Water_and_the_environment → *Water_management,*

one quickly reaches into rivers, lakes and reservoirs. Luckily it is easy to cut off major irrelevant branches early in the hierarchy.

Wrong Hierarchy. We were surprised to reach football teams. This happens along this chain:

Food_and_drink → *Food_politics* → *Water_and_politics* →
Water_and_the_environment → *Water_management* → *Water_treatment* →
Euthenics → *Personal_life* → *Leisure* → *Sports* → *Sports_by_type* → *Team_sports*
→ *Football.*

The above chain contains a wrong supercategory assignment: *Euthenics* is the study of the improvement of human functioning and well-being by improvement of living conditions. *Personal life*, *Leisure* and *Sports* are correctly subcategories of *Euthenics*. But *Water treatment* should not be a supercategory of *Euthenics*. This issue was fixed on June 12, 2014 by removing *Euthenics* from *Water_treatment*. However, similar problems still exist elsewhere.

Partial Inclusion. *Food_and_drink* has child *Animal_products*. Only about half of the children of *Animal_products* are relevant to the FD domain: *Animal-based_seafood*, *Dairy_products*, *Eggs_(food)*, *Fish_products*, *Meat*. Some are definitely not appropriate to FD:

Animal_dyes, *Animal_hair_products*, *Animal_waste_products*, *Bird_products*, *Bone_products*, *Coral_islands*, *Coral_reefs*, *Hides.*

Finally, there are some mixed subcategories that may include both relevant and irrelevant children: *Animal_glandular_products*: milk and its thousands of subcategories is relevant, castoreum is not; *Insect_products*: honey is relevant, silk is not; *Mollusc_products*: clams and oysters are relevant; pearls are not.

Non-human Food or Eating. Food and drink explicitly includes animal feeding, thus not all are foods for humans, e.g. *Animal_feed*. The subcategory *Eating_behaviors* has some appropriate children, e.g. *Diets*, *Eating_disorders*, but has also some inappropriate children, e.g. *Carnivory*, *Detritivores.*

5   Top-Down Expert Pruning

Supervised pruning of irrelevant categories becomes more efficient as experts are presented 'heavier' categories first; therefore we used a heuristic measure for the number of Wikipedia articles reachable from a certain category and provided them to the expert in descending order for judgement. This way, if an irrelevant category is removed, we can expect a drastic decrease of the number of nodes. The expert judged 239 of the top 250 categories in the list as irrelevant to the EFD topic. After removing them, we obtained a more focused hierarchy containing 17542 unique categories, therefore achieving a 50-fold decrease, with an hour effort from a human expert. At this step, we consider that a consensus among several experts is not needed, because only clean mismatches were removed. Examples of removed categories:

Natural_materials, Natural_resources, Water_treatment, Education, Academia, Academic_disciplines, Subfields_by_academic_discipline, Scientific_disciplines, Real_estate, Civil_engineering, Construction, Water_pollution, Property, Land_law, Intelligence, etc.

Some of these categories seem simply irrelevant, like *Civil_engineering*, others could potentially lead to articles relevant to FD, like *Natural_resources*. The path from FD to Natural_resources goes through *Agriculture, Agroecology, Sustainable_gardening Natural_materials* (length 5). However, the category is too broad and too distant to matter, and whatever relevant articles it would link to, should be retrievable by alternative, shorter paths from the FD root. For example, *Natural_resources* leads to Salt via *Minerals* and *Sodium_minerals*. However, there is a shortcut from FD directly to Salt via *Foods, Condiments, Edible_salt*, so there is no need to pass by *Natural_resources*, which in turn adds to the hierarchy many irrelevant subcategories.

The new cardinalities per level are shown in Fig. 3(a). Figure 3(b) reveals the levels at which the curation has the largest effect: starting with level 8, the decrease is larger than 50 % and from level 11, the decrease is larger than 90 %.

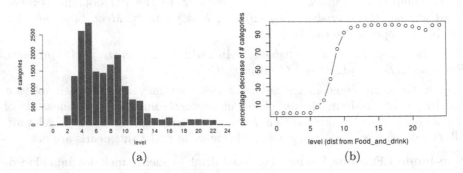

(a)   (b)

Fig. 3. (a) Number of categories per level after expert curation. (b) Decrease of number of categories per level after expert curation.

The refinement of the FD hierarchy was performed by an expert using the specially designed drill-down UI shown in Fig. 4. It starts with the *root* category and displays a node's child categories ordered by our heuristic measure of weight and all articles directly linked to the node. The user can drill-down on categories to expand them in the same way and quickly mark them as irrelevant which removes them from the repository and UI.

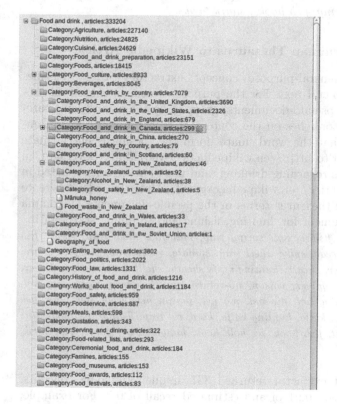

Fig. 4. Visualization interface for the FD categorization.

Fig. 5. Shark hook, an object from the Horniman Museum http:// www.horniman.ac.uk/coll ections/browse-our-collec tions/object/136887.

6   Bottom-Up Data-Driven Enrichment

A data-driven approach for estimating category relevance was described at Step 2 of our method (see Sect. 3.2). To demonstrate the approach, we considered the Horniman Objects Thesaurus, consisting of about 1500 concepts used for describing Horniman museum artefacts (700 are currently used in objects).

The Horniman thesaurus is a shallow hierarchy consisting of four levels. At the second level, the classification is most informative: *agriculture and forestry, domestication of animals, food processing and storage, food service, hunting, fishing and trapping, narcotics and intoxicants: drinking.* For example, the object *shark hook* (Fig. 5) belongs to the following path: *tools and equipment: general, hunting, fishing and trapping, fish hooks, shark hooks.*

6.1   Mapping the Horniman Thesaurus to Wikipedia Articles

We use an Ontotext general-purpose concept extractor[13] that identifies Wikipedia concepts in general text. For the purpose, we concatenated all the-saurus terms into several pseudo-documents, grouped by the second level category. The concept extractor relies on the context of each candidate for disam-biguation, in the sense that the word 'mate' form the thesaurus entry 'mate teapot' would be mapped to http://en.wikipedia.org/wiki/Mate_(beverage), in the context of other terms regarding drinking, and not to other senses, listed in the disambiguation page http://en.wikipedia.org/wiki/Mate. In order to create context, we delimited the thesaurus terms in the pseudo-documents by comma (','). Eg., the pseudo-document for 'hunting, fishing and trapping' starts with:

'hunt and fishing trap, fishing net, spring trap, mantrap, mole trap, spear, fish spear, eel spear, elephant spear, spike wheel trap, spindle, snare trap, marmot snare, bird snare, sinker, net sinker, sheath, hunting knife sheath, shellfish rake, clam digger, sample, arrow poison, reel, quiver, poison, no-return trap, fish trap, nose clip, net, hunting net, hand net, fishing net, dip net, pig net, pigeon net, scoop net, line, fish line, lure, fly, cuttlefish lure, knife, hunting knife, keep, rat trap, fishing rod, float, line float, net float, fishing float, fish hook, ice-hole hook, halibut hook, gorge, pike hook, salmon hook, shark hook...'

Evaluation. The concept extractor returned 337 unique Wikipedia concepts, with an estimated precision 0.91 of and estimated recall of 0.7. For example, *shellfish rakes*: correctly identifies https://en.wikipedia.org/wiki/Shellfish, but incorrectly returns the redirect https://en.wikipedia.org/wiki/Train for rake, instead of https://en.wikipedia.org/wiki/Rake_(tool).

6.2   Scoring FD Categories w.r.t. Mapped Horniman Concepts

Of all 337 concepts, 219 are in the FD hierarchy. Using our scoring scheme, we 'activated' 451 categories on the path to the FD root. The highest-scoring are shown in Table 2.

Qualitative evaluation of the scoring system: note that we retrieve Wikipedia categories concerning the broad topics of the Horniman thesaurus that were not explicitly input to our method: agriculture, domestic animals, food processing

---

[13] Customized version of http://tag.ontotext.com/.

Table 2. The highest scoring categories w.r.t. the proposed scoring scheme.

Category	Score	Category	Score
Cooking_utensils	1.00	*Crops*	0.99
Teaware	0.99	*Spices*	0.98
Serving_and_dining	0.99	*Agricultural_machinery*	0.98
Cooking_appliances	0.99	*Commercial_fish*	0.98
Drinkware	0.99	*Eating_utensils*	0.98
Staple_foods	0.99	*Food_storage_containers*	0.98
Tropical_agriculture	0.99	*Serving_utensils*	0.98
Gardening_tools	0.99	*Animal_trapping*	0.98
Fishing_equipment	0.99	*Food_and_drink*	0.95
Cooking_techniques	0.99	*Recreational_fishing*	0.95
Cookware_and_bakeware	0.99	*Breads*	0.95
Crockery	0.99	*Hunting*	0.95
Kitchenware	0.99	*Dairy_products*	0.95
Spoons	0.99	*Food_ingredients*	0.95
Fishing_techniques_and_methods	0.99	*Food_preparation_appliances*	0.95

and storage, hunting and fishing, drinking. Figure 6 shows all the categories up to the FD root that get 'activated' by the bottom-up scoring, meaning that they get a positive score.

Category scoring is also useful for ranking results of a semantic search, provided that enough relevant data is collected and mapped onto the hierarchy. If a user queries a concept, the tool can return a list of Wikipedia categories relevant to the concept, ranked by relevance to the FD domain. For example, if a user searches for 'fork', the category 'Gardening tools' 0.998 will appear higher in the results than *Eating_utensils* 0.982, because more concepts from the Horniman museum are mapped to *Gardening_tools*.

7 Comments and Future Work

We presented ongoing work on developing a FD categorization, with the purpose of classifying Cultural Heritage items from Europeana. To this end, we introduced a lightweight, SKOS categorization that borrows Wikipedia categories related to FD. Our preliminary results show that Wikipedia categories are rich enough to provide a good initial coverage of the domain. In fact, we showed that there are a large number of irrelevant categories that need to be removed by supervised curation. We developed an interactive visualization tool that allows experts to remove irrelevant categories and update the knowledge base.

We also presented a bottom-up, data-driven method for scoring categories with respect to concepts identified in Cultural Heritage collections, such as Horn-

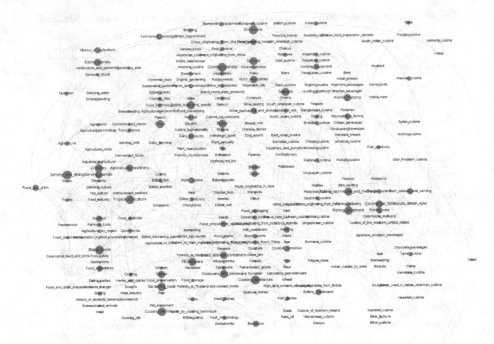

Fig. 6. Paths to *Food_and_drink*, activated by the bottom-up scoring scheme.

iman museum artefacts. We showed that by using this scoring scheme, a sub-hierarchy of FD is supported by evidence and thus confirmed to belong to the domain. This of course does not mean that the remaining categories are not food-and-drink relevant. Clearly, as more resources (e.g. recipes, books, see Sect. 2) are being processed and mapped to our classification scheme, more evidence will be gathered, for more accurate estimation of relevance of categories.

We evaluated the scoring schemes qualitatively, by showing that the categories that are 'activated' with large scores are those that describe the main topics of the Horniman thesaurus terms, namely agriculture, food serving, fishing and hunting, etc. These topics were not explicitly input to our framework, only the concrete terms like spoon, bread, cup, fishing hook, etc. A quantitative evaluation is future work, after the semantic search for FD concepts is open to the public. Then, we plan to submit various scoring schemes with various decay parameters and compare them based on user feedback.

Despite the reasonable coverage of the domain, we identified concepts – or sets of concepts – that belong to FD, but are not found under the FD root. For example, some hunting weapons are not accessible directly from the FD root. Horniman items representing spears could not be tagged, and they should, being tools for obtaining food. We have added a number of Wikipedia parent categorizations to enlarge the FD hierarchy, e.g. placing "Hunting" under FD, "Livestock" under "Agriculture" (which is under FD), etc. We also split some articles and added categorizations and labels (redirects) to match specific objects that we encountered. For example:

- Created pages "Shepherd's crook" and "Tumbler (glass)" by splitting text from existing pages. Added label "Crook"
- added to "Leash" the note "Leashes are often used to tether domesticated animals left to graze alone" as justification for adding category "Livestock".

We may add "private" secondary roots to the categorization: a direct, custom connection of type **broader** to the *Food_and_Drink* root is a possible way to add secondary roots.

A big challenge for the EFD project is building a multilingual categorization for up to 11 languages. Our prototype is currently limited to English, but we believe extending it is not hard, as we will take advantage of the 'parallel' Wikipedias for other languages. A possible approach for language X is to use all Wikipedia articles currently mapped to the English FD, get their correspondents in language X and start building the hierarchies bottom-up, to the corresponding FD root in language X. Thus, we ensure that all concepts from the English categorization would be covered by the categorization in language X. Of course, we would keep in mind that language-specific concepts may not be covered in English and thus may need to be added. The richness of the FD categories in Wikipedia and the availability of inter-language links makes this possible.

Acknowledgements. The research presented in this paper was carried out as part of the Europeana Food and Drink project, co-funded by the European Commission within the ICT Policy Support Programme (CIP-ICT-PSP-2013-7) under Grant Agreement no. 621023.

References

1. Agirre, E., Barrena, A., De Lacalle, OL., Soroa, A., Fern, S., Stevenson, M.: Matching cultural heritage items to Wikipedia (2012)
2. Alexiev, V.: Europeana Food and Drink Classification Scheme, Europeana Food and Drink project, Deliverable D2.2 (2015). http://vladimiralexiev.github.io/pubs/Europeana-Food-and-Drink-Classification-Scheme-(D2.2).pdf
3. Cheng, CP., Lau, GT., Pan, J, Law, KH., Jones, A.: Domain-Specific ontology mapping by corpus-based semantic similarity
4. Fridman Noy, N., Musen, MA.: Domain-specific ontology mapping by corpus-based semantic similarity. In: Workshop on Ontology Management at the 16th National Conference on Artificial Intelligence (AAAI 1999) (1999)
5. Medelyan, O., Manion, S., Broekstra, J., Divoli, A., Huang, A.-L., Witten, I.H.: Constructing a focused taxonomy from a document collection. In: Cimiano, P., Corcho, O., Presutti, V., Hollink, L., Rudolph, S. (eds.) ESWC 2013. LNCS, vol. 7882, pp. 367–381. Springer, Heidelberg (2013)
6. Medelyan, O., Milne, D., Legg, C., Witten, I.H.: Mining meaning from Wikipedia. Int. J. Hum. Comput. Stud. **67**(9), 716–754 (2009)

7. Miles, A., Bechhofer, S.: SKOS simple knowledge organization system reference. In: W3C Recommendation (2009)
8. Mousavi, H., Kerr, D., Iseli, M., Zaniolo, C.: Harvesting domain specific ontologies from text. In: ICSC 2014, pp. 211–218 (2014)
9. Mousavi, H., Kerr, D., Iseli, M., Zaniolo, C.: OntoHarvester: an unsupervised ontology generator from free text. CSD Technical report #130003, University of California Los Angeles (2013)
10. Parekh, V., Gwo, J.: Mining domain specific texts and glossaries to evaluate and enrich domain ontologies. In: Proceedings of the International Conference of Information and Knowledge Engineering (2004)
11. Pinto, HS., Martins, JP.: A methodology for ontology integration In: Proceedings of the 1st International Conference on Knowledge Capture, K-CAP 2001 (2001)
12. Ribeiro, R., Batista, F., Pardal, J.P., Mamede, N.J., Pinto, H.S.: Cooking an ontology. In: Euzenat, J., Domingue, J. (eds.) AIMSA 2006. LNCS (LNAI), vol. 4183, pp. 213–221. Springer, Heidelberg (2006)

Analysing Entity Context in Multilingual Wikipedia to Support Entity-Centric Retrieval Applications

Yiwei Zhou[1]([⊠]), Elena Demidova[2], and Alexandra I. Cristea[1]

[1] Department of Computer Science, University of Warwick, Coventry, UK
{Yiwei.Zhou,A.I.Cristea}@warwick.ac.uk
[2] L3S Research Center and Leibniz Universität Hannover, Hannover, Germany
demidova@L3S.de

Abstract. Representation of influential entities, such as famous people and multinational corporations, on the Web can vary across languages, reflecting language-specific entity aspects as well as divergent views on these entities in different communities. A systematic analysis of language-specific entity contexts can provide a better overview of the existing aspects and support entity-centric retrieval applications over multilingual Web data. An important source of cross-lingual information about influential entities is Wikipedia — an online community-created encyclopaedia — containing more than 280 language editions. In this paper we focus on the extraction and analysis of the language-specific entity contexts from different Wikipedia language editions over multilingual data. We discuss alternative ways such contexts can be built, including graph-based and article-based contexts. Furthermore, we analyse the similarities and the differences in these contexts in a case study including 80 entities and five Wikipedia language editions.

1 Introduction

Entities with world-wide influence, such as famous people and multinational corporations, can be represented differently in the news, in Web pages and in other documents originating from various cultures and written in different languages. These various representations can reflect language-specific entity aspects as well as views on the entity in different communities. In order to enable a better representation of the language-specific entity aspects in the information retrieval systems, methods to systematically identify language-specific entity contexts — i.e. the aspects in the entity descriptions typical to a specific language — need to be developed.

For example, in the English news, the entity "Angela Merkel", the Chancellor of Germany, is often associated with US and UK politicians such as Barack Obama, or David Cameron. Also, recent discussions of the European importance, such as Greek financial situation are included. On the contrary, although the German pages also include European topics, they frequently focus on the

© Springer International Publishing Switzerland 2015
J. Cardoso et al. (Eds.): KEYWORD 2015, LNCS 9398, pp. 197–208, 2015.
DOI: 10.1007/978-3-319-27932-9_17

domestic political topics, featuring discussions of political parties in Germany, scandals arising around German politicians, local elections, finances and other country-specific topics. For another example, in case of the multinational companies like GlaxoSmithKline (a British healthcare company), the aspects related to the local activities are prevalent in the reporting in specific languages. These aspects range from the effectiveness of the various vaccines developed by the company to the sports events sponsored by this company in a specific country. The knowledge of such language-specific aspects can support entity-centric retrieval applications. These applications can include e.g.: (i) creation of a comprehensive overview of the language-specific entity aspects in the document collection; and (ii) targeted retrieval of entity-centric information in a specific language context.

In order to obtain a comprehensive overview over the language-specific entity aspects and their representations in different languages, language-specific background knowledge about this entity is required. In this paper we choose Wikipedia as a multilingual knowledge base to obtain such background. Wikipedia — a multilingual encyclopaedia available in more than 280 language editions — contains language-specific representation of millions of entities and can provide a rich source for cross-cultural analytics. For example, recent studies focused on the manual analysis of the controversial entities in Wikipedia and identified significant cross-lingual differences (e.g. [19]). As entity representations in different Wikipedia language editions can evolve independently, they often include overlapping as well as language-specific entity aspects.

In this paper we focus on the problem of creating language-specific entity contexts to support multilingual entity retrieval applications. We use Wikipedia as a knowledge base to build such language-specific entity contexts. We discuss different ways of building these contexts using Wikipedia, including *article-based* and *graph-based* approaches and propose a measure to compute the context similarity. Furthermore, we use this similarity measure to analyse the similarities and the differences of the language-specific entity contexts in a case study using 80 entities of four different entity types and the representations of these entities in five European languages. Our experiments show that the proposed *graph-based* entity context can effectively provide a comprehensive overview over the language-specific entity aspects.

2   Creation of the Language-Specific Entity Context

In this section we define the language-specific entity context, present a measure of the context similarity and discuss alternative ways to extract such contexts from the multilingual Wikipedia.

2.1   Language-Specific Entity Context Definition

We define the language-specific entity context as follows:

Definition 1. *The context $C(e, L_i)$ of the entity e in the language L_i is represented through the set of aspects $\{a_1, \ldots, a_n\}$ of e in L_i, weighted to reflect the relevance of the aspects in the context: $C(e, L_i) = (w_1 * a_1, \ldots, w_n * a_n)$.*

In this paper, we consider entity aspects being all related entities, concepts and terms. We obtain such aspects automatically by extraction of *noun phrases* that co-occur with the entity in a given language. In addition, we can also consider the names of the linked articles as an additional source of the entity aspects. The weights of the aspects are based on two factors: (1) the *language-specific aspect co-occurrence frequency*, i.e. the frequency of the co-occurrence of the aspect and the entity in a language, and (2) the *cross-lingual aspect co-occurrence frequency* — the number of languages in which the entity context contains the aspect. The first weighting factor prioritises the aspects that frequently co-occur with the entity in a particular language. The second factor assigns higher weights to the language-specific aspects of the entity not mentioned in many other languages. Overall, given a multilingual data collection containing the languages $L = \{L_1, \ldots, L_N\}$, the weight $w(a_k, e, L_i)$ of the entity aspect a_k in the language-specific context $C(e, L_i)$ is calculated as follows:

$$w(a_k, e, L_i) = af(a_k, e, L_i) \cdot log \frac{N}{af(a_k, e, L)}, \tag{1}$$

where $af(a_k, e, L_i)$ is the *language-specific aspect co-occurrence frequency* of the aspect a_k in the entity context of e in the language L_i, N is the number of languages in the multilingual collection, and $af(a_k, e, L)$ is the *cross-lingual aspect co-occurrence frequency*.

In case the aspects are represented through the manually-defined links, their relevance can be high, but the frequency low compared to the noun phrases; Therefore, we assign them with an average *language-specific aspect co-occurrence frequency* computed for the noun phrases.

2.2 Context Similarity Measure

In order to compute the similarity between language-specific entity contexts, we use the vector space model. Each axis in the vector space represents the aspect a_k. We represent the context $C(e, L_i)$ of the entity e in the language L_i as a vector in this space. An entry for a_k in the vector represents the weight of the aspect a_k in the context of the entity in the language L_i. Then the context similarity of e's contexts in the languages L_i and L_j is computed as the cosine similarity of the context vectors:

$$Sim(C(e, L_i), C(e, L_j)) = \frac{C(e, L_i) \cdot C(e, L_j)}{|C(e, L_i)| \times |C(e, L_j)|}. \tag{2}$$

In order to allow for cross-lingual similarity computations, we represent the aspects in a common language using machine translation. To simplify the description in this paper, we always refer to the original language of the entity context, keeping in mind that the similarity is computed in a common language representation.

2.3   Article-Based Context Extraction

Wikipedia articles representing an entity in different language editions (i.e. the articles that contain the entity name as a title) can be a useful source for the creation of the language-specific context vectors. Thus, we first propose the *article-based* context extraction approach, which simply uses the articles representing the entity in different language editions of Wikipedia. We use all sentences from an article representing the entity in a language edition as the only source of the *article-based* language-specific entity context. One drawback of this approach is the possible limitation of the aspect coverage due to the incompleteness of the Wikipedia articles. Such incompleteness can be more prominent in some language editions, making it difficult to create fair cross-lingual comparisons.

For example, when reading the English Wikipedia article about the entity "Angela Merkel", a lot of basic aspects about this politician, such as her background and early life, her domestic policy and her foreign affairs, are provided. However, not all aspects about Angela Merkel occur in this Wikipedia article. We can observe, that other articles in the same Wikipedia language edition mention other important aspects. For example, in the Wikipedia article about "Economic Council Germany", it mentions Angela Merkel's economic policy: "Although the organisation is both financially and ideologically independent it has traditionally had close ties to the free-market liberal wing of the conservative Christian Democratic Union (CDU) of Chancellor Angela Merkel.". Even the English Wikipedia article about an oil painting, "The Nightmare", which does not seem connected to "Angela Merkel" at the first glance, also mentions "Angela Merkel" as: "On 7 November 2011 Steve Bell produced a cartoon with Angela Merkel as the sleeper and Silvio Berlusconi as the monster." The aspects contained in the examples above do not occur in the main English Wikipedia article entitled "Angela Merkel". As this example illustrates, just employing the main Wikipedia article about the entity can not entirely satisfy the need to obtain a comprehensive overview over the language-specific aspects.

2.4   Graph-Based Context Extraction

To alleviate the shortcomings of the *article-based* method presented above and obtain a more comprehensive overview of the entity aspects in the entire Wikipedia language edition (rather than in a single article), we propose the *graph-based* context extraction method. The idea behind this method is to use the link structure of Wikipedia to obtain a comprehensive set of sentences mentioning the target entity and to use this set to create the context. To this extent, we use the *in-links* to the main Wikipedia article describing the entity and the *language-links* of these articles to efficiently collect the articles that are probable to mention the target entity in different language editions. We extract the sentences mentioning the target entity using state-of-the-art named entity disambiguation methods and use these sentences to build language-specific contexts.

To illustrate our approach, we use the extraction of the context in the English edition of Wikipedia for the entity *Angela Merkel* as an example. For the

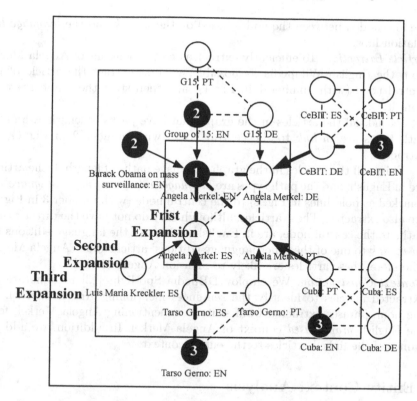

Fig. 1. An example of the graph-based context extraction from the English Wikipedia for the entity "Angela Merkel".

Wikipedia article in English about Angela Merkel, there are several *in-links* from other articles in English that mention the entity to it. Besides that, there are also *language-links* from the articles representing Angela Merkel in other Wikipedia languages to this entity's English Wikipedia article.

In Fig. 1, we use the arrows to represent the in-links, and dashed lines to represent the language links. The black nodes represent articles in English, while the white nodes represent the articles in other languages.

Overall, the creation of the *graph-based* context for Angela Merkel using these links includes the following steps:

1. *Graph Creation.* We create a subgraph for Angela Merkel from Wikipedia's link structure in the following way: We first expand the node set from the article in English about the entity (the central node) to all language editions of this Wikipedia article; Then, we further expand the node set with all the articles having *in-links* to the nodes in the node set; Finally, we expand the node set with all the articles having *language links* to the existing nodes, if they have not been included into the node set yet. Different types of edges

are also added between the nodes based on the *in-link* and the *language link* relationships.

2. *Article Extraction.* To efficiently extract as many mentions of Angela Merkel from the English Wikipedia as possible, we first extract the article of the central node (with number 1 in Fig. 1), and then start the graph traversal from it.

   Second, all the articles in the graph that have paths of length 1, and the path types are *in-link* to the central node (with number 2 in Fig. 1), are extracted;

   Third, all the articles in the graph that have paths of length 3, the articles are in English, and the path types are *language-link — in-link — language-link* (marked as bold lines in Fig. 1) to the central node (with number 3 in Fig. 1), are also extracted. These articles, although they do not have the direct *in-link* paths to the central node, are in English and one of the language editions has an *in-link* to one of the other language editions' article about Angela Merkel; Therefore, these articles are likely to mention Angela Merkel.

3. *Context Construction.* We employ DBpedia Spotlight [13] to annotate the extracted articles to identify the sentences mentioning Angela Merkel. All the noun phrases extracted from sentences mentioning Angela Merkel, form the English *graph-based* context of Angela Merkel. In addition, we add the names of the linked articles to the entity context.

3   Entity Context Analysis

The goal of the entity context analysis is to compare the *graph-based* and the *article-based* context creation methods. To this extent we analyse the similarities and the differences of the contexts obtained using these methods in a case study.

3.1   Dataset Description

To facilitate our analysis, we selected a total number of 80 entities with worldwide influence that evenly come from four categories as our target entities. These categories include: multinational corporations, politicians, celebrities and sports stars. For our study we selected five European languages: English, German, Spanish, Portuguese and Dutch, as our target languages. For each category, we included entities originating from the countries that use one of these target languages as official languages. As our approach requires machine translation of the contexts to enable cross-lingual context similarity computation, we chose Google Translate — a translation service that provides good quality for the involved language pairs.

Based on the approach described in Sect. 2, we created the entity-centric contexts for the entities in our dataset from the five Wikipedia language editions listed above using the *graph-based* and the *article-based* approach. The average number of sentences extracted from the main Wikipedia article describing the entity using the *article-based* approach is around 50 in our dataset. Using our *graph-based* context extraction method that utilises Wikipedia link structure to collect sentences mentioning the entity from multiple articles, the number of sentences referring to an entity was increased by the factor 20 to more than 1000 sentences per entity in a language edition, on average. This factor reflects the effect of the additional data sources within Wikipedia we use in the *graph-based* method for each entity processed. The total number of sentences collected by the *graph-based* approach is 419,289 sentences for the whole dataset under consideration.

3.2 Context Similarity Analysis

The cross-lingual context similarity resulting from the *article-based* and the *graph-based* context creation methods, are presented in Tables 1 and 2, respectively. To enable cross-lingual context similarity computation, we translated all context vectors to English. Due to the space limitations, we present example similarity values for four selected entities (one per entity type) for the seven language pairs. In addition, we present the average similarity and the standard deviation values based on all 80 entities in the entire dataset.

Table 1. Cross-lingual context similarity using the *article-based* context creation method. The table presents the similarity for four selected entities of different types, as well as the average similarity and the standard deviation for the whole dataset of 80 entities. The language codes representing the original context languages are as follows: "NL" — Dutch, "DE" — German, "EN" — English, "ES" — Spanish, and "PT" — Portuguese.

Entity	*Article-based* cross-lingual similarity						
	EN-DE	EN-ES	EN-PT	EN-NL	DE-ES	DE-NL	ES-PT
GlaxoSmithKline	0.43	0.34	0.29	0.29	0.31	0.22	0.26
Angela Merkel	0.68	0.66	0.84	0.54	0.60	0.59	0.66
Shakira	0.71	0.58	0.84	0.75	0.48	0.64	0.58
Lionel Messi	0.71	0.86	0.81	0.89	0.71	0.68	0.82
Average of 80	**0.50**	**0.47**	**0.46**	**0.43**	0.38	0.36	0.39
Stdev of 80	0.16	0.20	0.23	0.22	0.18	0.19	0.22

From Table 1, we can observe that using the *article-based* context creation method, the average similarity of the language pairs including English is always higher than that of the other language pairs. Using these computation results, we can make several observations: First, as the *article-based* contexts are more similar to English than to other languages, it is possible that the English edition builds a reference for the creation of the articles in other language editions in many cases. This can be further explained by the large size of the English Wikipedia that has the largest number of users, articles, and edits compared to

Table 2. Cross-lingual context similarity using the *graph-based* context creation method. The table presents the similarity for four selected entities of different types, as well as the average similarity and the standard deviation for the whole dataset. The language codes representing the original context languages are as follows: "NL" — Dutch, "DE" — German, "EN" — English, "ES" — Spanish, and "PT" — Portuguese.

Entity	*Graph-based* cross-lingual similarity						
	EN-DE	EN-ES	EN-PT	EN-NL	DE-ES	DE-NL	ES-PT
GlaxoSmithKline	0.72	0.73	0.59	0.61	0.63	0.62	0.55
Angela Merkel	0.64	0.62	0.42	0.60	0.75	0.82	0.51
Shakira	0.91	0.94	0.90	0.88	0.94	0.91	0.94
Lionel Messi	0.63	0.76	0.77	0.68	0.70	0.62	0.76
Average of 80	0.53	**0.60**	0.56	0.52	0.53	0.48	**0.61**
Stdev of 80	0.25	0.22	0.21	0.24	0.24	0.25	0.20

other language editions[1]. Second, as other language pairs are less similar, the overlapping aspects between the English edition and the other language editions appear to be language-dependent. Finally, although the cosine similarity values can be in the interval [0,1], the absolute similarity values achieved by the *article-based* method reach at most 0.5, even for the language pairs with relatively high similarity, such as English and German. Such relatively low absolute similarity values indicate that although the articles contain some overlapping entity aspects, they also include a significant proportion of divergent aspects.

In contrast to the *article-based* method, the *graph-based* method collects a more comprehensive overview of the entity aspects spread across different articles in a language edition. From Table 2, we can see that the most similar context pair is are the Spanish and the Portuguese. Intuitively, this could be explained by the closeness of the cultures using these two languages, and a more comprehensive overview of the covered entity aspects in both languages compared to the *article-based* method. We can also observe that the average similarity values significantly increase compared to the *article-based* method and can exceed 0.6 in our dataset.

From a single entity perspective, some entities may achieve higher than the average similarities for a language pair, when more common aspects are included in the context on the both sides. For example, this is the case for EN-NL, DE-ES and DE-NL pairs for the entity "Angela Merkel". Other entities may have lower similarities for some language pairs, especially when distinct aspects are included into the corresponding languages contexts, such as the EN-DE, ES-ES, and EN-PT pairs for "Lionel Messi".

To illustrate the differences in the language-specific *graph-based* entity contexts, we select the highly weighted aspects from the context vectors of the entity "Angela Merkel" constructed using the *graph-based* method, as shown in Table 3. In this table, the unique aspects that appear with high weights in all contexts of

---

[1] http://en.wikipedia.org/wiki/List_of_Wikipedias.

the entity "Angela Merkel" are underlined. We can observe, that the aspects that appear with high weights only in the non-German context — e.g. "England", "Kingdom" and "Dilma Rousseff" — are more relevant to the Angela Merkel's international affairs in corresponding countries. In contrast, the aspects that appear with high weights only in the German context — such as "German children" and "propaganda" — are more relevant to the Angela Merkel's domestic activities.

Table 3. Top-30 highly weighted aspects of the entity "Angela Merkel" in language-specific *graph-based* contexts.

English	angela merkel, battle, berlin, cdu, chancellor, chancellor angela merkel, church, edit, election, emperor, empire, england, france, george, german, german chancellor angela merkel, germany, government, jesus, john, kingdom, merkel, minister, party, president, talk, union, university, utc, war
German	academy, angela merkel, article, berlin, cdu, cet, chancellor, chancellor angela merkel, csu, election, example, german, german chancellor angela merkel, german children, germany, government, kasner, merkel, minister, november, october, office, party, president, propaganda, ribbon, september, speech, time, utc
Spanish	administration, angela merkel, berlin, cdu, chancellor, chancellor angela merkel, coalition, council, country, december, decommissioning plan, decreed, election, energy, france, german, german chancellor angela merkel, german federal election, germany, government, government coalition, grand coalition, merkel, minister, october, party, president, spd, union, year
Portuguese	ali, angela merkel, bank, cdu, ceo, chairman, chancellor, chancellor angela merkel, china, co-founder, coalition, csu, dilma rousseff, german chancellor angela merkel, germany, government, government merkel, koch, leader, merkel, minister, november, october, party, petroleum, president, saudi arabia, state, union, york
Dutch	angela merkel, angela dorothea kasner, bundestag, candidate, cdu, chancellor, chancellor angela merkel, coalition, csu, december, fdp, fist, french president, german, german chancellor angela merkel, german christian democrat politician, german federal election, germany, government, majority, merkel, minister, november, october, party, president, right, spd, state, union

Overall, our observations confirm that the *graph-based* context provides a better overview of the different entity aspects than the *article-based* method. The *graph-based* method can determine the similarities and the differences of the language contexts, independent of the coverage and completeness of any dedicated Wikipedia article. The results of the t-test confirm the statistical significance of the context similarity differences between the *article-based* and the *graph-based* methods for all language pairs except the EN-DE. This exception can be explained by a relatively high coverage of the German Wikipedia pages with respect to the aspects of the represented entities in our dataset.

The analysis results also confirm our intuition that, although the editors of different Wikipedia language editions describe some common entity aspects, they can have different focus with respect to the aspects of interest. These differences are reflected by the complementary information spread across the Wikipedia language editions and can probably be explained by various factors including the culture and the living environment of the editors, as well as the information available to them. Our *graph-based* context creation method is capable of capturing these differences from different language editions by creation of comprehensive language-specific entity contexts.

4   Related Work

Due to its coverage and diversity, Wikipedia has been acting as an outer knowledge source to build semantic representations of entities in various areas. Examples include information retrieval [4,10,14,17,22], named entity disambiguation [1,2,8,11], text classification [6,20] and text clustering [9].

To extract an entity context, many researches directly used the Wikipedia article about the entity [1,2,4,7–10,14,17,20–22]; some works extended the article with all the other Wikipedia articles linked to the Wikipedia article of the entity [6]; Others extended the article with the anchor texts and words in a fixed-sized window around such anchor text [12]; Further works only considered the first paragraph of the article [2] . Different from these approaches, our *graph-based* method do not only employ in-links and language links to broaden the article set that is likely to mention the entity, but also performs a finer-grained process: Annotate the sentences that mention the entity, such that all the sentences in our context are closely related to the target entity.

As to the context of the entity, [1,11] defined it as the tf-idf/word count/ binary occurrence values of all the vocabulary words in the target entity content; [2] defined it as the binary occurrences of entities; [18] defined it as as number of occurrences of entities; [4–7,9,10,14,17,20,22] defined it as the tf-idf similarities between the target entity and some entities in Wikipedia. In this paper, we employ aspect weights that have a different interpretation of the frequency and selectivity than the typical tf-idf values and take co-occurrence and language specificity of the aspects into account.

Following [21], some researches [9,12,14] also employed category links from the entity's Wikipedia article. Since the category structure is language-specific, it does not provide enough insights to compute similarity scores directly.

With the development of multilingual Wikipedia, researchers have been employing it in many multilingual applications [3,15,16]. Similar to the English-only contexts, each dimension in a multilingual context represented the relatedness of the target entity with the set of entities in the corresponding language. As different language editions of Wikipedia express different aspects of the entity, in our research, we take a step further to analyse the differences in the language-specific entity contexts.

5   Conclusions and Outlook

In this paper we presented the notion of the language-specific entity context and proposed a measure to compute the context similarity across different languages. Furthermore, we compared different ways of context creation including the article-based and the graph-based methods. A Wikipedia article describing the entity in a certain language can be seen as the most straightforward source for the language-specific entity context creation. Nevertheless, such context can be incomplete, lacking important entity aspects. Therefore, in this paper we proposed an alternative method to collect data for the context creation, i.e. the graph-based method. This method enables us to obtain a more comprehensive overview of the entity representation in a Wikipedia language edition as a whole. Our evaluation results show significant differences between the contexts obtained using different context creation methods and suggest that the graph-based method is a promising approach to obtain a comprehensive overview of the language-specific entity representation independent of the Wikipedia article describing the entity. In our future work, we plan to focus on the development of the context-aware retrieval applications from multilingual data sources.

Acknowledgments. This work was partially funded by the COST Action IC1302 (KEYSTONE) and the European Research Council under ALEXANDRIA (ERC 339233).

References

1. Bunescu, R.C., Pasca, M.: Using encyclopedic knowledge for named entity disambiguation. In: EACL, vol. 6, pp. 9–16
2. Cucerzan, S.: Large-scale named entity disambiguation based on wikipedia data. In: EMNLP-CoNLL, vol. 7, pp. 708–716
3. Daiber, J., Jakob, M., Hokamp, C., Mendes, P.N.: Improving efficiency and accuracy in multilingual entity extraction. In: Proceedings of the 9th International Conference on Semantic Systems, I-SEMANTICS 2013, pp. 121–124. ACM, New York (2013)
4. Egozi, O., Markovitch, S., Gabrilovich, E.: Concept-based information retrieval using explicit semantic analysis. ACM Trans. Inf. Syst. (TOIS) 29(2), 8 (2011)
5. Gabrilovich, E., Markovitch, S.: Computing semantic relatedness using wikipedia-based explicit semantic analysis. In: IJCAI, vol. 7, pp. 1606–1611
6. Gabrilovich, E., Markovitch, S.: Wikipedia-based semantic interpretation for natural language processing. J. Artif. Intell. Res. 34(1), 443–498 (2009)
7. Han, X., Sun, L., Zhao, J.: Collective entity linking in web text: a graph-based method. In: Proceedings of the 34th International ACM SIGIR Conference on Research and Development in Information Retrieval, pp. 765–774. ACM

8. Han, X., Zhao, J.: Named entity disambiguation by leveraging wikipedia semantic knowledge. In: Proceedings of the 18th ACM Conference on Information and Knowledge Management, pp. 215–224. ACM

9. Hu, J., Fang, L., Cao, Y., Zeng, H.-J., Li, H., Yang, Q., Chen, Z.: Enhancing text clustering by leveraging wikipedia semantics. In: Proceedings of the 31st Annual International ACM SIGIR Conference on Research and Development in Information Retrieval, pp. 179–186. ACM

10. Kaptein, R., Kamps, J.: Exploiting the category structure of wikipedia for entity ranking. Artif. Intell. **194**, 111–129 (2013)

11. Kataria, S.S., Kumar, K.S., Rastogi, R.R., Sen, P., Sengamedu, S.H.: Entity disambiguation with hierarchical topic models. In: Proceedings of the 17th ACM SIGKDD International Conference on Knowledge Discovery and Data Mining, pp. 1037–1045. ACM

12. Kulkarni, S., Singh, A., Ramakrishnan, G., Chakrabarti, S.: Collective annotation of wikipedia entities in web text. In: Proceedings of the 15th ACM SIGKDD International Conference on Knowledge Discovery and Data Mining, pp. 457–466. ACM

13. Mendes, P.N., Jakob, M., García-Silva, A., Bizer, C.: Dbpedia spotlight: shedding light on the web of documents. In: Proceedings the 7th International Conference on Semantic Systems, I-SEMANTICS 2011, Graz, Austria, 7–9 September 2011, pp. 1–8 (2011)

14. Milne, D.N., Witten, I.H., Nichols, D.M.: A knowledge-based search engine powered by wikipedia. In: Proceedings of the Sixteenth ACM Conference on Information and Knowledge Management, pp. 445–454. ACM

15. Nastase, V., Strube, M.: Transforming wikipedia into a large scale multilingual concept network. Artif. Intell. **194**, 62–85 (2013)

16. Nothman, J., Ringland, N., Radford, W., Murphy, T., Curran, J.R.: Learning multilingual named entity recognition from wikipedia. Artif. Intell. **194**, 151–175 (2013)

17. Otegi, A., Arregi, X., Ansa, O., Agirre, E.: Using knowledge-based relatedness for information retrieval. Knowl. Inf. Syst. **44**(3), 1–30 (2014)

18. Ploch, D.: Exploring entity relations for named entity disambiguation. In: Proceedings of the ACL 2011 Student Session, pp. 18–23. Association for Computational Linguistics

19. Rogers, R.: Wikipedia as Cultural Reference. In: Digital Methods. The MIT Press, Cambridge (2013)

20. Wang, P., Hu, J., Zeng, H.-J., Chen, Z.: Using wikipedia knowledge to improve text classification. Knowl. Inf. Syst. **19**(3), 265–281 (2009)

21. Witten, I., Milne, D.: An effective, low-cost measure of semantic relatedness obtained from wikipedia links. In: Proceeding of AAAI Workshop on Wikipedia and Artificial Intelligence: an evolving synergy, pp. 25–30. AAAI Press, Chicago, USA

22. Yazdani, M., Popescu-Belis, A.: Computing text semantic relatedness using the contents and links of a hypertext encyclopedia. In: Proceedings of the Twenty-Third International Joint Conference on Artificial Intelligence, pp. 3185–3189. AAAI Press (2013)

Author Index

Alexiev, Vladimir 182

Belhajjame, Khalid 76
Bierig, Ralf 141

Cadegnani, Sara 17
Calì, Andrea 30
Cochez, Michael 36
Cristea, Alexandra I. 197
Cristea, Valentin 88

del Carmen Rodríguez-Hernández, María 17
Demidova, Elena 153, 197
Draszawka, Karol 51

Ermolayev, Vadim 36

Gabbay, Dov 108
Gossen, Gerhard 153
Grigori, Daniela 76
Guerra, Francesco 17, 51, 94

HaCohen-Kerner, Yaakov 64, 108
Hanbury, Allan 141
Harmassi, Mariem 76
Holzmann, Helge 153

Ifrim, Claudia 88
Ilarri, Sergio 17
Ioannou, Ekaterini 94
Ivašić-Kos, Marina 133

Kitanović, Olivera 167
Kompatsiaris, Ioannis 64
Kotzyba, Michael 1
Kozikowski, Piotr 94
Krstev, Cvetana 167

Liparas, Dimitris 64
Lupu, Mihai 141
Lynch, Thomas W. 30

Martinenghi, Davide 30
Mocanu, Mariana 88
Moumtzidou, Anastasia 64
Mughaz, Dror 108

Nürnberger, Andreas 1

Obradović, Ivan 167

Platis, Nikos 127
Pobar, Miran 133
Pop, Florin 88

Rekabsaz, Navid 141
Risse, Thomas 153

Sabag, Asaf 64
Souza, Tarcisio 153
Stange, Dominic 1
Stanković, Ranka 167
Szymański, Julian 51, 153

Tagarev, Andrey 182
Terziyan, Vagan 36
Tološi, Laura 182
Torlone, Riccardo 30
Triantos, Thanos 127
Trillo-Lado, Raquel 17

Velegrakis, Yannis 17, 94
Vrochidis, Stefanos 64

Wallace, Manolis 127

Zhou, Yiwei 197

Printed in the United States
By Bookmasters

Classical Vector Algebra

Every physicist and engineer, and certainly every mathematician, would undoubtedly agree that vector algebra is one of the basic mathematical instruments in their toolbox.

Classical Vector Algebra should be viewed as a prerequisite for, and an introduction to, other mathematical courses dealing with vectors, and it follows the typical form and appropriate rigor of more advanced mathematics texts.

The vector algebra discussed in this book briefly addresses vectors in general 3-dimensional Euclidean space, and then, in more detail, looks at vectors in Cartesian $\mathbf{R}^3$ space. These vectors are easier to visualize and their operational techniques are relatively simple, but they are necessary for the study of Vector Analysis. In addition, this book could serve as a good way to build up intuitive knowledge for more abstract structures of n-dimensional vector spaces.

Definitions, theorems, proofs, corollaries, examples, and so on are not useless formalism, even in an introductory treatise – they are the way mathematical thinking has to be structured. In other words, an "introduction" and "rigor" are not mutually exclusive.

The material in this book is neither difficult nor easy. The text is a serious exposition of a part of mathematics that students need to master in order to be proficient in the field. In addition to the detailed outline of the theory, the book contains literally hundreds of corresponding examples and exercises.

Textbooks in Mathematics

Series editors: Al Boggess, Kenneth H. Rosen

An Invitation to Abstract Algebra
Steven J. Rosenberg

Numerical Analysis and Scientific Computation (2nd Edition)
Jeffery J. Leader

Introduction to Linear Algebra: Computation, Application, and Theory
Mark J. DeBonis

The Elements of Advanced Mathematics, Fifth Edition
Steven G. Krantz

Differential Equations: Theory, Technique, and Practice, Third Edition
Steven G. Krantz

Real Analysis and Foundations, Fifth Edition
Steven G. Krantz

Geometry and Its Applications, Third Edition
Walter J. Meyer

Transition to Advanced Mathematics
Danilo R. Diedrichs and Stephen Lovett

Modeling Change and Uncertainty: Machine Learning and Other Techniques
William P. Fox and Robert E. Burks

Abstract Algebra: A First Course, Second Edition
Stephen Lovett

Multiplicative Differential Calculus
Svetlin Georgiev, Khaled Zennir

Applied Differential Equations: The Primary Course
Vladimir A. Dobrushkin

Mathematical Modeling the Life Sciences: Numerical Recipes in Python and MATLAB™
N. G. Cogan

Classical Analysis: An Approach through Problems
Hongwei Chen

Classical Vector Algebra
Vladimir Lepetic

Financial Mathematics Volume II: A Comprehensive Treatment in Continuous Time
Giuseppe Campolieti and Roman N. Makarov

www.routledge.com/Textbooks-in-Mathematics/book-series/CANDHTEXBOOMTH